The Saddest Pleasure

A JOURNEY ON TWO RIVERS

A GRAYWOLF MEMOIR / 1990

The Saddest Pleasure

A JOURNEY ON TWO RIVERS

Travel book as memoir,

memoir as novel,

novel as polemic.

BY MORITZ THOMSEN

Graywolf Press / *Saint Paul, Minnesota*

Grateful acknowledgment is made for use of passages from *Open Veins of Latin America: Five Centuries of the Pillage of a Continent* by Eduardo Galeano, published by Monthly Review.

Publication of this volume is made possible in part by grants from the Bush Foundation, the National Endowment for the Arts, and the Minnesota State Arts Board. Graywolf Press is the recipient of a McKnight Foundation Award administered by the Minnesota State Arts Board and receives generous contributions from corporations, foundations, and individuals. Graywolf Press is a member agency of United Arts, Saint Paul.

Published by G R A Y W O L F   P R E S S
Post Office Box 75006
Saint Paul, Minnesota 55175
All rights reserved.

I S B N 1-55597-124-5

Library of Congress Cataloging-in-Publication Data

Thomsen, Moritz
The saddest pleasure : a journey on two rivers :
a memoir / by Moritz Thomsen.
p.   cm. -- (A Graywolf memoir)
1. Brazil--Description and travel--1981-
2. Thomsen, Moritz--Journeys--Brazil.   I. Title.   II. Series.
F2517.T48   1990
918.104'63--dc20   89-27450

9   8   7   6   5   4   3

For Clay and Barbara Morgan

Table of Contents

Introduction

A travel book may be many things, and Moritz Thomsen's *The Saddest Pleasure* seems to be most of them – not just a report of a journey, but a memoir, an autobiography, a confession, a foray into South American topography and history, a travel narrative, with observations of books, music, and life in general; in short, what the best travel books are, a summing up.

Thomsen, the most modest of men, writes at one point, "Though I have written a couple of books I have never thought of myself as a writer. I had written them in those predawn hours when the land still lay in darkness, or in days of heavy winter rains when the cattle huddled in the brush dumb with misery. . . . I had always considered that all my passion was centered around farming." The books he refers to are *Living Poor* (1971), the best book I have yet read on the Peace Corps experience, and *The Farm on the River of Emeralds* (1978), which is a sort of sequel, and describes a maddening and exasperating series of reverses as part-owner in a farm (with an Ecuadorian) on the lush and muddy coast.

To my mind, this farmer is a writer to his fingertips, but he is an unusual man and his writing life has been anything but ordinary. Writing for him is a natural and instinctive act, like breathing. It is obvious from this book and his others that he loathes polite society and shuns the literary world (meeting João Ubaldo Ribiero in Bahia he is meeting a kindred spirit). He is no city slicker, he is not possessive or acquisitive; he mocks his physical feebleness, he jeers at his old age and his sense of failure. He wishes to write well and honestly, he is not interested in power. A great deal of foolishness or a little wickedness makes him angry. He always tells us exactly what he thinks, in his own voice. He is the least mannered of writers, and he would rather say something truthful in a clumsy way than lie elegantly.

I liked him the instant I met him, and even then, eleven or twelve years ago, he seemed rather aged, frail and gray-haired, wheezing in the thin air of Quito. I knew he was a good man and that he was tenaciously loyal and that he was a serious writer. He was in his middle sixties and had published his Peace Corps book, and he told me he was working on several others, including a memoir of his father. He hated his father, he said, and since literature is rich in such hatreds, I encouraged him in his memoir. He tantalized me with stories of his father's odious behavior – the time he hanged his wife's pet cat, the time he tied a dead chicken around a collie's throat with barbed wire because the collie had been worrying the hens. I think I've got that right. His father was a poisonous snob and a liar, and he made poor Moritz's life a misery. And clearly it went on for some time. We read in this travel book of how, at the age of forty-eight, Moritz was still being berated by this paranoid maniac for joining the "communistic" Peace Corps. The only other person I have met in my life who hated his father as much was a German who told me that his father had been a member of the precursor of the SS, the SA – *Sturm Abteilung* – and, long after the war was over, was still ranting. Indeed, Thomsen Senior and this Nazi would have got along like a house on fire.

I am happy to see this monster in the narrative. Whatever else travel is, it is also an occasion to dream and remember. You sit in an alien landscape and you remember all the people who have been awful to you. You have nightmares in strange beds. You remember episodes that you have not thought of for years and but for that noise from the street or that powerful odor of jasmine you might have forgotten. Details of Thomsen's life emerge as he travels out of Ecuador, through Bogotá and around Brazil – his childhood dreams, his shaming memory of a shocking incident one long-ago Halloween, his years in the war (twenty-seven combat missions flown in a B-17 in 1943 alone), his father's death and funeral, his disastrous farming ventures, and the outrages he witnessed in various coastal villages in Ecuador.

By the end of this book, you know Moritz Thomsen intimately, and what is more important, he is a man well worth knowing. In many respects this is a self-portrait, but in this case the artist is painting himself naked. He is candid. He withholds nothing. When we get a glimpse of his body he is never sentimental: he describes poor, weak human flesh. In Rio, for example, he is in a room with a mirror. He has no mirror in Quito. "I am looking at myself for almost the first time in ten years, and can see at last that I had been truly broken by that time in the jungle and that old age." He was sixty-three at the time of the trip, but he had been very ill beforehand. His illness and his sense of failure make him morbid, of course, but also ghoulishly humorous. He gives most people a lot of latitude, but he is always hard on himself. He laments that he doesn't look Latin. He reflects on his own appearance: "Pure gringo, but more bum than working man."

Moritz Thomsen is rare in an important way. He is a true Conradian, and his distant literary ancestor is someone like Axel Heyst in *Victory* – although I should quickly add that Axel Heyst's father was a different sort of devil from the elder Thomsen. In the 1960s many middle-aged men and women joined the Peace Corps. It was not unusual for a man in his forties or fifties to head off to Africa or South America to teach school or show people how to raise chickens. Three little old ladies and an elderly gent were in my own Peace Corp group, which left the States in 1963 bound for Nyasaland in Central Africa. People at home said, "Lordy, I don't know how they do it," but the fact was that they didn't do it very well. Moritz Thomsen underplays his Peace Corps successes, but the records show that he was an exemplary volunteer. That is not his rarity; he is rare in having stayed on, and twenty-odd years later he is still in Ecuador, still committed to the place and the people, still an anarchist at heart, and still poor.

He is the man – there are not many in the world – who stayed behind. Americans seldom do. You meet the odd German, the tetchy Englishman, the panicky Hindu, the refugee Pole, or whoever; but seldom do you see the cultured, civilized, widely read American in the Third-World boondocks. Throughout his books, Thomsen says, but never explicitly, that going away made him a person, made him a writer. His subject is not suffering humanity, but rather loneliness and fellowship. He sees himself as the ultimate tramp, but then so was Henry David Thoreau, so was W.D. Hudson, so was Gauguin, so, for that matter, is the courageous Wilfred Thesiger, in spite of his Eton tie. Because Thomsen stayed behind, he saw the dust settle, the sun drop behind the mountains, and another generation of vipers appear in the government. He is watchful, patient, and, in his way, very strong. He remembers everything. His writing is not that of someone who is merely visiting, but that of a man who has taken root; and after the initial uneasiness he feels in traveling – his hatred of planes, his superstitions, his irritation with other passengers or officialdom, his worry about lack of money, his deep loneliness and isolation – he begins to drift and relax, and he begins to encounter Brazil. In this sort of travel there is catharsis, but few travelers are so honest in their reactions or so skillful in documenting them. He is happier in the hinterland and on the river; his writing begins to sing. It is not a coincidence that it was on his river trip that he described the diesel rhythm of the boat as "slow and languorous, like the heartbeat of a sleeping woman."

"I'm going to wind it up. Call it a day."

"Whatever for?"

"I'm too old to travel, for one thing."

"Which Frenchman said, 'Travel is the saddest of the pleasures'?"

"It gave me eyes."

An imaginary Maud Pratt talking to an invented
Graham Greene. PICTURE PALACE *by Paul Theroux.*

Sem árvores, sem Deus.

Fundamental Bahian Candomblé *precept*

The Saddest Pleasure

A JOURNEY ON TWO RIVERS

PART ONE

Despedida

Among a long list of bizarre social customs that enchant and irritate a North American who has come to live in South America, one of the most revealing about national differences is the *Despedida*. The despedida is a highly ritualized leavetaking arranged by friends and family when you prepare to set out on a journey. Because Latins, or at least Ecuadorians, those Latins whom I know best, are family oriented in a most morbid way and because they have strangely mixed perceptions about time and history, they do not take lightly the announcement that a friend or a relation has decided to leave them for a time. Wandering in a foreign country, or for that matter, even moving to the next town strikes them as highly hazardous, as intemperate as Russian roulette.

Decently educated Ecuadorians after centuries of colonial exploitation seem unaware that conditions have changed somewhat since that first cursed rabble of Spanish scum invaded the continent confronting gushing volcanoes, a trembling earth, the sly perfidy of rascally Indians, cloudbursts of rain, swollen rivers, terrible disfiguring diseases. It is as though they still studied the old maps whose borders are adorned with medieval mermaids and sea monsters, frightful creatures with the faces of dogs, and great swishing flukes capable of shattering the timbers of the stoutest caravel. The news that you have chosen for whatever reason to take a trip hits the Latin nuclear family with a force of 8.5 on the Richter scale.

A well-organized despedida shares certain characteristics with an Irish wake; leaving is a little death the pain of which can only be dulled by drunkenness. Mourning, friends and family gather for an all-night bash. Increasingly maudlin and portentous, they wish you a safe trip in hopeless voices and enthusiastically drink from the bottles you have provided. As the night wears on some of the guests will predict your death by gun, blackjack, poisoned clams, or overturned canoe, and some will accuse you of cold-heartedness in leaving friends who so cherish you. "Bring me back a keep-sake," they will say. "You who are rich enough to travel; some little some-thing to remember you by — if, that is, you esteem us enough to ever come back to this poor land." Grandfather has been brought down and put in the center of the old black leather sofa; this is his chance to be listened to, to be believed. He recalls the campaign of 1913 — the wild Indians who puffed out silent curare-tipped darts of *chontaduro*, the thirty-foot snake who ate both horse and rider after crushing them together into one great ghastly aspic. Sores as big as butter plates on arms and legs, spreading and incurable cancers from the bite of the dreaded Conga. "And who is leaving us this time? Luis Umberto? Bring me the child that I may bless him."

A traditional middle-class despedida climaxes the following day at the airport when, as the moment of departure approaches, the traveler is sur-rounded by a dozen close family members; they begin to shriek with fore-boding. Mama is always there, the star, dressed in the mourning black that anticipates the crash of your airliner and the deaths of all aboard. She jeal-ously fights off aunts and cousins and jabs viciously at the traveler's fiancé. Everyone mills about making the sign of the cross and calling on the Virgin Mary for her intercession in this foolhardy move from which no good can be expected to come. Dripping handkerchiefs mop at wild, swollen eyes, and sobbing matrons push back through again for one more embrace, an embrace so sensual and clinging as to raise the specter of incest. The male members of this tragic group, the uncles, the brothers, the godfathers, stand at the fringes. They stare at the floor, take deep drags on their cigarettes, and clench and unclench the muscles in their jaws. They are just a few seconds away from a total breakdown that would destroy forever the macho image they have spent a lifetime cultivating. These black-eyed Latins, hawk-nosed, inscrutably proud, caught up in the drama of the moment, are feel-ing an almost uncontrollable impulse to sob like children.

No matter that Luis Umberto is going only to Miami or New York, no matter that the trip is for only five days and that on Friday of that same week he will be back with his cargo of electric hair dryers, tape recorders, and color television sets.

·   ·   ·

During the twelve years that I have spent in Ecuador, I have, in the matter of despedidas, been lucky. Too busy farming, too poor to make trips, I hoed the weeds in my own bean patch. Ecuador was strange and crazy enough so that I felt no urge to see new country. The farm was in the jungle, my neighbors were black, wild things happened that I would never understand. I didn't need to take trips; in a sense I would always be a tourist in my own house. There was hardly a morning that I didn't awaken with a feeling of disorientation; surprised and joyful at finding myself involved in a highly improbable scenario. Outside the window were hummingbirds, banana leaves scraping the screen, the rushing sound of the river or the rain forest sound of dripping water, the calls of naked children fishing in hand-carved canoes.

How carefully I had made my plans – the immigrant's visa, the permission to own land, the Ecuadorian partner who, as I grew older, would gradually take over. I had constructed an impregnable line of defenses that would see me through to the last day, and I even visualized my own death as a kind of triumph as I dropped in the sun with a machete in my hand, falling with a burst heart in the center of a small circle of lopped-off vines. No, my only despedida would be that final one as I was slid into a crypt tightly wrapped up like a little beribboned packet of souvenirs lying forgotten in a dresser drawer.

How cleverly I had constructed the Ecuadorian section, that last movement of the somewhat banal, hopelessly romantic symphony that was my life. If the first three movements had not been entirely my own work and owed as much to economic catastrophes and the madness of men like Hitler, there was no question in my mind that the fourth movement had been hand-crafted out of my own desires, obsessions, and illusions. Well-played it would tend to make sense of all the rest as I buried the past or made some kind of half-sense out of it.

Suddenly everything had collapsed; the careful plans had come unraveled. I was standing on the podium wildly waving my hands, urging the violins to give out with a little more vibrato when my partner, Ramón, had taken charge – scattering the score, shattering the instruments, overpowering the chords with screams of fear and anger. Ramón, my best friend, my partner, that jungle-wise black who was supposed to support me through the crises of my sixties and at the end see me decently buried, had lost his nerve. He had driven me off the farm. The details were so outrageous that now, almost a year later, I still cannot bear to think about it.

Kicked off the farm, I went to live in Quito. I spent a month in a hospital fulfilling Ramón's predictions, got cured of what, after all, had not been cancer, and came out into that dull emptiness that envelops a man who has been retired before his time and against his will. I had no work, no obligations, no schedule. I found a small apartment with a view of a cement wall from its three windows and a long row of potted geraniums. I bought a bed, a table, and four plates; three more than I needed. How awful it was to be of no use to anyone, to awaken in the mornings and be unable to think of a single reason for crawling out of bed. One day out of desperation it occurred to me that finally I might make a trip.

I arranged everything in near secrecy – tickets, visa, traveler's checks. The trip was a symbol of rejection, humiliation, and uselessness; I dreaded the idea of a despedida, one that would be nothing but a public admission that I was running away. I told friends I was leaving but was careful not to mention the date. I wanted to slip away and disappear for a time. The sudden emptiness of my life struck me as shameful, and I was embarrassed to reveal an unhappiness that I couldn't hide; it seemed to be an unhappiness that I had brought upon myself. I felt vaguely guilty, as though by coming to live in South America and abandoning my own country, that country of Lyndon Johnson and Richard Nixon, I was being paid back finally for running from a corruption that I should have stayed to combat in whatever fashion.

And so early one morning I am roaming around in my apartment putting the last of the things away and drinking a last cup of coffee. It is still dark outside. My bag is packed. I am playing music appropriate to the occasion; very loud. My plane takes off in four hours, and almost no one knows when I am leaving. I have beat the Ecuadorians at their own game (almost my first victory over them in almost a year), I have cheated them out of that public orgy of screaming and sobbing that gives them so much pleasure.

Suddenly the doorbell begins a horrible buzzing in the kitchen, a six o'clock chattering that makes the windows vibrate and sets up little circles of waves in the coffee cup. Puzzled but unsuspecting I walk out through the patio and open the iron door to the street. "Despedida, despedida," call children's voices from the darkness, and into the light Ramón and his wife, Ester, and their two children, Martita and Moncho, walk toward me with their enormous and heart-breakingly beautiful black smiles. Once again my careful plans have shattered, and I am to be given that thing I least need – a goddam despedida.

My frustration melts in the delight of seeing the children again. Leaving the farm had meant leaving the children, and this, perhaps, had been the thing that hurt me most. In a sense those kids were mine; in a sense they were the only two people in the world I loved who had returned my devotion. "But how did you find out I was leaving today?" "Aha, that's a secret, a secret."

As we walk back to the apartment the brazen trumpets of Walton's *Belshazzar's Feast* welcome them.

A lot of hugs and kissing; the children, blushing, dance around. Ester goes into the kitchen to make breakfast, the children run out to buy bread, eggs, strawberry jam, and butter; they come back with four eggs, four little biscuits hard as rocks, no jam, no butter, and are sent out again, giggling. Ramón in his ranch boots sits on the couch shivering from the cold of Quito and decides not to try and talk against the music. He and Ester have been quarreling about something, probably money, because when the children come back from the store Moncho goes into my bedroom and laboriously types out a message which he folds and hands to his father. "Papa, you are a bad man. You are treating mama very bad." Ramón reads the note without expression and hands it to me, and I kneel down and say to Moncho above the music, "Don't worry, Moncho; your father treats everyone very bad." He goes back into the room where the typewriter sits alone on the now empty table and types out a message for me. "Martin, take me with you." Ramón holds out his hand for the note, reads it, and says, "Take me with you, too."

We sit and listen to the music; much too loud to talk against, it disguises the tenseness that exists between two people who don't have anything to say to each other. It is filling that emptiness between now and the plane's take-off. Snarling trap drums, crashing cymbals, angry strings buzzing like bees, a fanatic chorus, brassy trumpets blatting out coarse Old Testament sounds. I have just written a book about Ramón, of how when I was in the Peace Corps I had found him on a jungle beach and with my money and his intelligence made him into a man of such competence that my presence on the farm became superfluous, made him into the king who would depose me. Now when he asks me, probably not caring much, what the music is about, I am ready for him and neurotically ready to prove that if the music is about me, it is sure as hell about him too.

"Listen, I'll translate. Praise the God of gods. Praise the God of iron." The orchestra rushes out with clanking iron sounds. "Praise the God of wood; praise the God of brass; praise the God of gold." With a golden clashing the music thunders out nicely mixed with the smell of frying eggs and in the little silences the sound of Martita typing out a note to someone.

"Babylon was a great city," I translate – and begin to translate freely, carried away, because it is not Babylon we are praising now but the jungle farm that Ramón now manages alone and from which I have been exiled. "Its merchandise was of gold and silver. Spices, oils, fine linen. And bananas," I add resentfully. "Pineapples, oranges, cattle, acres of green pasture, slaves, and the souls of men." Ramón nodding his head looks at me intently; my voice has broken on "the souls of men." Though Ramón is black and was born as poor as the poorest of our workers, with his new money and power he has developed a benign contempt for Negroes; on the farm I was continually criticizing his patronizing attitude, his tendency to treat the *macheteros* as though they were children. Still, I realize that many of them wish to see Ramón as a great *patrón*, the big daddy who will solve their problems. What does that look of Ramón's mean? Is the music beginning to agitate the edges of his vulnerabilities?

The music is getting pretty wrought up and passionate and I have to guess at some of the words. "But the king is an arrogant man; he has no pity; he is proud and petty and his head is as hard as a block of ebony. He has forgotten God.

"And now as they sit feasting, the fingers of a man's hand appear, and the king sees the fingers writing on the wall. And this is what the hand wrote: '*Mene mene tekel upharson'.*" In awe the full chorus translates, and I translate for Ramón. "Man, you have been weighed in God's balance, and man, you have been found guilty.

"And in that same night, Belshazzar, the king, was murdered and his kingdom divided."

For the dozen of years that I had worked with Ramón I had tried to make him shudder under the impact of powerful music. No luck. He is not at home with rhythms that don't set his feet to tapping. But now at last, I think, he has been moved. He contemplates the destruction of a kingdom, and his head gives a couple of trembles, a mini-shudder. Watching him, wondering what he is thinking – if I am the king who has been brought down or if he sees himself as a king now in danger of being judged – Ester appears out of the kitchen with plates upon each of which a single fried egg is centered.

We eat, and a few minutes later as the music ends Ramón says, "What I *really* enjoy is a nice tango," and smiling, he half closes his eyes, sweeps up a beautiful girl from the empty air and moves his shoulders in sensuous delight. Martita brings me the letter she has written. She wants presents from Brazil, nice things: earrings, little gold ones like little girls wear; a black doll; seashells; a pot of flowers; a party dress. Moncho asks for nothing but sits solemnly cutting off very small bites of egg white (he has always hated the yolks). But he is not hungry and gives up. They have been driving from the farm since two in the morning, and Moncho is sleepy. Moncho is eight years old.

So. Ramón has understood nothing; he doesn't see himself or anybody but a king as a king.

From the kitchen where Ester is washing the four plates come the low preliminary moans of a good woman warming up for the delights of a despedida, but now I discover something pleasant: Ramón doesn't want a despedida any more than I do. He is still a country type, nervous in the city traffic, and he wants to get back to the empty country roads. He drives me out to the airport a couple of hours before I want to arrive, with the intention of simply dropping me off at the door and fleeing back to the jungle. He had arrived at six and would like to get out of Quito by eight. But at the airport the children, who have never seen jets and in fact have scarcely ever seen Quito, beg and pester and finally Ramón, who secretly loves jets with a terrible passion, gives in. We park the car and all of us go up on top of the building and watch the planes coming in and taking off. Ester's eyes begin to water.

We stand at the railing of the observation deck facing into the sun, our backs to Pichincha, which is cut and quartered into small, brilliantly green Indian fields of corn or alfalfa, beans or potatoes. On the lower slopes the duller, larger plantings of eucalyptus glow like groves of olives, and up near the peak smashed against the mountain lies a great silver cross, an army plane that had got lost in the fog. In front of us lies the runway with a hump in its center like a humping dog's back.

It is the howling of jets that now defines the beginnings of journeys and announces with a sneer the mediocritazation of the world's cities to which one must now travel with diminishing anticipations. I sense this before the trip begins and have resentful feelings for these fat aluminum bullets that have destroyed the romance of distant places and have shrunk the world to the size of a pumpkin.

The hysterical screaming of this mornings' crop – that unearthly howling as one by one they build up power on the apron to slowly turn and move away from the airport building and crawl through the grass like sluggish larvae coming to life under the sun's heat, that blast of hot kerosene wind that washes over us, makes of this particular farewell something portentous and awful. For months the situation between Ramón and me has been tense and complicated, and now the screaming of the jets is so shattering with its message of farewell, of swift, final, and violent endings – of death – that we are both shaken. In a harsh w?y it symbolizes the ending of that relationship, which we have discussed often enough but without any feeling of reality. The screaming jets making melodrama of life like second-rate background music to a banal movie build up in a dishonest way a load of emotion that is counterfeit.

But when little children with big eyes are involved the most shameful tear-jerker can jerk tears out of me. I begin to feel a kind of distress mixed with disgust as I consider the probability that I will break down at the next plane's shrill announcement. How I resent the ease with which I can be manipulated to publicly display something phoney, an emotion of grief constructed of almost nothing but a weird whooshing noise and a blast of hot wind. I am leaving for a couple of months to wander aimlessly through Brazil and then return. No big deal.

"When are you coming back?" Ramón asks. "I mean, what day? So we can meet you."

"Maybe I won't come back," I tell him. "Maybe I'll find a little farm on the Amazon."

A shriek from Ester but Ramón's face is expressionless.

But how cheap, how obscene to try and hurt Ramón in front of the children, to exhibit emotions that will frighten or confuse them. I realize this as Martita, hearing something tense in my voice and looking deeply into my face, begins to whimper. I have never been completely convinced about the honesty of Martita's emotions, which are sometimes pretty extravagant, and now I sense the possibility that she is half-playing a role and trying to do what is expected of her. But Moncho is no actor; he always comes on clean and pure like a golden arrow straight to the heart. Now he grows pale and grabs convulsively at my hands; his eyes are scared. They don't know how to handle this trip, and they are confused about what part I now play in their lives. That tension, that special kind of sadness that now exists between Ramón and me, a defeat that colors our infrequent meetings when we sit around and don't say much, has shaken the ground beneath their feet. And so just as I feel the tears about to come, I cut the moment short. "It's time for me to check in," I say. "No more despedida." I shake hands with Ramón, hug Ester, and kneel to the children. As they kiss me I whisper in Moncho's ear. "I was just fooling your father; I'm not going to buy a farm anyplace, and I'll see you in a couple of months. I'll send you postcards." Then I get up and without turning around, walk away. God, how I hate farewells. I am making a trip because there is an emptiness in my life that needs to be filled with something fresh and moderately intense, but I had not anticipated feeling something so goddam intense so goddam early on this first morning even before take-off. The unexpected appearance of the children has frustrated my plans for a quiet, undramatic getaway. As I haul my bag to the ticket-counter to be weighed and checked I begin to dread this trip and the little tricks it might have up its sleeve.

The Quito airport in the years since I have used it has turned chic and slick; international travelers now have their own waiting room. I check out of the country at a cash register and am "finalized," then herded through a one-way hall like a cattle chute. I am the first international traveler and I sit alone in a sunless room rich in yellow plastic, silent and chilly in this early morning.

Beneath the melodrama of that goodbye that had brought tears to my eyes, lying deep and half-hidden, there is a real kernel of fear and grief. I am sixty-three years old now, have been very sick, and I see myself as a statistic that proves that old men forced into retirement are especially vulnerable to death's kiss. I am living with the kind of emptiness that perhaps only death can fill. Three days before this flight that is coming up, for the first time in my life, I have had a will drawn up. Death is very much on my mind; if I no longer see it as that flashy and operatic affair with the machete and the jungle vines, if the possibility now exists that it may come in a squalid way on a street in Rio or a cheap hotel room at the edges of the *sertão,* I still regard it in a friendly way. A few years before I had almost died in a highway accident and so I know that death is beautiful and pleasant and that actually my death has nothing to do with me. With the deepest part of my mind I know that dying, the most important event of one's life, is almost the only event in which one is totally uninvolved. Still, dying is a spooky business, and only those who remain behind to contemplate it will be involved, or more accurately, those who remain who love me. The children. If I don't especially want to die it is because I don't want those two to suffer; not even for the two weeks it will take for them to accept their loss and once more fill with life at life's demands. Two weeks? One week, then.

It has been forty-five years since I took a trip whose only object was pleasure. It was a trip around the world with my family. I had accepted the idea of this ultimate cruise as being not especially out of the ordinary; it was just one more part of that middle-class world to which I belonged, a little something that I had coming to me. That trip lasted almost a year; it was 1935, the depth of the Depression; hundreds of millions of people were without work, revolutions were brewing in every country we visited, Hitler and Mussolini had come to power, and the crews of those luxury liners were Harry Bridge's radicalized seamen who waited on us with a scarcely concealed loathing. What I remember most about that year was my own feeling of unease, an awareness of obscene privilege, and the conviction that we were probably the last of the travelers who would eat such rich food from the heaviest of silverware, the heaviest porcelain, the most heavily starched white linen. Gradually the ships we took turned into the tumbrils that were carrying us toward a guillotine. Surrounded by waiters and mess boys, dancing at night to a jazz orchestra, lying for hours in deck chairs, playing bridge until it was time for cocktails, floating above the blood red seas of sunset off the coasts of China, Malaysia, India, Arabia, or Egypt we became completely incongruous, as isolated, as unnecessary to the suffering world as some mysteriously moving cancer that erupts on the body's flesh, now here, now there. In the river before Shanghai, docked in Manila or Penang or Alexandria we stood at the railing waiting for cups of hot bouillon and watching naked wretches below us as they loaded or unloaded cargo, or we had ourselves pulled through oriental streets by panting men, men as thin as reeds. I was nineteen, and I knew nothing except that I was being poisoned by what I saw. And finally I realized one thing: that we were parasites drifting through a vile world that was ready to crack up: everything I saw confirmed my conviction that another, more terrible war was about to break over our heads.

Lou Gehrig, fatally ill, sat with us at the captain's table as far as Singapore. In Bombay a famous writer came aboard; he wrote for *Cosmopolitan* magazine and claimed to be the highest paid writer in the world. Edison Marshall. No one had ever heard of him; years later I would see his name on the screen credits of pirate movies starring Tyrone Power. We watched vultures eating dead bodies in Bombay, and somewhere off the coast of Ceylon, hidden in the shadows of a life-boat I had watched my father, half-mad with jealousy because my step-mother was dancing tangos with the ship's barber, climb up the railing on the sun deck as though he intended to throw himself into the sea. I don't think it occurred to me that I might stop him. Crossing the Pacific I had read *Look Homeward, Angel*; crossing the Indian Ocean, *Anthony Adverse*.

Now with the same lack of enthusiasm, and this time with death in the blood I am getting ready to take another trip; it will be similar in its uselessness but carried out in a different style. It has been years since I first denied my middle-classness and began trying to live in another way. This trip will not offend my sensibilities. Dollar meals if I can find them; five dollar hotels, if they still exist. No guided tours, no visits to historical monuments or old churches. No taxis, no mixed drinks in fancy bars. No hanging around places where English might be spoken. I know after twelve years in South America that my gringoness is apparent to the stupidest Latin American, but I will try and hide this unfortunate fact (which, perceived immediately, robs me of all my human qualities) by wearing cheap walking shoes and the pants and shirt of a working man. Waiting alone in the semi-darkness of the international lounge I find myself staring into a mirror. Oh God, I will fool no one. Pure gringo, but more bum than working man.

However, there is one thing in my favor that makes this little disguise unnecessary. I am sixty-three, white haired, not very well preserved. I have become that person who is of no interest to anyone and about whom no one will have the slightest curiosity. I have become to all intents and purposes invisible.

Well, let us learn something about Brazil, this country through which I am about to walk in my twelve-dollar rubber-soled work shoes. I paw through my briefcase and take out Eduardo Galeano's *Open Veins of Latin America* and flip through the pages, reading at random:

"According to the United Nations the amount shared by 6,000,000 Latin Americans at the top of the social pyramid is the same as the amount shared by 140,000,000 at the bottom. There are 60,000,000 campesinos whose fortune amounts to twenty-five cents a day."

.   .   .

"The Brazilian anthropologist Darcey Ribeiro estimates that more than half the aboriginal population of America, Australia, and Oceania died from the contamination of first contact with white men."

.   .   .

"The price of the tide of avarice, terror, and ferocity bearing down on these regions [South and Central America] was Indian genocide; the best recent investigations credit pre-Colombian Mexico with a population between thirty and thirty-seven and a half million, and the Andean region is estimated to have possessed a similar number; Central America had between ten and thirteen million. Aztecs, Incas, and Mayas totaled between seventy and ninety million when the foreign conquerors appeared on the horizon; a century and a half later they had been reduced to three and a half million. In 1685 only 4,000 Indian families remained of the more than two million that had once lived between Lima and Paita, according to the Marquis of Barimas."

. . .

"Some authors estimate that in the period of the rise of rubber no less than half a million Northeasterners succumbed to epidemics of malaria, tuberculosis, or beriberi. Says one, 'This grim charnel house was the price of the rubber industry.' . . . In 1878, 120,000 of Ceará's 800,000 population headed for the Amazon and less than half got there; the rest collapsed from hunger or disease on the *sertão* trails or in the suburbs of Fortaleza."

. . .

"Between 1964 and mid-1968 fifteen auto and auto parts factories were swallowed up by Ford, Chrysler, Willys Overland, Simca, Volkswagen, and Alfa Romeo. In the electric-electronic sector, three important Brazilian concerns passed into Japanese hands. Wyeth Laboratories, Bristol Myers, Mead Johnson, and Lever Brothers gobbled various laboratories, reducing national production of drugs to one fifth the market. Anaconda pounced on nonferrous metals and Union Carbide on plastics, chemicals, and petrochemicals; American Can, American Machine and Foundry, and other colleagues took over six Brazilian machine and metallurgical concerns; the *Companhia de Mineracaos Geral,* owner of one of Brazil's biggest metallurgical plants, was bought for a song by a Bethlehem Steel, Chase Manhattan – Standard Oil consortium. A parliamentary commission set up to investigate the matter reached some sensational conclusions, but the military regime closed the doors of Congress and the findings never got to the Brazilian public. . . . The commission found that in 1968 foreign capital controlled 40% of the capital market in Brazil, 62% of external trade, 82% of ocean transport, 67% of external air transport, 100% of motor vehicle production, 100% of tire production, more than 80% of the pharmaceutical industry, about 50% of the chemical industry, 59% of machinery and 62% of auto parts production, 48% of aluminum and 90% of cement production. Half of the foreign capital was that of U.S. concerns, followed by German. . . . An OAS document reports that no less than 95.7%, 80% in the case of manufacturing industries – of the funds U.S. enterprises require for their normal functioning and development in Latin America comes from Latin American sources in the form of credits, loans, and reinvested profits."

From the darkness at the far end of the lounge a cash register bell makes a single statement, the fluorescent lights, blinking and stuttering, finally wash the room with their cold, heartless light, and a minute later when I look up from the book, I am no longer alone. As though to prove that I am actually invisible, it is only with the arrival of this second person that the waiting room becomes operational.

Motionless on a plastic couch across from me, staring at the floor, sits a woman in her middle twenties. She has straight, sun-streaked hair caught up and clipped at the back, great very clear, very dark brown eyes, and she is dressed with the practical smartness of someone who knows how to travel; tan slacks, a faded safari jacket; at her feet a basket loosely stuffed with woven tapestries from Otavalo. She is beautiful, but what is more impressive than her smartness or her beauty is her grief. In that half hour as the room gradually fills with travelers she sits in a catatonic stillness, frowning at the floor, looking at no one and lost in the profound and desolate meditation of a woman whose love affair has just ended very badly. Looking at her I feel the pity that one feels at the sight of a wounded animal, and I fight the impulse to sit down by her and take her hand. Impossible, of course; she is firmly locked within her impregnable grief. Studying her face I realize that I know no one who could be worthy of her – and begin to glow with the power of a new insight: that the world has changed, that men have changed, that men can no longer match the potentialities of the women they pursue and, having won, cannot permanently cherish.

On the cover of Galeano's book a woman, South America, lies bleeding on the ground, pierced by the swordlike leaves of a cactus. The lounge is filling, and I put the book away. Galeano's Brazil is not the Brazil that I had read about in Lévi-Strauss or Tomlinson or Amado or Machado de Assis. The snakes, the jaguars, and the blood-sucking insects of Wallace and Herndon have been transformed into American businessmen; the jungle vines that strangle the forests, into a rampant capitalism. That war that I had seen coming in 1935 while I watched that naked, old-fashioned colonialism begin to writhe in its first death throes had changed nothing; economic domination had simply taken another, more threatening form. Galeano's Brazil on a gigantic scale begins to resemble Ecuador. No wonder I am so anxious to disguise my nationality; reading those passages in the back of my mind I had been nagged with feelings of guilt and shame as though, in a way that I have never bothered to examine, I am involved to some degree in this continental rape.

The lounge is full of people now, and part of the crowd is an athletic team of some kind. They look like Chileans or Argentinians, a half-dozen young men, *futbolistas* or tennis players. They are dressed nicely but carry themselves stiffly as though flannel trousers and sports jackets were vaguely troubling innovations in their lives. Though they all arrive together, they separate in the waiting room and treat each other as strangers. Pondering this I am given my second insight of the day. My God, yes, on this continent where such things are taken seriously, whatever they have been playing, they have lost. Something about making a trip has triggered my imagination and I find myself inventing the lives of perfect strangers, giving them jobs, problems, passions. From the way their clothes fit or from the tie they have selected to interpret themselves to the world I feel as though I can create a whole detailed background for them.

Suddenly just as the public address system announces that the Air France flight will be an hour late, I am confronted with something chillingly slap-stick to set beside the grieving woman.

From out of the men's toilet the tallest of the athletes emerges. He is handsome and sports a twelve-dollar haircut that frames his face and makes of it something angelically renaissance. Gray flannels; a navy blue blazer with brass buttons. He is obviously the captain of the team. As I look at him I receive my last insight from Quito – an insight that redefines the word and gives back to it the original meaning. His pants are unzipped from A to Z; from a flagrantly blazing space a large expanse of scarlet underwear and a little boiling out of pubic hair can plainly be seen. It is not just two o'clock at the waterworks; it is high noon.

Easy to flesh out the details: lost in the contemplation and manipulation of his gorgeous locks the team's captain standing before the rest room mirror has forgotten another, less important detail. I throttle that first impulse to rush over and warn him; I have not involved myself with the beautiful, grieving woman, and I have no intention of becoming involved in this vulgar comedy. Let one of his teammates step in. He wanders to a window and gazes out at the runway, and I begin to remember a day in 1944 when I was just about his age and dressed just as improbably as a captain in the Army Air Force. I was standing beside the tracks in a Chicago railroad station waiting to get on a train to someplace. A very embarrassed gentleman sidled up, stood directly in front of me as though to screen me from the crowds, and whispered, blushing, "Excuse me, excuse me, sir; your fly . . . " I had never felt authentic with my wings and ribbons, and in that moment as I clutched at my crotch, moaning – that childhood nightmare of public nakedness made real at last – I felt as though I had been found out : a charlatan, a man just back from combat, trembling at the edge of a crackup but posing as a war hero.

I suppose that I am going to have to get involved.

But I stall for another ten minutes. If I get up I will immediately lose my seat. Air France, perhaps preparing us for the tawdriness that lies ahead, has packed fifty of us into a small room with twenty seats. Finally when the team captain turns from the window and exhibits his underwear to the inside travelers, I get up and go over to him. When I have told him, enjoyed that look of horror on his face (it is always fun to tell someone something that he doesn't know), observed his cheeks go pale and then blaze with color, listened to his absolutely incredulous voice saying, "Oh, for the Jesus Christ," I walk discreetly away with a smug feeling – the little old white-haired gentleman bringing his dollop of order to a fucked-up world.

Much later a voice in the ceiling asks us to prepare to board, apologizes for the delay, wishes us a funsy trip, and hopes that very soon we will travel again with Air France. We file past a row of Ecuadorian soldiers who slap us here and there for guns and open our briefcases for brief glances. Halfway to the plane in a move that has nothing to do with conscious thought, I stop, turn, and with wild, eager eyes search hungrily along the top of the building where a hundred waving people are lined up. How far away Quito seems. Martita and Moncho have gone, of course; they are probably halfway back to the farm by this time. The desolate, grieving girl, still frowning, still searching the ground for answers, passes me. Behind her the unhappy young man; he holds a tennis bag across his front. As he approaches I smile to acknowledge the special relationship that binds us together, smiling carefully in a friendly way without a trace of mocking. He gives me back a look of such rage and loathing, so disoriented, so accusing, that I take a step backward to let him pass.

The trip is about to begin, and I am beginning it exhausted. I have already made an implacable enemy. Feeling even before I have left the city where I live that I have come a terrible distance and would like nothing better than to hole up for a day in a quiet hotel, I climb the long steps and enter an enormous plane as fat, tasteless, and crowded as a cattle truck. It smells of ozone, the bodies of tired travelers, half-eaten ham sandwiches, and vomit.

Quito – Bogotá – Manaus – Rio

Quito to Bogotá is a short hour's hop and it has an inconsequential air about it – Times Square to Columbus Circle. After flying in the war almost fifty years ago I still hate airplanes, still cherish short flights that are silly little celebrations, all take-offs and landings with nothing in between.

We climb to altitude, cruise there for a second or two, and begin the descent. Halfway to Bogotá a small army of attendants dump trays of incredible, inedible, and identical food into our laps. Some of us, faint with hunger, dabble at the fruit cup but contemplate with horror that biggest hump of something crouched in the biggest hole and covered with a glistening brown sauce that looks as though it had been recently poured through a cow. Up until this moment I had always thought the word in French was *merde*. Not at all, the menu informs me.

Later, sadder, still hungry, nose pressed to window, I study the wing and behind and below it the razor slit of a view: clouds in many amusing colors, shapes, and sizes; a red river, badly flooded, curving swiftly through hills of red earth; a deserted adobe town with rain-darkened tile roofs; a red mountain fiercely bare of trees – and finally, the glistening pastures of Bogotá. We come in fat and slow; earthbound, turned from gull to worm or goose or whale, we squirm and wiggle and come to rest like an old hen settling down over a hatch of eggs. Cold rains sweep the countryside, the big doors open, and splashing through puddles we all run for cover.

Bogotá is famous for its villainy, its thieves, and the ever new and sparkling ways that people can be robbed. Scarcely a tourist travels through Colombia, if you listen to an Ecuadorian, without some horror story: watches ripped from wrists on the main drag; Leicas razor-bladed out of camera bags; passports and cash whisked out of pockets as some careless Latin lout apologizes for having almost knocked you over and solicitously dusts your tie, your lapels, your breast pocket, your backside. It is said that the police plant dope in your luggage or "find" it in your pockets. But they are good scouts, they don't want no problema, and you can buy your freedom. Lately, in a dazzling new development, dozens of tourists have begun showing up in Quito having arrived by bus from Bogotá. They are found wandering half-naked in the streets, incapable of speech. Days later when they have begun to recover their senses and are questioned they all pretty much tell the same story. "The last thing I remember is this nice man in the bus who gave me cookies." It is not only the six-year-olds in Bogotá who should be warned about taking candy from strangers. "And listen," a friend warns me, "you'd better watch your things in the airport, too."

My revenge on Bogotá will be to ignore it. For a long three minutes, absorbing their essences, I stare hard at Colombians as they move through the long airport halls—and decide to ignore them, too. I will wait my eight hours in the airport building for the night flight to Rio, trying to temper my sensations like a bear preparing his psyche for a long hibernation. But this trip, which has scarcely begun, has already changed me. Familiar things— chairs and windows, the woman mopping the floor, the farmer with a rubber poncho, have become slightly more interesting; not only do I see things in cleaner, truer colors, but certain aspects of my character have become magnified to an alarming degree. I have become as strange to myself as that range of mountains across the horizon that I am looking at for the first time. I detect vast new capacities for impatience, resentful anger, and cynicism. What a grouchy traveler I'm going to be. The faces of strangers that had been at one time pleasantly blank or vaguely benign, faces that had held the possibility of virtue, have begun to assume hostile or corrupt expressions. I prepare to fight back.

The airport building is handsome and chilly and though reasonably new is in the process of being repaired. Signs hung over the unmoving escalators and the locked doors of toilets apologize for the inconvenience. Gusts of rain rattle against the windows, the pastures of Bogotá appear and disappear in clouds, the runway is a lake that has stolen all the light from the sky.

In the restaurant I pay three dollars for a chicken sandwich and a small bottle of beer. The cagey country rube, I find it a little difficult to both eat and keep my hands on the luggage. I push the big blue canvas bag under the table and straddle it with my feet, and it cowers there, faintly throbbing, aware of the menace in the air. Later in the airport bookstore buying postcards to send to Moncho and Martita I find Anthony Burgess's *The Last of*

Enderby and feel that I have been, finally, struck with grace. It is a book I have been looking for for years, this final volume in a wonderful trilogy about a not quite first-rate poet. Smiling with anticipation and then pouting with anger because this slim paperback is priced at six dollars instead of one ninety-five, I buy it and sit with it through the afternoon and evening. But even Anthony Burgess, whom I love, has ripped me off this time. Old Enderby is not Enderby anymore; six months in America have ruined him completely. Enderby into Burgess into a cranky, peevish Evelyn Waugh.

No more three-dollar sandwiches for me, the bastards. At seven o'clock I try the cheaper restaurant that is half-hidden at the far other side of the airport building. It is a long distance, and I am sweating when I get there, appalled that my tawdry collection of clothes and books can weigh so much. The restaurant is gay and lively; cheap music floods the room, the tables are splashed with spilled beer, scraps of food, and crumpled napkins. It pulses with that chaos and inefficiency that, if there is time to enjoy them, delight one in South America. At times. I sit at a table with Burgess for half an hour, but no one comes to wait on me. The invisible man. To hell with it. I stagger back to my end of the building and ask to be isolated in the International Traveler's Section to wait for the free midnight snack of assorted plastics that will come once we are airborne.

As night falls the wet runways catch and mirror an incredible sunset of brilliant pinks and blues so that below and above us we are drenched in light. For a few moments corrupt, chaotic Colombia shines as magically beautiful as paradise. Dragging my bag, which has now begun to weigh several hundred pounds, rushing to capture the light before it fades, I feel those sharp constrictions in my lungs like a teaser in the theater of next week's movie – a preview of how I'm going to die. But right now that light is more important than life itself and I keep going and keep going and sneak outside and snap a picture. Ten seconds later the light begins to wash from the sky, and I stand there panting and sweating, feeling good however, as though I'd won something, as though I'd captured something ephemeral that will now be mine. A little later sitting in a big, cold room and thinking about the cigarettes that are going to kill me, I smoke three in a row to calm my nerves.

Tonight I will be flying with Lufthansa. I like neither Germans nor airlines but now, forced to be fair, let me note a little touch of humanity. The manager of Lufthansa, a young German, seeks me out in the international lounge. "Terribly sorry about this. The airfield in San Jose is closed due to cloudbursts of rain. Your flight will be an hour late."

I thank him for his trouble, and a half hour later he is back – this time with a small bottle of champagne. "Really, really, I'm terribly sorry about this; your flight will be *two* hours late." He hands me the wine and I forgive Lufthansa everything.

I have been locked into the duty-free area and am surrounded by a hundred booths displaying cameras, watches, radios, and tape recorders, perfumes, soaps, lotions and creams, leather goods, cigarettes, and a thousand different kinds of booze. Colombia has emeralds and an emerald Mafia and here are a dozen stores filled with golden doodads and jeweled stuff, the gems as pale green as mint candies. I walk up and down through the empty hall examining everything carefully in the brightly lit cases, delighted to discover that there is absolutely nothing there that I would wish to own. I had spent forty years modestly collecting this kind of garbage and then, let us hope, grown wiser, the next twenty years giving it all away.

Nine o'clock, ten o'clock, eleven o'clock. The room slowly fills with travelers and outside airplanes from far away arrive for thirty-minute stops. Twelve years in the jungle had isolated me from the flow of time's changes, from the muddying of life's waters. Now parading before me a new and special kind of people pace back and forth, stretching their legs. I am being sent back to school for a refresher course.

From the planes, which rest on the tarmac before staggering on in the night to Miami or Rome or Madrid, come the courtesans, the rich men's whores, who rush into the duty-free alleys, their practiced eyes appraising to the centavo the value of the displayed crap. There are four or five in every plane. They whip past the leather goods and the bottles of colored liquors and come to a full stop before the displays of emeralds. They are fantastically beautiful; dressed in long silk sheathes of white or wearing black kneehigh boots with four-inch heels or mink capes that hide everything but their asses, their hair black, long, and lustrous, their eyes mysterious deep pools of blue or purple. Watching them with anguish, one can only be drawn down to the contemplation of their thighs. They have only one function; they are manufactured creatures out of the dreams of men with new money and the juvenile bad taste of street kids who learned about love from the MGM musicals of thirty years ago.

Certainly, they are not really human beings, but I am not unmoved by this pornography – the long flawless limbs, the perfect skins, the exotic cheekbones, the wrenchingly beautiful and empty eyes.

Walking behind the women, trying to keep up, looking cool or trying to look cool, come the owners of these gorgeous animals. The men are not a very impressive lot, though one cannot deny that they have taken on a kind of reflected grandeur. There is a fat corruption in their faces; they look like what they probably are—dealers in marijuana and cocaine, wheeler-dealers who are buying up farm land for shopping centers and fancy condominiums, politicians or military colonels in mufti. Overweight and faded, probably under doctor's orders, probably not much liking themselves if they ever stop to think about it, they slide through the hall. Though it is fast approaching midnight some of the men appear with Canon cameras with telescopic lenses jutting out of their stomachs like slightly misplaced erections.

Could I have seen this kind of a show in the airports of the 1960s? Perhaps in Los Angeles where the first models of the new world culture are produced.

Second class, same classroom: Political Science. From where I sit it looks as though at eleven thirty the only honest cop in the building is replaced by a more cooperative gent. Duty-free airport stores should sell only to passengers who are leaving the country, but suddenly I notice great quantities of wrapped packages about the size of portable radios or tape recorders being carried out of this quarantined area. There are four young men, one cop, and about thirty packages involved in tonight's operation. How slick and blatant it is. The faces of everyone take on a new malignancy.

Whores and gangsters, cheap Japanese watches, gawdy rings and bracelets, corrupt cops and contrabandistas, dope. A one day's journey has put me in the middle of a new world that I had never imagined. What I had expected was a journey into romanticism, into the slower, timeless world of the near past; perhaps even so far as childhood, which one, perhaps falsely, remembers as a place of purity, strong colors, excruciating authenticities.

What I know now in a sudden rush is that that old world has gone; things have changed way past my capacity to understand or accept. I am like some Rip van Winkle who has awakened and wandered into a present that fills him with confusion and despair. Moving so abruptly from a Stone Age jungle, a medieval Quito, to a modern airport is too long a trip to make in one day for actually it is not the present that I am being allowed to see but that future toward which everything that I have seen today is tending. The world's airports do not reflect the present, they are fantasy palaces stunning in their sameness and sterility, and they are fulfilling the aspirations of the people who most use them—the people I am watching tonight, the new tastemakers disseminating their vulgarities into the most isolated and poverty-stricken areas of the world. It is my two children who have made me see this tinseled show in moral terms; an awful realization hits me: I have stumbled into the future, into that world that Moncho and Martita are going to have to live in.

Knowing this now, a weird and frightening thing begins to happen in the most private parts of my body. Just as over Berlin and flying through meadows of spent flak, the body in its terror repudiated the reality of the moment and the testicles would rush into one's body, and the penis would shrivel, and the sphincter would come unhinged, out of pity and terror for the children, these same things happen again. Obscenity is now defined in purely physiological terms. I get up quickly and go into the men's toilet.

I have lived too long with poor people to sit now in the middle of all this jewelery and the electronic crapola and the whores and the gangsters who want to own it, eating overpriced food, listening for eight hours straight to Muzak's plastic masturbatory music not to feel a profound disorientation. I have seen that smile of total joy when a poor man is offered bread; women weeping because someone has loaned them the five dollars they need to take their dying child to a doctor. I have seen people react with happiness at the thought of owning the very simplest of things: a piece of rope, a pot, a fishhook: have walked through villages of fifty houses where the most valuable thing was a fifteen-dollar radio.

How can those little children of Ramón's thread their way through this new flood of vulgarities that is about to engulf them without losing the way, without becoming infected by this future of instant gratifications and easy, false solutions? Maybe Moncho can; he is a pure kid who sees into the heart of things, but Martita is a little girl and with the bad taste of the young is easily captivated by sleazy things that glitter.

We are sitting out here under a night sky; the music is playing, all the lights are on, the planes come and go, everything but the toilets is pulsing and throbbing. Surrounding us are the black pastures of Bogotá and dimly lit farm houses, and suddenly the airport becomes a fort under siege.

A spiky-haired blond guy has been moving closer. Twisting his head while pretending to scratch his neck he has read the title of my book and discovers that he has a friend in this crowd of South Americans. He sits down one seat away from me, looks into my face in a brotherly way, smiles, and says, "Hi there. Have you found Jesus?"

I sit and stare at him with my mouth open, unable for a second to make a sound. So he's a gangster too; pimping for Jesus. Ecuador is full of guys like this, and many of them have asked me the same question, and so I am ready. "Why shit, Sam, *found*? I didn't even know he was lost." My answer doesn't faze him; he looks at me, giggling. "That was the one thing I should have guessed," I say finally. "You're a missionary, right? You're going to Manaus and the brothers will meet you in a speed boat, right? You're going up the river and save souls for Jesus? Right?"

"Yes, yes," Spiky-hair says. "You're very observant. This is my first trip out. I got the call, my marching orders, God's voice telling me to save the heathen, a clear voice, just as clear as yours. Go out and bring me in my sheep. Ten points for every soul."

"God said *that*?"

"Well, you know, in a manner of speaking." My face must seem angry and incredulous to him; he begins to giggle again.

"If you get ten points for an Injun soul, how much is the soul worth of a good red-blooded American?"

"We're all equal in the sight of God. Still, I think someone like you who is clearly in the grip of Satan might be worth a little extra. And excuse me for saying it; no offense meant."

"That's O.K. And I don't mean to be offensive either, but let's not talk about God. Missionaries just depress the shit out of me."

There is a very long silence as we search for common ground, and just before the silence becomes unbearable, "Used to be one of my favorite writers when I was a boy," the missionary says, tenderly patting the Anthony Burgess lying on the seat between us. "What an imagination."

"Yes," I say, warming to him now. "What a great writer. The way he loves words, the way he builds scenes."

"*The End of Enderby*," the missionary says thoughtfully, thinking back. "Is that the last one, where the kingdom falls, where that other planet crashes into Mars?"

"Maybe you're thinking of another Burgess," I suggest, remembering another writer of animal stories that had enchanted me when *I* was young. "Papa Skunk? Reddy Fox? Reginald Racoon?"

"His Tarzan books were the best; then he went on that interplanetary kick."

Ah yes, I think. Edgar Rice Burgess. He was one of my favorites, too. There is another long silence as we both swing through the trees. And then he asks, "You going all the way?"

"All the way to where?"

He looks at me and giggles, but he gets up and starts to move away. "You're right, all the way to where? That's good. Well, wherever where is, have a good trip, you hear?"

"You, too. Be careful out there; don't get your head shrunk."

"Oh, no, that's gone out of style; we've taught them not to do that anymore."

"Don't you believe it. I just happen to know of a Catholic priest on the Napo who collects missionary heads like coyote pelts. He's got hundreds. You can just bet he's working with secret Vatican funds."

"You must be kidding," the missionary says, beginning to look thoughtful.

"Not a bit. On the Napo. Three hundred dollars a head, but he'll pay up to six hundred if they let him pick out the ones he wants."

"Good heavens, you must be kidding," he says. And then, "Oh, them doggone Cat Lickers; you know I wouldn't put it past them."

"Listen, if you want to be a really first class specimen I'd let my hair grow out another few inches."

"Oh goodness," he says moving off, "you must be kidding." His face is troubled, but looking out past the booths of digital watches, the Betamaxes, and the economy-size bottles of cologne, it suddenly clears. Two blonde spiky-haired types have just entered the room carrying bags and briefcases. The missionary smiles and rushes toward them. "Hi, Jesus lovers," he calls. Watching them as they talk together I am reminded of a horror film — Invasion of the Body Snatchers.

And remember with affection the friend of a friend of mine. He worked for the Texaco Oil Company in the Amazonian jungles of Ecuador, and on weekends with nothing to do would dress up in the dark serge suit, the white shirt, and the dark tie of a Mormon missionary; he carried the missionary's briefcase, he emptied his face of reason, his black oxfords were highly polished. He would burst into the drinking places of small villages and pounding on the bar, begin to yell. "Hey, goddamn it, bring out the bottles; where the goddam hell are the women? What the hell kind of a goddam stinking joint *is* this?" He must have been a good man combating as faithfully as he did the missionary menace.

·　　　　·　　　　·

Sometime in the early morning hours, flying at 35,000 feet, the plane rises on an upsurge of hot jungle air; it is a kind of celebration, a kind of liberation. We are now leaving the sad, corrupt, Colombian mountains and sliding down over the flat endless jungles that drain into the Amazon. It is only my need to put a period to the end of a long day that has made me see being tossed into the air as a joyful thing. But it is a joyful feeling totally unlike the whump of flak breaking against the wings, and jolted fully awake I press to the window and the enormous blackness outside. Nothing, nothing, not a glimmer of light. A huge blackness. We are an hour out of Bogotá perhaps; on the map we are descending over the Rio Negro to Manaus where the waters of two rivers meet but will not mix – the yellow flood of the Amazon and the Negro, the color of Coca-Cola. Out of these black waters have developed those species of bright-colored, fluorescently glowing fishlets with stop signs, flashing beacons, warning stripes, and danger signals painted across their bodies that brighten the aquariums of the world.

Abruptly awakened I suddenly find it absolutely incredible to be sitting in the darkened cabin of this plane surrounded by sleeping people and flying across an empty continent. Apparently the pilot (let us hope) and I are the only two people in South America who are fully awake. Manaus, the river Negro, the rivers Amazon, Tabatinga, Jari, all the old magic of these names comes awake, and I sit at the window, thinking of where we are and scarcely believing it.

We are flying over an immense, an oceanic land, the world's last mysterious and only half-tamed area. It is a staggering endlessness of looping rivers, islands that appear and disappear in a day, savannas, lakes and swamps, gently rolling jungle or jungle as flat as a pool table, flooded, hostile to man, stretching away to the horizon. And as we pass over it *at this very instant,* unbelievable and horrifying things are happening. We are flying over the diamond and the gold hunters, those obsessed wanderers sleeping under thatched lean-tos or in the open on river sand bars or in dark huts without windows and without air, isolated against the menace of the night. Government officials, missionaries, anthropologists, colonists, and the captains of riverboats – they all want something from the Indians; they can't keep their hands off the Indians. Some of them are sweating and sleepless, some of them have malaria and are afraid – contemplating their isolation, the chances they took, the way the luck changed. Over a black lake the clouds are parting and starlight will shine over the silent mirror of the waters. Perhaps it is a lake without a name, perhaps it is as large as Belgium. *At this very instant* a jaguar is dropping down upon the sleeping body of an animal, a man; thirty-foot boas are slowly moving in their thousands through the branches of a thousand trees. In a certain place, in a hundred certain places, the rivers are boiling as schools of piranhas tear at something dying in the water, and in certain places ten miles square, down there somewhere where the leaves of trees hang as motionless as death, the cry of a night bird is the only sound in that profound stillness; the only sound except for that plane up there above the clouds rushing through the night.

And I am stuck there at the window rushing back into my childhood, a little boy again, searching downward for a lit candle or the glimmer of starlight on a river or even a darker blackness below the clouds and amazed at how the past has come surging back out of that unilluminated blackness. Blind, I know exactly what we are passing – the slow curling rivers looping back upon themselves; the green of the land spotted with crimson and yellow blossomed trees and as tightly textured as my grandmother's petit point; the mile-high granite upthrusts of bare, black rock pushing up through the trees; and scattered through the endless spaces small hidden gatherings of open-sided, palm-thatched huts. For many hours, since the courtesans of Bogotá had enflamed my imagination with their long, slim legs my thoughts have crept around the edges of sexual and moral concepts. Now once more I begin to see this invisible land below me as I had imagined it many years ago. At thirteen, bursting with the lusts of puberty, my sexual fantasies had transported me to South America. It was on the Amazon where I had imagined that one would find the ultimate barbarity, some utter shamelessness, some wild and wonderful freedom where, if I ever went there, I would be able to test the extents of my cowardice and the extreme limits of my capacity to live at the edges of perverse behavior. What these limits were I couldn't imagine, but believing my parents, who characterized me as a despicable lad (I was continually being caught in drain pipes and broom closets playing doctor with friends and cousins of either sex), I suspected that my potential might lie out there a thousand miles in the heart of unspeakable territory.

Those unspeakable practices out of my imagination and out of my boyhood, so buried and confusing that I hardly dared consider them, or when I did, set me to lusting or shuddering with revulsion, they seem rather boring now. They were morbid and exhausting exercises in the cultivation of a self-loathing that would match other despicable qualities that my father recognized in other nonsexual activities. My handwriting, for instance, a crabbed and spastic performance (it still is) used to drive my father into sustained tirades of carping invective that could only be regarded as being sane by being broadly interpreted. Still, I tended to feel that my handwriting betrayed the sexual maniac, and when he would order me to write in a notebook two thousand times, "One must write with the wrist instead of the fingers" (stealing the madness of someone named Palmer), I spent whole weeks of afternoons filling up the pages with my fingers and not only with little resentment but almost with a kind of enthusiasm, as though my father with his adult wisdom would cure me of my dirty thoughts. About this time, inspired by something I had read in Stekel or Havelock Ellis, I had engaged in something loathsome and chilling with a cantaloupe out of my grandmother's refrigerator. No wonder nobody could read my writing.

In my youth there were no real sins but sexual ones, and by the age of twelve I had already been damned for years to the fires of hell for being a super-enthusiastic masturbator. Still, even then I felt that there were more intense pleasures awaiting me than this lonely practice, which required such intense imagination. When my sexual meditations were involved with the Brazilian jungles, having little fuel to fire my erotic imaginings, I often put myself in a circle around a campfire with a hundred naked Indians. We sang Boy Scout songs waiting for the bright flames to die and then late, late at night (about ten) we would all engage in a contest to see who could masturbate the fastest. Several years later in my middle teens, when dusky nubile girls had begun to march across the landscape of my dreams, I would transport myself by astral travel to the banks of the Xingu. Several times a week I wiggled and heaved in a squirming, squealing mass of naked humanity where I hoped to achieve that cataclysmic one, that ultimate eternal orgasm that would cleanse me forever, that would leave me as not much more than a modest pool of pulsing sperm and a lifeless husk as empty and pure as the shed skin of a spring snake. It seemed to me then, and perhaps this illusion still lives dimly at the edges of my imagination, that the quality of an orgasm is determined by the number of people involved in bringing one to it.

Until my sophomore year in high school words like Brazil and Amazonia had been powerful aphrodisiacs; even now they held a certain exciting power.

The plane begins to descend a hundred miles out of Manaus. Manaus, another dirty, exciting word, that wild town of the wild rubber hunters, fantastic orgies, beautiful imported ladies of pleasure where, who? – Jenny Lind? Caruso? – sang heartbreaking songs to weeping men in the world's most improbably placed opera house (ugly, ugly). At last, Brazil is coming close. Almost ahead at ten o'clock the undiscovered bones of Fawcett and his son lie bleaching on a burned-over savanna; at eleven, four hundred miles away a few remaining tubercular Indians are being given gifts: sugar laced with arsenic, blankets dipped in a solution of diphtheria (government blankets, government sugar); at two o'clock, if you can believe it, those loving, buggering Indians of Schneebaum are out there loving and buggering; at three, up the river toward Ecuador, heads are being shrunk and the lips sewed shut, and the wizards of the Pastaza and the Marañón are quaffing *huayasca* and turning into leopards. Around us are the mourning ghosts of Bates and Wallace, who worked furiously but left unidentified another fifty thousand species of bugs and plants. And isn't there another ghost out there, a kid in khaki shorts and tennis shoes who peeks through the slats of palm fronds at humping bodies and manipulates himself to the rhythm of jungle bongos?

A glitter of lights toward the horizon, a string of lights that shapes a river's shore; a distant series of lightning flashes and then darkness again. Fifteen minutes later the jolt of a bad landing more Air France than Lufthansa, the taxiing, and the long relieved silence of another safe landing.

Thirty minutes in Manaus. Most of us disembark and walk through the airport building. It is new, but it is also three a.m. and few if any of us are moved to cries of enthusiasm for its clean, crisp architecture. How cold they keep it; like the Goose Bay terminal in Labrador—in January. I walk through the empty resounding halls and shiver. Through a window a little huddle of Jesus lovers can be seen waiting for luggage.

Across a barrier by the airport's main doors I stop and stare out through the large glass windows to the parking lot, cement highways, and acres of raw, red earth. It is my first glimpse of Brazil. We are now, taking a world view, in the very middle of that immense and spreading proliferation of demonic wildness at the very heart of the Amazon jungle—and it is all represented by one tree that stands at the edge of the parking lot passionately lit by a street light. It is a mango with large, tough, almost black leaves, and as I stand there staring at it, accepting this solitary tree and with my imagination filling in the cement areas with jungle, jungle cats, jungle sounds, a yawning taxi driver opens one of the doors. Into that chill building rushes a great warm, soft, languorous movement of tropical southern air that is simply amazing in its power to seduce. It is the sweet air of Brazil, the reality of Brazil that I had failed to reproduce when I constructed out of my passion those orgasmic landscapes of adolescence. Christ, I had got it all wrong. This air is all warm and sensuous innocence. As it rushes over me, instantly I am educated to the foolishness of having for a lifetime associated this land with my youthful erections.

I am filled with relief and delight, but below the delight lie other more complicated, less delightful realizations. In some very small but definite way I am changed in that moment as though a subtle realignment of my cells had taken place. That vague menace of being able to dabble in delight-ful sensuous adventures has faded away like drifting smoke before this great embrace of innocent air. But I fear the realization has come too late; I may have wasted my chances by accepting those banal fantasies for a harder, uglier reality that may have more truly reflected my own potential.

Standing in that swell of Brazilian air that welcomes and that promises sweetness and languor but no sin I am half-content to be freed from my illu-sions. I will not be tested in Brazil. I am an old man, and I have let all my chances slip away. No, I have been as incapable as every ex-Protestant lapsed middle-classer of living in the shadow of monumental vices or, caught up and fully alive at last, swirled around in the whirlwinds of wrenching passions. Like everyone, I have walked through life with timid steps trying to obey without respect its more-than-often stupid rules. People of the middle class, though I deny that this word describes me now, turned cowards by their possessions, do not live deeply. I can feel myself dropping into something that is very like a post-coitus triste but, not fair, not fair, without the compensatory spasm of coitus.

Most of my friends in Quito are, like me it seems, only half-alive. After dinner a week ago a group of us sat and played a game clockwise around the table — "The Worst Thing I Ever Did." (Kay trying to remember says completely seriously, "But I don't think I ever did anything bad.") By chance I had to confess first and, having played the game before, could tell without thinking back about a Halloween night when I was ten years old. A tiny white-haired woman had come to a door whose bell I had rung. She called into the darkness where I crouched, hiding, "Come on in boys and girls; I have cookies and ice cream for you." I had stood outside her vision and thrown an egg at her — heard it smash against her face — and rushed away wildly in horror and self-loathing. (Fifty-three years later I can still hear that dreadful sound; my flesh still crawls.)

Telling about this in a voice that trembled it had never occurred to me to mention instead an early afternoon in 1943 when I had led some groups of bombers to a now-forgotten German target where either three or thirty thousand people were reported to have been killed. I have truly forgotten both the target and the number of dead — out of guilt, I suppose, but more especially out of that constant terror that we all lived in during those months that left a tremendous blankness in our minds. When I stand before that old charlatan, God, am weighed on the scales, found wanting, and am hurled into hell's fires, it will not be those thousands of people that I killed, it will be that goddam egg.

The door in the airport opens again; another wave of incredibly soft air washes into the building. Now, in memory, I perfume it with the scent of *maracuyá*.

The old white-haired gentleman, his lungs filled with the air of childhood and feeling reasonably good considering the hour, walks more or less briskly back to his seat in the plane. A sleepy stewardess lays a blanket across his shoulders. Sitting there, trying to add it all up he does feel rather like a quite superfluous old man, a vaguely ridiculous figure who from now on will address young people with diffidence, not caring much but half-expecting to be ignored or gently mocked. It is the first time that he really knows that he has spent his life; his pockets are almost empty; there is no second chance. A good part of his real life from now on will surge up out of his memories.

PART TWO

Rio I

The international airport in Rio de Janeiro has been built on tidelands miles from the city; the fare by taxi is fifteen dollars, about what the average Brazilian worker makes in a week (about what I have budgeted for an entire day including tips and cigarettes). A Brazilian friend in Quito – Edgardo, a pleasantly half-goofy archaeologist whose passion is old bones, has told me how to beat the rap. He is even more close-fisted than I am. "Catch the airport bus to the Dumont airport; it's right in the center of the city. That will cost you about forty cents; then you hop a taxi to your hotel for about a dollar."

Outside the door I choose to leave by is the only bus on the whole length of the curving drive. Locked up and deserted but it says Dumont. I sit down by it on the sidewalk embracing my blue canvas bag, which, scarcely one day along on this trip, has begun to disintegrate; the zipper is pulling away from the canvas. Glancing into its guts I observe Joseph Conrad and Anthony Burgess engaged in a furious combat of disorderly pages. Edgardo's information is only partly correct: there is a bus for Dumont but it will not leave for another two hours. I don't know this, but it really doesn't matter; I am not going anyplace, and, as it turns out, that two hours on the sidewalk will be the happiest time that I spend in Rio. I will see nothing that disagrees with that sparkling city I have constructed in my imagination.

Ah, Rio at dawn. The air is as soft and as caressing as in Manaus; it seems to hold a profound and dreamlike quiet. Smells of the sea and tropical flowers hang in the air, and across an empty space hidden by elevated highways I invent the salt marshes and the deserted tidelands of the inner bay.

In the distance swelling black walls of solid granite push out of the sea. The sky is the most important thing; it is immense and glows with an incredible soft pinkness, and across it little naive pink clouds as harmless as newborn lambs wander, waiting for the sun. These are the sea-clouds that rise like mist out of very tranquil and sun-dazzled oceans. Why is the sky so beautiful, why this little pang of anguish? Of course; this is the sky of Esmeraldas, the sky above the farm, that sky of the doldrums with its promise that nothing will ever change—that lying sky that promised me that I would not grow old. What lovely pain in the purity of tropical dawns, in the softness and languor that wipes out the past.

Sprawled on the sidewalk like a skid-row wino, and as though I had drunk a bottle of Thunder Bird, as happy as one, I wait for the bus doors to open. I am very sleepy. I sleep in little bursts as the sky changes from tender pink to garish yellow and as the humming sound of a great city coming awake obliterates the silence. At seven thirty the bus driver and a dignified black lady who sells tickets invite me to go with them, but just as I am gathering myself together to make the change I glance down the walk to observe with shock and confusion the first of the ghosts who will walk near me in this great city. From out of the airport my father, ten years dead, emerges. Same face, same heavy shoulders, same massive chest, same short arms, the arms of a wrestler. My God, even his suitcase is the same; it is one of those heavy brown leather bags that went out of style when trains went out of style. He walks to the curb, hails a taxi, and without seeing me, drives past. Shaking my head to clear it I get up and climb into the bus; what, I wonder, is the ghost of that unhappy man doing here?

Now, like a stone thrown into a whirlpool I am dropped into the heart of Rio. The place jumps to an awful rhythm; cars and people rush through the streets. Noises (though car horns are forbidden), excremental smells, dust, blaring music, torn up avenues, whole torn up sections of town. Excavations, board walks, blocks of streets with leaky water pipes and the gutters gushing full; thousands of men in red and yellow plastic construction hats stand in hundreds of holes dug into the streets and fuss with a wild tangle of plastic piping and electric cable. Looking down into the holes is like observing open heart surgery. (The patient is not going to recover.) Rio, like New York or Chicago, like Calcutta or Paris, is plainly a city that no longer works very well, but observing the frenzy it looks as though they were trying to fix it in a single day.

It has been about forty years since I slept in a thirty-dollar-a-day hotel—if I ever did—and I am furious with the taxi driver who caught me at

Dumont and has brought me here pretending to be unable to understand my request for a ten-dollar room. I will sleep for a while and then go out and find another place. But first, and this may be my last chance, I am curious to know why certain beds are so expensive. A paper band stretched across the top of a dust-speckled drinking glass; a paper band across the toilet bowl with its proud printed message in three languages that I may put my ass in intimate contact with the seat without fear of contracting foul and incurable social diseases; the gush of bright orange water from the hot water tap and the orange stalactite that hangs like a runny nose from the shower head; the air conditioning that roars and shakes and chills; the classy oil painting above the bed, a drunken Vlaminck, white Paris houses, mud in the streets, one of three thousand ordered by the hotel to fill its rooms with beauty; a small refrigerator that holds two bottles of cola, two bottles of *guarana*, two cans of beer; a tray with miniature bottles of whiskey, vodka, gin, San Raphael along with chocolate bars, packages of strangely named cigarettes, cashews, and crunchy looking stuff that looks like sawdust. I am beginning to feel a new kind of emptiness in this tremendous city and fight the impulse to fill it with potato chips, soy bean meal disguised as something rare and tasty, and a slug of something jolting. Instead I take off my clothes, shower, and go to bed. In the street below the window Rio rocks and rolls, and I am rocked to sleep somewhat in the same manner as an Old Testament maiden caught in adultery.

In the early afternoon, refreshed but still jet-lagged and disoriented, I walk down into the streets. I head away from the wide avenues and the tall buildings into a modest barrio with tree-lined streets and low three-story buildings. They are shabby, tired, brave, painted in soft colors — rose, subtle greens like an organic stain, faded blues and yellows — roofed with blackened tiles that once were orange. Dates carved into their facades proclaim their indestructibility: 1903, 1898, 1912. The trees and the fronts of buildings from which chunks of plaster have begun to peel away absorb the street sounds. This is more like it.

For the next couple of hours I climb steep steps up to the second floors of a dozen hotels. Like some rural character out of a Faulkner novel, I am incredibly slow to realize that I am visiting the "hot pillow" hotels whose rooms are rented by the hour. Blue and red lights glow in dark hallways; mermaids, tigers, jungle sunsets, murals in fluorescent Day-Glo colors on the walls; piped-in music thickens the air. I have come to one of the barrios of Rio devoted to love. Though I walk down a dozen different hallways whose doors have been flung open to display the emptiness of the rooms, I am repeatedly told that the hotel is full, and I am not entirely unhappy about this for all the beds I glimpse are round. Kind hotel managers writing on little cards that will direct me to another place are also advertising their establishments on the flip side: "Hotel Flora and Fauna of the Amazon. Try our famous circular beds." "The Fine Arts Hotel. You won't be disappointed in our exquisite round beds with mattresses of foam rubber." I am not aroused; I have been vaccinated sixty-three times against this fever, and the beds look like the giant plastic hamburger buns of Oldenburg, unreal in the small airless rooms where the windows are hung with heavy dark drapes that hint sadly of lasciviousness and the one night pantings of uncontrollable lust. Walking past them I feel my scrotum tightening in a kind of confusion, an incipient impotence. What can you do on a round bed that you can't do on a square one? Spin? Tell time?

"It will be very difficult to get a room here if you are unaccompanied," an old man tells me, finally. I wander where he points – a busier street with stoplights and a rush of traffic, and five minutes later in a small hotel called something like "The Blood of the Good Jesus" I am offered three rooms: the most expensive facing the main street where the manager has to shout to be heard and the cheapest at the back of the building on the top floor with a big window that looks out over an artsy confusion of pink tile roofs loaded with horny pigeons. The room is reasonably quiet, with a washbowl I can pee into at midnight and a good square bed honestly aligned with the compass headings. The shower is almost next door; there is no soap, but there is toilet paper in the toilet-paper holder. Seven dollars a day.

Back at the Crystal Palace the manager is disinclined to believe the tenth-floor maid, who reports that I have left untouched that tray of booze and salted snacks. But he takes my money finally, and I stagger off down the street. Five blocks, ten, panting, pausing to rest. The blue bag doesn't like this move and has made itself awkward with new bumps and bulges; from time to time it lurches out of control and attacks people.

So here I am at six o'clock safely locked away, dizzyingly unaccompanied, gazing down at the tile roofs, the jutting brick chimneys, the fragile and peeling latticed doors of my neighbors. With the darkness the pigeons disappear into cross-shaped holes cut out for them in the brick walls below the rain gutters. The softness of the air has turned into pure nostalgia; the air and the trees are the only things connected to nature. I try to savor it in a solemn and personal way for it is only the air of Brazil that connects me to the past. The sun goes down. I stand at the window feeling the real beginnings of loneliness, or rather, feeling the beginnings of a desperation that I had anticipated and come looking for.

At seven I wander up a strange street looking for a restaurant; at eight I find one that serves something more than coffee, orange juice, and sandwiches. Sitting at an outside table I order what I think is a tossed Italian salad but am brought instead a small washbowl full of potato salad, five pounds of boiled and sliced potatoes lightly covered with oil and parsley. I eat what I can but concentrate on the beer, which is good and very cold. Inside the restaurant under large slow-moving fans the white tablecloths move; the lovely fans of another century.

When I push the still-almost-full bowl of salad away from me, immediately a Negro who has been standing against the wall and made invisible by some large potted plants appears by the next table and with the fierce power of his concentration impales me on his look. He stares into the bowl of salad, brings one hand to his mouth and implores me with the other hand, the palm up, open and vulnerable. He is about thirty years old and dressed in clean but tattered clothes; there is a fineness about the delicacy of his cheekbones that reminds me of Ramón. I offer him the salad; he takes it and sits at the next table, hunched over the food, eating rapidly. The waiter from whom I expect disapproval comes by the table and smiles at me, nodding. "Will you give him a beer, please?" But the Negro who has heard me, says, "Please, just a cola." We do not look at each other again for there is something unspeakable in that desperate hunger that lies between us like an accusation.

Walking in the street I consider with confusion that good feeling I had had at offering a hungry man my garbage.

There is a block-square plaza to cross on the way back to bed; it is pretty at night with a big statue in its center and black marble designs curling through the white marble pavement. Large shade trees stand at each end of the park in double rows.

A group of youths is leaning against benches or sitting on steps and smoking at one end of the plaza. At the same instant that I enter it three police cars as big as grocery vans park in the street by the youths and a dozen policemen herd them together and surround them. From a safe distance I watch identification papers being produced, apparently not one of them of any value. I would like to go closer where I could plainly see the faces of the cops to see if some quality or element of fascism would be evident in the movement of their eyes, the set of their jaws, or the kind of moustache they had selected to interpret themselves to the public, but I keep my distance. My passport and my money are hidden in the bottom of the suitcase; I am breaking the law by walking about without those pieces of paper that will prove that I am honorable and not a threat to the military, who rule the country. And if they wanted to take me in, no document in the world would spare me. From where I stand all I can see that they have in common is their slimness. The cops are as swift and slim as snakes. The young men, negligent and bored, acting as though this happened every night, some of them yawning and stretching their arms, are pushed into the cars and driven away. The whole thing takes about three minutes; it is like an unimportant scene from a horror movie, and I have the feeling that I am the only one who has even bothered to watch.

One hundred feet farther on a crowd has gathered around something of interest, and I push in to investigate. A short pot-bellied middle-aged black man with many gaps between his teeth and wearing a very narrow-brimmed straw hat is giving a performance. Shirtless and sweating he is sailing straw hats out into the air at a crazy slanting angle and trying to catch them when they return. He is a completely inept performer; when the hat does from time to time slide back along its trajectory he usually fails to catch it. Half the time the hat, wobbling erratically, falls to the ground ten feet in front of him; many of the hats become entangled in the lower branches of a *matapalo*, and small boys fetch them down with sticks. The crowd laughs at the man but in a friendly way, as though enchanted with his incompetence. Each time he tosses a hat out he lets out a sharp squeal; each time he misses he squeals again; they are identical squeals tuned to the deceptions of life, and the crowd seeing in him their own failures likes him better when he misses. I define him to myself as a brave and desperate man who, without talent but out of need, has taken to the streets to earn a few cruzeiros. How did the idea come to him? Is he a man easily led into hare-brained schemes? Within my definition of him he is too sad to watch. When he kneels on the ground and begins to mix inflammables together, I move away. As I leave he is lighting a torch and preparing to spray flames out of his mouth, but I am unwilling to see this poor devil fuck up and set his face and hair ablaze. He needs, whether he has it or not, six more months of hard practice. I would like to give him something, but don't know how and feel besides that it may be a sin to encourage him.

There is another crowd at the other end of the plaza. Just as I reach its edges and am trying to peer over the heads of the people, there is the sound of splintering wood and the wildly screaming voice of a furious man. A small slice of watermelon flying through the air slaps against my leg. The wet ploppy sound of the melon and the feel of it like a violation of privacy momentarily paralyze me. The crowd, as though it were being exploded, moves out into a much larger circle that now puts me toward the center of it, alone with a man who is in the process of losing his mind.

I am too startled to be frightened or to move away for a few seconds. It is too much like watching a newsreel of government troops firing point-blank into a crowd of civilians to be quite real; it is real though I am not quite part of the action. I stand there in amazement as the crowd scatters and the screaming man, beside himself, scoops up slices of watermelon, peeled and unpeeled grapefruit, and bunches of bananas and hurls them into the faces of the people. He is in violent motion, and I cannot recall any of his physical qualities though I seem to remember, impossibly, that his hair was standing on end. As he throws away his capital he is also kicking at anything lying upon the ground: two orange crates, a little pile of rags, a little plastic airplane bag, and a white enameled tray made from the top of an old freezer. When everything is dispersed except one crate, he stands still for a moment considering how he may further express those feelings that have not yet been discharged, and now with tremendous force with one bare foot he kicks violently at the orange crate, breaking out its bottom and entangling the rest around his leg. He flinches with pain and looks distractedly at his bloody toe as though he were amazed to discover that he was still capable of feeling, and then howling he rips away the box and throws the pieces at us.

When he takes a kitchen knife from a back pocket, the knife probably that he had used to peel the grapefruit, I move away quickly, watching the people now who are scattering into little groups. They have sad, bemused expressions on their faces; only one man in that whole crowd of a hundred laughs—a loud, gasping, frightened and uncertain laugh that says contemptuously but without conviction, "Not me, I am tougher than *that*."

The mad man rushes into the crowd, yelling curses, dancing, and waving his arms. As he leaves his territory a dozen small children, shrieking like birds, rush across the empty space and scoop up the grapefruit and the bananas.

Just across the street from the hotel, leaning close against a lamppost and facing toward a dark tree-covered side street, is a lighted candle, an open box full of matches, and, lying balanced across the matches, a large unlit cigar. In that dark street it looks exactly like a shrine—which is exactly what it is—a Macombo shrine reverently placed against one of life's curses.

The pink and orange walls, the pink tile roofs that shone from my window have sunk now into the pool of night, but looking out as I undress, looking out past this blackness below the sill, I see spread across my horizon some five or six blocks away a circle of some twenty square enormous buildings, most of them fully lighted. They hadn't been there two hours before. All night as I sleep off and on, the illuminated buildings glowing with a cold, blue, silent light sit out there like a wall putting limits across this poorer part of town. About four in the morning one by one the buildings go dark, and I sit at the window thinking of another time as one building, floor by floor, blinks off and blends into the night.

Trying to sleep, remembering the squeals and the screams and the imploring and unjudging look of the hungry man, I begin to remember back about ten years to that time when I first began to live under the weight of such things.

.   .   .

And another cry of rage is ringing in my ears, a screaming that I listened to one night, words shrieked out in a Spanish that I could understand.

In 1969 I had come back to Ecuador after four years in the Peace Corps to buy a farm with Ramón. I had been gone about ten months, some terrible things had happened, and I had returned to an Esmeraldas that had forever changed; the whole province had become politicized and it was as tense as a stretched wire.

To the north of town in a small jungle village near the sea, a village just a few miles from Rioverde where I had lived as a volunteer, two cops from my town who had been invited as guests had senselessly shot and killed a seventeen-year-old Negro kid at the town's big yearly fiesta. The people were maddened and one cop had his head cut off by a furious farmer swinging a machete; the other cop was badly cut up but managed to escape. Two days later a squad of police came out from Esmeraldas in a large motorized canoe; others arrived by horseback. They rounded up the people of that town very much as those kids had been rounded up in the Rio plaza, and they were subjected to the naked brutality of a rural police force that feels it can control the populace only with terror. I will skip the details for I am still unable to write sensibly about certain things that happened to people that I knew, but to hint at the quality of the things that went on in that town for the next few days, I will mention only that the leader of the town, the *teniente politico,* who was suspected of knowing where the murderer of the cop was hiding, was tied up outside his house and given glasses of hot horse piss to drink at frequent intervals. The news of these outrages spread over the province; it is the kind of thing that commonly happens in South American villages, the kind of thing that is never printed in the newspapers. The people in the village were blacks; the cops were imported *mestizos* from the sierra, and the racial implications were infuriatingly obvious.

Two weeks later and three days before I came back to Ecuador to buy a farm with Ramón, the body of a young Negro was found where it had been dumped on the garbage heap outside the city on the high slopes that fall toward the river past San Mateo. His naked body and his ripped testicles were tightly wrapped in barbed wire. Ramón's wife, Ester, had known the man. As a teen-ager he had been a petty thief, she said. He had been caught a couple of times by the police and even without their extreme methods of interrogation had confessed and been imprisoned. In his twenties he had decided to reform his life. He built a little kiosk on the street out of waste balsa chunks, and old corrugated iron, bought an electric juicer, and sold glasses of iced fruit juice. He was making it in a small way and among his neighbors had begun to live down his youthful reputation. When he was picked up by the police for the last time he had, unfortunately, nothing to confess. He was too stupid or too dazed to oblige the police by confessing what they needed to hear, and in their enthusiasm they killed him; it was probably a mistake.

When I drove down from Quito in our brand new pickup I met Ramón and he told me what was happening in the town; the place was getting ready to explode. It was very late, and the two of us drove out into a poor part of town where we had heard that someone lived who had a farm to sell. I waited in the pickup while Ramón went into the house to talk; and it was absolutely marvelous to be back and to be sitting once more in the sweet night air of the tropics. The usually vibrant streets were silent and deserted and it was strange not to hear music blaring out from all the shacks. After a time I began to hear a crowd of people moving up the street behind me, and ahead two blocks I could vaguely make out some kids piling old tires at the crossroad and setting them ablaze. On another street toward the center of town I could hear the shouts of another gathering crowd. I didn't particularly want to leave Ramón but felt it was dangerous to be parked on these streets that were filling with black smoke and the smell of burning rubber and the gathering crowds of yelling men, but just as I started to drive off Ramón appeared. "Get down to the parking lot at the hotel," he said. "The lot with the high walls. You can let me off anyplace, but you get off the streets, you hear. Go to your room and stay there; I'll see you tomorrow."

"Well, shit," I said, "you stay off the streets, too. Oh shit, Ramón, it looks like it's finally happening."

I was frightened but exhilarated. I had been only four years in the country but I had seen enough to hate the government and its timidities and inefficiencies, the corruption of the police, and the shameless way the people were raped by the ruling families. I hoped that it was finally happening, that the whole poisonous and feudal system that enslaved the country would come crashing down. I had always dimly felt that when the people of Ecuador would gather together to topple the ever-changing but identical regimes that kept them slaves, that the terror would begin among the wild free Negroes of the coast, those men of spontaneity, vengeance, and emotion. If in their ignorance and their passion they would be unable to construct a new and fairly decent social system, at least they were capable of burning down the old one.

"Is it finally going to happen now?" I asked Ramón, but he glared into the night without answering.

We turned the corner and met a crowd of people filling the street and marching toward us. "Oh shit," Ramón said, "pull way over to the curb." We sat there with the lights off and waited, the only car on the streets in the whole town, I think. The crowd came up to us and, splitting, flowed around us on both sides. I had imagined being engulfed by a crowd of older people with the intense, fanatic faces of revolutionaries; it even crossed my mind that as a foreigner this crowd might associate me with the crimes that had been committed against it. The sound of shattering windows, rocks crashing against the hood, the thought of being drowned in their spit or being beaten bloody by their fists lived in my imagination as a possibility. I was clutching the steering wheel to keep from trembling, and Ramón was fumbling beneath the seat for a tire iron or a jack handle. We were suddenly put into a situation over which we would have no control, like bodies about to plunge over a fall of water that could either throw us up unhurt along the lower banks or tear us to shreds. How I hated this bright new pickup in this moment. The situation was further complicated by my feelings for this mob; in a sense and on a theoretical level I shared their anger; if they had torn me to pieces, a couple of small shreds would have condoned the act.

But the faces were mostly high school students; some of them I even knew and many of them were friends of Ramón. They were kids between thirteen and seventeen. On both sides of the car they were sticking their heads through the windows to greet us. "Hey, Ramón, *compañero*, you better come with us; we're going up and burn the police building." "Hey, Martín, you came back. Remember me? Arturo from the Rina." "Ramón, your daddy came back; well, don't forget me when you're rich."

They passed us and the sound of their marching faded away.

"So. What do you think now?" Ramón asked. "Are those little kids going to bring down the government?"

"Well, they did it last year in Quito," I said. "The students and the truck drivers."

"Yes, and are we any better off now?" Behind us there was the sound of shots and dull explosions, and Ramón said, "Let me off here. The army has arrived. And you head for the hotel. Fast."

By the time I had parked the car the biting stink of tear gas hung in the air. A block and a half away at police headquarters the cross-street was blocked off by parked police cars and twenty to thirty cops with machine guns. I stood on a far corner for a minute and watched a crowd of kids approaching from one direction and heard the yells of another group coming up another street. Both groups halted about half a block away from the police building in the face of the cool and arrogant contempt of the police, who sat in the cars smoking cigarettes or stood on the roofs of buildings negligently watching the youngsters. From the army headquarters south of town, army trucks had arrived and were now moving very fast up the deserted back streets. There were sounds of gunfire both from the north and south of the city's center.

There were still a very few people on the main street, and as I approached the hotel I watched two black kids ahead of me snatch up a large bolt of dress material from a storefront and go rushing away down the street swinging knives before them and yelling. They disappeared down a side street toward the river, toward that poorest part of town, an island called on the maps at low tide Isla de Piedad where the houses were built on high stilts and surrounded by water at high tide, that part of town called by the people *Mire-culo*, "look at the ass," because there were no toilets in that whole section and the people had to shit on the river's bank just off the main street, the malecon.

I stood in the doorway for a few minutes and watched the steel shutters in all the shops coming down; the hollow popping of tear gas cannisters had begun up by the police headquarters. The sweet tropical air of Esmeraldas had turned obscene and poisonous.

Suddenly there was a concentrated burst of rifle fire from the direction of police headquarters, a great sigh of despair from many mouths mixed with a few panic-stricken and childish screams, and a minute or two later a strong overwhelming wave of gas. The owner of the hotel appeared in the doorway and when he saw me cried, "Señor, what in God's name are you doing out here?" and pulled me inside. (Later, thinking of how he had grabbed me, I remembered being jerked off the streets of London twenty-five years before as I stood on the sidewalk under a rain of metal fragments and spent flak cartridges in the last of the German air raids, and the rage of the warden who had discovered me there watching it all in my innocent ignorance.) I stood in the hotel lobby, my eyes weeping from the gas, and the hotel owner with a dampened handkerchief held over his face darted out into the street and brought the iron shutters clashing down.

For a few minutes it was quiet. "Order has now been restored," the hotel owner said, his face pale. "The bastards said they would do it with guns if they had to, but who could have believed that they weren't just talking tough? Those are our children out there; how do they dare?"

It is strange that I have never been able to remember anything about the room I slept in that night; there is usually not much to remember about hotel rooms where you sleep alone except your relationship with the window, but I cannot remember that room as having had a window. My memory tells me that I spent that night in a tightly shut steel box.

Scattered firing went on in the streets for at least an hour; army trucks roamed up and down; how clearly I heard it in that closed-in prison of a room. Finally, it was silent—no gunfire, no trucks, no tear-gas cannisters, no cars, no human voices. But I was fully awake and perhaps as fully awake as I had ever been in that town. I had come back to a place that I thought I knew, to discover that either I had never understood it or that it had completely changed and that that tranquil coastal town throbbing at night to the beat of music and through whose streets one wandered, caught up in lust for the slim, proud black girls and made vulnerable and passionate by the softness of the night air as clinging as black arms, was now a town that boiled with repugnances and rage. It had always been that way, of course, but the rage had always been secret and disguised as resignation. And tomorrow it would be disguised as resignation again for the town had lost; it had been overwhelmed by the power of guns and by the determination of the military to ruthlessly terrorize the people in the first beginnings of their revolt.

I was still wide awake at twelve o'clock when out of that late midnight silence that had gone unbroken for more than an hour a man began to scream. It is this scream that I remember as I sit in Rio and watch the buildings putting out their lights. How it resounded in that tightly closed room in Esmeraldas, how it resounded, that cry that is still echoing ten years later in another country. "Bread, you sons of bitches. Work, you sons of bitches. Ay, ay, ay. Not justice. Fuck justice. Just work so I can feed my children." I lay in bed listening to the man with the tears streaming down my face.

An hour later, half asleep at last, that screaming man became entangled with my perceptions of Ramón. They became identical; Ramón was a poor man without power, education, or influence; he could never make it in this country of poverty without some outside help. In an unexpected way those midnight screams had helped me to see that I would be engaged in a worthwhile thing to work with Ramón, to help him reach his full potential. In my sleep I determined that I would never let him down.

The next morning Ramón came by the hotel, we had breakfast, and drove twenty-five miles out of town to a farm that was for sale. We drove out every day for ten days more and stood on the bank of the river and dreamed about buying that piece of ground – and finally did. That naive idea that I had brought back with me to Ecuador, that we would find a place of innocence and simplicity where we might build an authentic life out of the spare essentials, had been pretty much shattered. We were buying a farm in a land cut every which way by hidden faults of rage, frustration, and contention, a land under terrible pressures that heaved and trembled with potentialities for violence and destruction. We settled down in that war zone, our senses awakened to its dangers and its impermanence, made more aware than ever before by the realization that we were living on the lip of change and that tomorrow it might all be swept away by the loveliness of simple things: leaves, sunlight, the flow of water, the harsh, brutal simplicities of poor lives.

Three days after that violent night in which one or two students were shot, my body in its own unique way informed me that I had experienced a devastating trauma. I have come very gradually to recognize the delayed physical symptoms of events that shake my soul. I have always reacted the same way to those big things in life that fill me with fear and make me wonder if I have stepped into a situation that I can't handle: the skin peels off my body. It is as if by suppressing certain emotions and dulling my true feelings, fevers occur that boil away my flesh. A half-dozen combat missions over Germany each left me as peeling and flakey as though I had spent twelve hours under a desert sun. All through my honeymoon I peeled, and peeled again, and when I went broke in California I had left the farm as red and raw as a lightly basted Chihuahua.

.   .   .

At six a.m. I come awake in Rio, brought back to the present by the local pigeons who are hurling themselves off the edges of buildings and clapping their wings together as they soar heavily away to cadge breakfast; they sound like dish towels drying on a line and whipping in a strong wind. The pink and orange brick walls of yesterday are purple in the shadows, and yellow where the sun is gaining its first foothold on the walls. The encircling skyscrapers of light on the horizon have gone away.

I lie naked under the flow of morning air and look at myself reflected in a six-foot mirror at the foot of the bed. It has been a long time since I have studied myself so carefully and with such horror. It is all there, the things I had suspected but not thought much about—the sagging stomach, my ass flabby with grossness, my shriveled sex, a timid rosebud peeking out through tired pubic hair. How cruel my mouth looks with most of my teeth sitting over there in a glass of water. It has been a year since I left the farm where I didn't even own a mirror; in Quito under a dim light I could make out that face that needed shaving; I am looking at myself for almost the first time in ten years, and can see at last that I had been truly broken by that time in the jungle and that old age, when it came, came as swiftly as a street bully who with blows and blunt instruments shatters a man in a moment. This is what Ramón had seen when he told me that I must leave the farm. Well, well, no wonder. I have been betrayed by my gross body, this aging stranger who lies staring at me so resentfully and which in no way is a reflection of how I see myself. "There he is, your double; why can't you be friends with him?" It is an idea instantly repudiated.

It is only that wrinkled and exhausted-looking rosebud, hinting at impotence and withdrawal, that I accept as truly indicative of the psychic blows that I have suffered since leaving Quito two days ago. I have been wounded, perhaps permanently by moving too quickly from the primitive corruptions of feudal Ecuador to the monumental corruptions of the more modern world. Still inside that old man's body, which is hardly mine and which I must reject, I feel a little teen-age glow of curiosity and anticipation; it is too dimly felt to have a center or an object yet. How stupid of my partner to have seen only the white patchy hair. I will not be destroyed by a fucked-up world; it is the pigeons who send me this message. Their clapping, which

sounds now like a bunch of trained circus seals slapping their flippers together as they honk with delight, sounds like applause, sounds as though
they were applauding *me*. As well they might. I have survived another day.

In the next couple of weeks what I have long suspected forms itself into
the kind of a theory that a tourist might usefully use as a traveler's guide:
famous sites seen by too many eyes are robbed little by little of their power
to excite or dazzle; each pair of eyes has taken something away. Public
things are diminished by lying helpless under the public gaze.

With H. Stern's free map of Rio, a map as simplified as a first-grade ex-
planation of Darwin's theory of natural selection, I go out into the streets. I
am looking for beautiful views, sweeping landscapes, sandy curving
beaches, jutting black granite upthrusts, mountains with tremendous
statues of Jesus on top—all of the famous things that were the unseen but
deeply felt background for Fred Astaire and Ginger Rogers when they
danced to glory in the Rio penthouses. I have got to justify this trip by some
quickening of the blood.

Heading by foot for Copacabana I end up five hours later in the Santa
Teresa district, a barrio of high cement apartment houses surrounded by
steep jutting hills. Half-dead, my feet aching from ten miles of cement, I
limp back to the hotel determined to try again the next day. Somehow I
have veered off course by about ninety degrees, though I have seen Jesus
from many different angles (yet always with his back to me). The next
morning at a slower pace and bearing left I get as far as Botafogo before my
way is blocked by hills and dead-end streets—and exhaustion. The out-
standing feature of the Botafogo district is its many high cement apartment
houses. I walk back to the hotel stopping from time to time to drink beer
and arrive late in the afternoon weaving drunkenly.

On the third day, spotting a bus that says Copacabana, I whip out past
the modern art museum, the war memorial, the yacht club, the sweep of
the harbor, Sugar Loaf, and find myself standing on the Copacabana beach,
a perfect curve of sand upon which timid breakers—exhausted as though
they had been worn away to little slapping lake waves by the postcard
cameras—slap. Behind the beach a mile or so of high cement apartment
houses. This is supposed to be that spot where there are more people to the
square inch than any other place on earth. But this morning the beach is almost deserted except for some youths tossing a ball and a handful of very
old, very red and paunchy men, their chests white with tangled hair, jog-
ging and gasping at the water's edge. Apparently everyone is still in his
cubicle being dense.

Over everything is the light mist that rises from the sea and softens detail, the light of nostalgia, that golden patina that suffuses the paintings of Rembrandt and that Spengler says is a symptom of this age's final plunge into decadence. Above me, facing me at last, Jesus looks down, Jesus in the form of a cross as crude as two crossed sticks of wood. It is all very nice but it looks more intense on the postcards with their brighter, cleaner colors and with the panting old men replaced by the bare asses of coffee-skinned Cariocas. I look and look but there are no bare asses on that whole stretch of almost-deserted beach. Well, I have seen Copacabana; we are not amused.

Back in town I decide to look at some of Brazil's art, but the Museum of Modern Art has been given over to the gringos: twenty or so Rauschenbergs made of stenciled cement sacks and fragments of torn paper boxes that make my old man's blood boil with apathy, and the traveling Raoul Dufy show sponsored by the French government that I have already seen in Quito. But the Dufys are marvelous and I go in to see them again – and to decide that in the strangeness of Brazil and in that spacious museum they are twice as beautiful as they had ever been in Quito's Banco Central. Those pure blues and greens; how they glow in Rio's light. Belas Artes, the more conventional museum on Rio Branco, is closed for cleaning; the place must have been filthy for it is still closed ten days later.

In less than a day I have done my duty as a tourist and am now confronted with the problem of time. My curiosity is too easily satisfied – or rather I have learned that the fascination of a strange place is centered in its people rather than in its views and monuments. Great bronze statues of generals on horses bore the shit out of me, and when they are placed in the middle of an avenue where they cause traffic jams and sudden death I am led only to consider for the thousandth time certain Latin irrationalities.

Because I speak no Portuguese and have chosen to move through those parts of the city where tourists do not go, I find after a few days of not speaking that I have begun to doubt my own existence. To be pushed and knocked about on the street becomes a pleasure; it is a proof that I take up space, that I am as solid as that lamppost, that I am one unit in a mob. It is a revelation to realize that so much of us is what is reflected in another's eyes, that our reality when we are unhinged from the normal interests or habits or passions that make up our life is made up in large part simply by how we are perceived by others. But how strange that this was not true on the new farm, that second farm that Ramón and I bought and where I went to live alone and where for days at a time I spoke to no one. There is an aloneness in a big city that is quite distinct from that solitude in a jungle where you are always more or less connected to the world by your contact with natural things.

I wander in the streets trying to avoid those sections of town where big office buildings ape New York. I look for streets with rows of trees to walk under, searching for green things. I visit the botanical garden and the zoo (almost breaking down when I find two little California quail penned up in a small cage half-full of their own shit. How delicate and vulnerable they look isolated from the condors and the hawks). I sit on park benches and watch funny red-haired Brazilian animals, half-squirrel, half-rat, as they lope and sniff. I spend an hour enjoying a mother cat who appears out of the black labyrinth of a matapalo with two kittens as wary as though they lived in a real jungle.

Sometimes, driven to make an effort that is against my inclinations, my sense of propriety, I will smile at passing strangers, trying to involve them with a desperate, whorish look to look back and acknowledge my existence. But their faces are preoccupied; they look through me as though I were transparent or as though I were some old and superfluous derelict about to put the bite on them for a cup of coffee. Still, at odd times when I am walking, people will stop me and ask directions; I am never prepared for this momentary involvement with humanity, and stunned, I usually stare back into their faces, making idiot sounds, sharing their lostness. Or I would manage to say apologetically, "*Yo no falo Português.*" A couple of times, laughing, not believing me, I was told, "But you *are* speaking Portuguese," and patted and squeezed, I would smile back. A real love affair.

Unlike Paul Theroux, despair does not make me hungry. On the contrary, as the days pass, deciding to go out and eat becomes more and more complicated. The truth is that I am not especially seduced by Brazilian cooking, and my Portuguese is so crude that apparently everything I say sounds as though I were ordering potato salad. Another reason for my anorexia is this: the kitchen of an Italian restaurant is directly below my fourth-floor window, and at seven a.m. when the day's spaghetti sauce is being prepared, the absolutely overwhelming aroma of chopped garlic comes crashing and booming into my room with all the subtlety of a fat Neopolitan mamita swinging a rolling pin. It is not that I dislike the smell of garlic, a most civilized perfume, but in this case it is so strong that one can almost see it. It burns my nose and throat as I stand in the doorway beginning to weep. Breathing the air in my room is like eating a hearty meal; more menacing, breathing that air I feel as though I am simply one of the ingredients in a complicated recipe in which all of us in the building are involved. At any moment, I will be asked to descend and offer myself up in bits and pieces to the day's spaghetti lovers. Before I leave the city I will have developed the nose of a Mississippi bloodhound and, lying in bed at night, will identify every plate that is being carried out into the dining area. Out of my loneliness toward the end I even feel that on those ropy vapors from below I have achieved a certain relationship with the Negro cook who sends these intense and choking messages up to me where I sit in my cell studying the pink tile roofs. On Saturdays I watch him climb a maizelike iron cage to a lower roof where he pulls the heavy cement lids from two cisterns and checks the week's water supply. Once he even looks at me as I hang from the window; I resist the urge to wave, to toss him cigarettes. I like his spaghetti.

Let me report in full my conversations in Rio; what will follow is practically everything that I say or is said to me during this time; if it seems painfully extensive try dividing it into fourteen days, and it probably comes out to fourteen thirty-second discussions. The cast of characters includes, beside myself, the owner of the hotel, the elevator man, a prostitute, and Orlando, an air-conditioning engineer from São Paulo, a guest in the hotel with whom I eat breakfast for a few mornings. After the first day I have begun to call the elevator operator Payaso, and while he seems to enjoy this name, it is not until almost the last day when I learn that this word, which in Spanish means clown, in Portuguese means something like the dead leaves cleaned out of a planting of bananas.

PAYASO: Is verrie goot, batatas fritas. Ha ha ha ha.
ME: Fried potatoes?
PAYASO: Sim, sim, sim, verrie goot, batatas fritas. Ha ha ha ha ha ha ha.
ME: ?
ME, to Orlando: Carmen Miranda? Villa-Lobos, Baden Powell? There's an awful lot of coffee in Brazil?
ORLANDO: You're speaking of the great ones. But we Brazilians have no memories. We think like this. (He holds up two fingers cutting time into one-inch pieces.) Miranda? Forgotten. Villa-Lobos? Nobody knows his music here. Baden Powell? He has left the country; he is not ours anymore.
ME: Pele?
ORLANDO: Yes, Pele; he has left us, too. We don't even get to drink our own coffee; it's graded into four qualities; the first three are all exported; we get to drink the shit. But, you know, it's a funny thing. A friend of mine

sneaked me out a pound of number one coffee; it was awful. We're so used to the shit, we prefer it.

M E, slapping the table and singing: Oh, there's an awful dearth of coffee in Brazil.

ORLANDO: Americans are funny. Now tell us a joke, a good American one.

ME: All right. Have you heard about the Arab who was so short that every time he farted he filled his boots with sand?

ORLANDO: The Arab? A short Arab? Sand?

ME: Yeah, see, a real short Arab. His ass was only inches from the sand.

ORLANDO: Sand? In his boots? Out in the desert? Down on the beach?

ME: More or less. (This is my joke, my gift to Brazil, and though I will tell it another half-dozen times I will never get a laugh.)

PAYASO: Batatas fritas, verrie goot, verrie goot. Ha ha ha ha ha.

ME: Jesus, what a Payaso.

PAYASO: Sim, sim. Payaso. Payaso com batatas fritas.

ORLANDO: I will tell you about our slavery; we are a people very easily brainwashed. We are a drugged people and no obstacle to the desires of the military. We like three things: *fútbol**, television, and Carnival.

ME: Yes, fútbol seems very political, though I don't understand just how.

ORLANDO: If we win the World Cup the government can pass a dozen more restrictive laws; no one will care; if we lose the World Cup, maybe they will let up on us a little.

ME: In other countries they say that the people are drugged with alcohol and sex.

ORLANDO: But of course. And the Catholic Church . . . and your terrible American music, that idiotic go-go disco music. We are a people easily seduced. While we were dancing to your beat the multinationals moved in; now our country belongs to Volkswagen, Phillips, U.S. Steel, Coca-Cola, Ford.

ME: Do you consider yourself an intellectual, one of the few people who knows these things?

ORLANDO: No, no. What I'm saying is common knowledge; Brazil is now owned by the United States. Everybody knows this.

ME: I've read that there are millions in your country who make less than twenty dollars a month, that there are millions of abandoned kids who live in the streets and steal and whore to live.

ORLANDO: All true, all true.

---

* *In South America soccer is called fútbol. – ED.*

M E: I've read someplace that Brazil is the only country in the world where people laugh while they're starving to death.

O R L A N D O, his face suddenly stricken with sadness: Is that what they say about us?

M E: You could call that an heroic quality. You know what Confucius say, If rape inevitable lie back and enjoy it.

O R L A N D O, staring out the window and after a long pause: Our history hasn't begun yet; you will see some ugly things one day, a people not laughing.

M A R I A D E L O U R D E S (almost all the whores and shop girls I talk to are named Maria de Lourdes): *Ola, caballero,* you *triste?* Come on, *triste,* we make fuckee-fuckee.

M E: *No falo Português pero comprendo* fuckee-fuckee.

M A R I A: Oh, Johnny, Oh, You *Yanki.* You gringo *Yanki.* Oh, you so beautiful.

M E: Yeah, uh huh.

M A R I A: Oh. *Johnny,* you Americano. My big lover he Americano. He come back some day. His name Johnny, too. He beautiful, too. You got cigarette?

M E: My name isn't Johnny, but I'll bet your name is Maria?

M A R I A: Sure, *claro,* my name Maria, Maria de Lourdes. Oh Johnny, come. Maria suck Johnny.

M E: Oh Jesus, Maria, at ten in the morning?

M A R I A: Ten o'clock, two o'clock, sunshine, moonshine. Is good. You come Hotel Concepcion; is not far. I make you verrie happie.

This conversation ends in hysterical laughter as I consider the name of the hotel, what she proposes to do, and on a bed that possibly isn't even round. I move away nervously as I tell her I'll see her later, that I like my hanky-panky in the dark.

H O T E L O W N E R: You from Quito, no? Is that the capital of Peru?

M E, deeply offended, though for most of my life if I had thought of Ecuador at all I had thought of it as being in Africa: No, goddam it, Quito is the capital of Ecuador.

P A Y A S O, who has been listening: Ecuador. Ecuador. Jesus, ha ha ha ha, who ever heard of Ecuador?

M E: *Mierda,* who ever heard of Puerto Alegre?

H . O .: What's it like your Ecuador?

M E: Beautiful, poor, screwed-up by stupid politicians. Like Brazil, no?

H . O .: Ah, Brazil. Every day of my life I thank God I'm Portuguese, not Brazilian.

M E: Well, isn't it the Portuguese who screwed up the country?

H. O.: Five hundred years ago we did it; now the Americans are doing it. You got more people in your embassy today than Pizarro had when he conquered the continent.

M A R I A: Charley, Charley, you bad man. I wait and wait; you no come back. You no like Maria?

M E: It's not that, Maria. It's my wife; she watches me closely, a very jealous woman.

M A R I A: Ah, Charley, you poor man. Well, I go. You give Maria cigarette. . . . No, naughty Charlie, you give Maria *two* cigarettes.

O R L A N D O: But of course the Americans own the country now; look at Ludwig, the best example. Imagine a secret forbidden country in the middle of Brazil bigger than Paraguay where Brazilians can't walk, with its own police. Owned by one man. My God, do you know what he's doing out there?

M E: Many people are terrified about what's happening in the Amazon. Is there this feeling in Brazil, that the world has reached some awful crisis, that maybe we're almost the last people in history?

O R L A N D O: You mean the bomb, the poison oceans?

M E: Yes, the whole thing, and now especially the destruction of the Amazon.

O R L A N D O, not speaking, lays his hand palm up before me and moves his thumb rapidly back and forth across his fingers.

M E: What's that, money?

O R L A N D O, nodding: Monee, monee. The whole world is committing suicide for monee.

These conversations when written down together seem highly tedious and banal, but spread over two weeks and interjected into the vast silences of my daily life they took on intense meaning, intense emotion. I imagined that I was reacting somewhat like some sheltered virgin in a nineteenth-century Spanish village who invents a whole fantasy life from a few plunked strings below her midnight window.

I ponder the words as I stroll through the streets or sit on park benches moving from bench to bench as the sun rearranges the park. I carry a pocketbook of Conrad's short novels with me now, but I cannot understand the words. I put the book away after a few minutes without being able to concentrate, confused by those balanced sentences. Conrad's stately preparatory pace does not mesh with the hysteria of Rio; it is like trying to pray on a roller coaster.

Staring vacantly into the passing crowds, suddenly without warning and with a little rush of joy, I recognize someone. Gloria from Esmeraldas is walking toward me – or some essence of Gloria. Maybe it is simply the way a woman has fixed her hair, or holds her head; perhaps, seen from behind it is simply the spreading tilt of her buttocks, tight in pants. Out of a dreamy emptiness I find myself watching Pedro or Tadeo, an old man with the sad wasted face of Plinio, a little girl with Martita's violently curling hair; Roldán, the super-macho leaning against a lamppost or staring with popped-out eyes at a passing girl. Ramón and Ester (it is miraculous to recognize two people at once) stand outside a restaurant while they stir the potato salad around in its bowl; and another time an angry Ramón jumps onto a moving bus and disappears before I can wave. They are all black people from the farm that walk the streets of Rio. The normal magnificence of black people makes white people too boring to contemplate. My eyes find no mystery in their pale skins, in the familiar symptoms of their disintegration or their mediocrity. They are as invisible to me for their color as I am to them for my age. And so many of the blancos are old; they look like first-generation European immigrants, their faces sullen with failure or disillusion. I do not want to look at old people and recognize myself.

Not wanting to see myself, I have pulled the wardrobe out from the wall at an angle so that in that room that is too small for two I will not have to awake to that naked old man in the next bed, nevertheless, I catch sight of a stern figure staring at me from the mirrors of storefronts. Amazed, I peer closely, for it is someone I scarcely recognize. I am not happy with this bag of flesh that so ineptly translates my qualities. No one, I decide, would want to talk to that old fart. Denying my own identity is a full-time job, and doing it I discover that I am full of myself – and bored. The days have to be filled, but how I hate having to think and think of how to fill them. I invent desires that I then find impossibly complicated to satisfy.

Sitting in a restaurant or on a park bench or in a movie house before the lights have dimmed, or standing, yawning, before some monument, suddenly for no reason a spotlight will snap on and illuminate me. Standing apart to one side I find myself watching as though I am a stranger – an aging man without purpose, moving through a strange city of millions, knowing no one and superfluous to the city's life, an old gent who has moved of his own free will into a situation that is pushing him to the edge of panic. He is comical, distasteful, ridiculous, and I feel exactly the kind of pity for him that I would feel for some actor in a play who has stupidly messed up his life and for whom I don't have much sympathy. What is more real than my situation is the cool detachment with which I watch myself. I am the most interesting thing going on in Rio, and even my boredom when observed clinically has a strange fascination. Still, while the whole thing swings between melodrama and comedy, I feel impelled to honor my emotions if I can honestly identify them.

In a sense I have manipulated myself into this isolation and have even sought it. I had refused the names of the friends of friends who had offered me introductions to "the best composer of protest music in Brazil" or "my sister, one of the very good engravers" or "the man who laid out the botanical gardens." I had come seeking loneliness for what I might learn from it and thought that having names to fall back on might delay or protect me from the full implications of the experience. I had figured that it would be like taking an Air Force survival course with bars of chocolate hidden in your pockets. I was, I hoped, like a man going into a surgery that would leave him, after a time of difficult recuperation, cured.

On about the fifth day in Rio I awake one morning to observe that all the skin has begun to peel from my body. I realize, and for the first time through this absolutely honest message that the body is sending me, that I am going through a monumental experience, as important as any in my life.

For a few days I pack around another little weight as I walk the streets of Rio. The sudden appearance of my father into my thoughts tends to confuse and complicate my perceptions of Brazil. There is a new connection here that I don't immediately make, which I am not really very interested in making. I have rejected almost all my past that is not involved with Ecuador and want to feel that my life only began to turn intense and interesting after I had decided in middle age to leave my country, to reject if I could my middle-class prejudices, and to be remade by confronting a strange and unfamiliar culture. I want to feel that if I am now facing a kind of crisis in my life that all its causes will be found in the immediate past. But something strange that I resist is coming to life. When I stroll through the more disreputable parts of town – the wharves, the cheap hotels, bars, and whorehouses across from the docks where the steamships lie, I have the funny feeling that I am somehow walking in the footsteps of my father, moving behind him on the rundown tree-shaded streets. I resent the arrival of this uninvited guest, there is nothing left for us to say, and I walk away from him when I spy him ahead of me sadly standing before a monument or coming out of a restaurant. In the day it is easy to channel my thoughts to other things when my father suddenly appears, brought back to life out of the most trivial scenes – a hamburger stand, a sailor's bar, a real estate agent's advertisement in a newspaper, but now for a couple of nights he stands before me as I sleep, vaguely menacing, vaguely pathetic, making promises that I know he will not keep. And in a final dream he is Pizarro riding across a plaza, sword in hand and slashing at the backs of Indians. That morning I awake with the connection made.

·   ·   ·

In the early 1900s, a dozen years before I was born, my grandfather, after a series of conferences with the infamous and now totally discredited dictator, Diaz, was awarded a concession in Mexico. Grandfather undertook to construct a railroad from Acapulco to an already-existing English line that terminated in Mexico City. He formed a company and called it the Mexican-Pacific. The Mexican government agreed to pay him one hundred thousand dollars a mile and would deed to him a strip of ground ten kilometers wide on each side of the completed line. He had built about ten miles when Zapata's guerrillas poured down out of the dry hills, politicized the railroad workers, blew up the tracks and the bridges, and began lying in wait for the paymasters who went in each Saturday with a line of mules loaded with silver Mexican pesos to the work camps. The laborers earned three dollars a week. My father, not yet twenty, had been one of the paymasters, and he, along with the English engineers and the superintendents, ran for it. Some of them got out of Mexico disguised as women, one as a priest. (This guy must have been a real dummy to have turned himself from a gringo into something that was even more despised, and maybe he was the one who didn't make it.) My father, who for months had been afraid to sleep in town and had gone each evening at sunset to a barge anchored in the middle of the Acapulco harbor, got passage on a small coastal steamer that took him to Los Angeles. He said that on this trip he ate stewed dog and that it wasn't bad.

It was the most exciting adventure of my father's life; it had been until 1930, when the banks went broke and family friends began jumping out the windows of high buildings, my grandfather's only business failure. Both of them for different reasons could never forget that place and on Fridays when we invariably ate at grandmother's house the talk at the table centered on that disaster. Stories about Zapata, the town plaza where every night until ten the girls with their chaperones would circle the outside perimeter in a clockwise direction and the boys, lifting their hats and bowing, would move against this magnificent flow; drunken knife fights in the *pulperías*, the police chief's beautiful daughter who languished with love for my horny nineteen-year-old dad. My grandfather's favorite story, though favorite is not perhaps quite the word, was about a week he had spent in London; he had seen what was coming and was within a day of selling the company to some English bankers for an enormous profit when the revolution broke. He woke up one morning with no buyers and nothing to sell. My *father's* favorite story, the point of which was to prove that Mexicans were lazy, inscrutable, and not too bright, concerned a pay raise that the company had ordered. The work had been going well, government soldiers had been sent in to keep the laborers in line, hundreds of women had moved into the camps and were cooking for the men. Grandfather decided to double their wages. "And you know what happened?" my father would always ask, beginning to laugh in an outraged and incredulous way as though twenty years later he still could not believe it and as though the laws of free enterprise by which he lived were shattering around him, "Instead of working six days a week those crazy greasers only showed up *three* days a week. There was nothing else to do; we cut their wages back to fifty cents and everything was hunky-dory. Ah, those guys, they could never see more than one day ahead."

By 1915, when I was born, the whole Mexican-Pacific business had been written off as a total loss. But in 1930 in the terrible beginnings of the world-wide economic crash that was trimming my grandfather's immense fortune down to a few modest millions, an amazing thing happened. The Mexican government wrote to say that they considered the Diaz contract valid and binding and that my grandfather was now owner of thousands of hectares—all the land at the outskirts of Acapulco, a six-mile strip of land along the coast, and all the flat agricultural lands north and inland from the town.

My grandfather, just two years away from the gallbladder operation that would kill him, formulated his last and most brilliant scheme. It was a pip, as my father would say. He would send agents to Germany, sign up hundreds of desperate and bankrupt farmers, transport them to the river valley on the Pacific coast, run off the few Mexican farmers who were squatting on his invaded land, and plant bananas and pineapples. He would be five days closer to the western American markets than United Fruit; his dream was, with the stolid, dependable, hard-working German farmers, to fight it out with United Fruit and bring that giant to its knees.

But in 1932 my grandfather died and this whole beautiful scheme, which each day became more dreamlike, was forgotten. His death coincided with the collapse of the banks. It was a great idea that had come too late for him and at a time when, whatever the merits of the plan, the banks would have been unable to help him. He was the only one in the family with true business genius – and he operated in those years when the west lay open and pristine in its abundance of wheat, fish, gold, and timber. He was irreplaceable, and after his death the function of the family was simply to try and save the remnants of his kingdom, a kingdom that collapsed around the heirs as though the whole intricate structure had been constructed of paper, as perhaps in part it had been.

Three or four days before my grandfather died I was sitting one morning in the dining room of his home eating breakfast when one of my aunts, still wearing a dressing gown and with little strips of plaster still stuck to her temples to keep her sagging face muscles firmer, walked silently into the pantry and began to use the phone. I was sixteen. I listened with some interest at first to her conversations; since she had chosen to make them from the pantry I knew they were supposed to be secret. What she was doing appalled me; that she was doing it in my presence appalled me more. A formidable woman engrossed in her public image might be excused for farting loud and clear in the presence of a two-year-old, but she would not cut loose in the presence of a teen-ager, and I felt as I listened to her now that she either held me in a kind of contempt or that she considered me a kind of co-conspirator. Her insensitivity in certain areas was monumental. I had known this before when, apparently incapable of realizing that she was deeply offending me, she would after lunch if the two of us were alone together, take out her false teeth, rinse them in her drinking glass, and slip them back into her mouth.

As I listened, pale and trembling in the face of her vulgarity and as the crack, snapple, and pop went out of my uneaten breakfast cereal, she called the three Seattle newspapers – the *Star*, the *Times*, and the *Post-Intelligencer* – and explained that since obituaries when written in haste to meet a deadline were often shoddy and incomplete and since her father would soon be going into a major surgery from which he might not recover, she felt it her duty to anticipate an unfortunate possibility and lay out the information that the family would wish to be included in those final honors to a pioneer and civic leader. She then read from a prepared and detailed list the companies that her father headed, the clubs to which he belonged, the honors he had received, the banks where he sat on the board of directors. She did not mention that he had run away from home at the age of twelve, the son of a Danish peasant too poor to feed his many children. This was a part of grandfather's saga that he loved to emphasize, but his daughters thought, since it hinted at common blood and shamefully humble beginnings, it gave to his immense wealth a vulgarity that stained and diminished their social pretensions.

As my aunt talked the maid came into the dining room and set a plate of something before me. Her cheeks were flushed with anger; like me she resented being allowed to witness something so outrageous and that by being performed in her presence made of her an object no more important than the stove or the sink. For a moment we avoided each other's eyes, then, since we were friends, we stared at each other, shaking our heads in disbelief.

It is very early morning of another day; I come out of my room and pause for just a second in the hallway; through a half-opened door I look at my grandfather as he lies in bed, an old man of eighty-one but still immensely impressive. The sheets are turned back and he is dressed in a heavy linen nightshirt, blindingly stiff and white. He has just finished making a telephone call and is hanging up the phone; in the hall, even here, I can smell the old-man smell of his piss. In another three hours he will be going to the hospital for an operation. He turns his head and we look at each other. "Good morning, grandfather." He nods his head slowly but does not speak; he is thinking of something else; in another twelve hours he will be dead.

After grandfather died the family lost interest in the Acapulco property. We were owners of all the land, the peninsula, which, curving, formed the northern boundary of the inside bay and the steep hillsides to the north that dropped into the ocean, but we had no idea of what to do with it. We weren't about to go out into the jungles and plant bananas.

A young German named Wolfgang Schoenborn showed up in Seattle one day. He made an interesting but ridiculous proposal to the family, which was, I believe, almost immediately accepted. A new partnership would be formed in which Wolf would have a half-interest. He would go to Acapulco, subdivide the land into lots, and turn the place into a summer resort for rich people, a tourist center for traveling Americans. We knew, of course, that he was insane and that his idea would come to nothing. Acapulco was much too far away over awful mountain roads; with luck perhaps ten tourists a month would suffer that journey to a hot, humid, squalid town. But what the hell, why not let him try; we had nothing to lose.

In the summer of 1935 during the vacation between my freshman and sophomore year, I had gone to Mexico. The family suggested that as long as I was there I might as well go down to Acapulco and see how that crazy

German was making out. I spent a month in Acapulco living on the beach in a small thatched hut just down a path from Wolf's almost identical shack. He had an Indian woman who came in each morning and made us breakfast; our other meals we ate in the town's only decent hotel, a little place on the rocks just out of town where, for fifty cents while you ate little swordfish with blue bones, Mexican kids would dive off a high cliff into wild water that surged and crashed against rocks. It was the simplest and most stylish life I ever lived until Ramón and I bought the farm some thirty-five years later.

But we were in the depths of the Depression; it didn't look like Wolf was going to make it. He had been there for a couple of years, had laid out a few roads that wandered through enormous bouldered country dry with cactus, alive with iguanas and rattlesnakes, those big coastal six-foot mothers. He was making a few sales to rich Mexicans and rich Americans and instead of bribe money was paying off the politicians with choice lots. While I was there the governor of the state of Guerrero had just begun demanding an enormous bribe in pesos; the politicians were moving in.

One morning Wolf and I drove across the peninsula to a little beach that was almost deserted. We swam and lay on the sand and then walked up to an outside bar under some palms. As we sat in the shade trying to become mildly drunk before lunch a Mexican kid about fourteen years old pulled a little rowboat into the water and idly paddled around in the clear water of this calm and enclosed bay. He was a boy, perhaps the very first of the Acapulco beach boys, who made a few pesos by rowing tourists around on little jaunts that had no destination. There was one odd thing about him: though he was dark and had the pure features of a Mexican, he was freckled and there was a wide strip of very blonde hair that ran all the way back from his forehead.

"Do you see that handsome boy down there?" Wolf asked me. "Does he remind you of anyone?"

"No," I said. "He looks stronger than most of the kids around here, but I'm not reminded of anyone."

"You should be," Wolf said. "He's your uncle."

While I listened Wolf then proceeded to give me the details of a love affair that my grandfather had had years before. He had tried to retire when he was seventy, had come to Acapulco on that trip that was supposed to sever him from the business world, had fallen in love. He had continued on with his trip for another ten days, but one morning, unable to bear a separation that was causing him such anguish, he had directed the captain of the ship to order him a seaplane. Somewhere off Cuba he had left the ship and flown back to Acapulco. One day Wolf even pointed out the woman with whom my grandfather had fallen in love. Her hair was graying now but in the loveliest way; she was the most beautiful woman I had ever seen. She was a pip, and she lived in a house that my grandfather had bought for her; one of the nicest houses in town.

A couple of months later back in Seattle I told my aunt the story about that kid in the rowboat – my uncle; her half-brother. I wanted to shock her, to crack open the facade of hypocrisy that enveloped the family in the brown drapes of German respectability. I was at that age when it seemed completely dishonest of us to pretend that we were a decent family when in truth we were a pack of individuals with extremely flawed and human qualities. And being descendants of the Danish bog men, carried around a few inhuman qualities, too. None of us had really known grandfather or wanted to. He had been that godlike figure of authority who completely dominated his children with the enormous sums of money that he kept dividing among them; he was that impeccably, darkly dressed old gentleman who presided at the head of those Friday night dinners. He wanted his family there on Friday nights, and by God they were there, the whole kaboodle, his children and their children, nobody really liking anybody else but kept in line by that forbidding figure who, like God himself, kept his family endlessly and placidly circling around him, little planets to his sun, little planets that had nothing in common except for that golden heat from the central star.

Ever since I had seen the woman that grandfather had loved, I had felt a new appreciation for him. I was proud that a man of seventy could still make a fool of himself, that he was still virile and lusting; I hoped that his capacity was contained in one of the genes that he might pass on to me. But mainly I admired his good taste. Assuming that he had had to buy that woman, I thought that he had done it in a princely way; he had paid through the nose for first-class merchandise, had done it with style, and had left her when the time came in a dignified way. I wanted to tell my aunt that, I wanted to say that grandfather had been a stylish guy and much more human and appealing than any of us had ever realized.

But the story I told did not seem to shock my aunt though she had listened to it with terrible attention, hardly breathing. Afterwards she studied me for a long time before she spoke, as though she were no longer quite sure if I were still that nonentity to whom she could confess to a new action so lacking in grace. Apparently I still was.

"I've never told anyone this," she said, finally. "About the day father died . . . you were there in the house with us, weren't you?"

"Yes," I said. "I was staying in the guest room just across from grandfather's room."

"He made a phone call that morning, very early, very early in the morning."

"Yes, yes," I said, suddenly remembering. "I came out just as he was hanging up the phone. I remember that it surprised me because it wasn't 7:30 yet."

". . . I was in bed," my aunt said. "And just by coincidence I had to make a call." She began to blush. (My aunt was a woman who was famous for listening in on phone calls, reading other people's mail, standing unseen behind half-closed doors.) "And I listened. He was talking to a woman, Father, speaking passionate words. He was speaking to a woman that he deeply loved. He was very frightened that day, you know. He would never have made that call from the house if he hadn't been frightened. . . . He was saying good-bye to her. He was telling her that she was being provided for."

"Who was it?" I asked. "Did you ever find out?"

"Some doxy, I suppose," my aunt said. "I never found out. But isn't it amazing? None of us ever knew; it never could have entered our minds."

"I'll bet she was no doxy," I said. "Grandfather was a classy gent; I'll bet she was a beauty."

My aunt was silent for a long time. "We were all in the room with him at the hospital," she said. "He said good-bye to mother, but he didn't say good-bye to *us*. He was afraid but not because he thought he might not see his children again. . . . And isn't it amazing that he would find on the street that affection that none of us ever gave him?"*

---

*AUTHOR'S NOTE. As usual (and I am still amazed about this), my aunt has pushed all the actors into the wings and is performing alone, center stage. She was that kind of a woman. Before I leave her and, by a vicus of recirculation, by swerve of shore and bend of bay get back to Brazil, I want to shamelessly interject this family riddle. It is our best family story, and though it has no apparent connection with anything in these pages, perhaps it lies at the base of those family eccentricities and confusions that so enraged me as a child.

When my grandfather first became rich, my aunt, who had been born on a Kansas wheat farm but was now inviting the Boeings to tea, decided that it would be appropriate to investigate the family roots; she was rather ashamed of my grandparents' German accents; she felt vague stirrings of noble blood surging through her veins and thought it likely that back there in another century there were things that we might claim—a royal emblem, a crest, some connection with ancient kings. She hired a genealogical expert in Europe who traveled to Tundern in Schleswig-Holstein and

That fall I went back to college, and sometime toward the end of the year or in the following spring my father on his way back to Seattle from a trip someplace stopped off for a night in Eugene, Oregon. He called me from his hotel. I went downtown and had dinner with him, and afterwards we went up to his room. He was coming down with a cold and went directly to bed. About seven thirty a couple of my friends who were curious to meet my father knocked on the door. They came in, my father offered them a drink of whiskey, which they refused, and the three of us sat on the floor at the foot of the bed and began to talk.

I need no trip to Brazil to help me remember what followed. Without realizing it, or realizing it dimly, I was about to offend my father in a way that he would never let me forget. Until he died some thirty-five years later, except for certain long stretches of time when he refused to communicate with me at all, he would bring up that evening at least twice a year. He needed no other evidence to prove that I had qualities that he detested and that damned me forever to his contempt.

A small room in a second-rate hotel. Brown wallpaper, heavy brown drapes. And there was my father lying in bed with a dozen little bottles of pills on the table beside him. He was having trouble breathing and sat propped up by pillows. Behind him an enema bag hung from a hook on the bathroom door, and his leather suitcase with his initials stamped in gold sat half-opened on the only chair. Now, writing this, I remember the names of my two friends – the Helgren brothers, two enormous, wholesome kids with flaming red cheeks. They were off a dairy farm in the Willamette Valley. Majoring, like me, in journalism, they wanted to be sportscasters.

I don't remember what we walked about until I began to talk about Acapulco. About sitting on the beach with Wolf, about the Mexican kid with the blonde hair and the freckles and how he paddled around in the

---

traced back the family history. Months later, the story goes, my aunt received (and let us hope that it came in an unmarked manila envelope) the family scoop. She had paid, the story goes, several thousand dollars for this information, and now after reading it she sat down and sent another large check to Europe to have the report destroyed. There was something in the family past that was impossible to reveal. She never spoke of it, never even admitted that she had tried to investigate our beginnings.

What was it? What could it have been? What lay back there in the past that was so hideous, that was so shameful that not even family members were allowed to know? It could only be one thing of course, but it took me years to figure it out. Were we descended from a line of horse thieves, traitors, degenerate Blue Beards? No. It was much worse than that; we were descended from Jews.

water in his little rowboat. "And do you know who it was, daddy?" I cried. "Do you know who it was? It was your half-*brother.*"

The Helgren brothers laughed, it was a marvelous story. One of them asked me how it felt to be twenty years old and have a fourteen-year-old uncle. My father said nothing; perhaps it was becoming a little more difficult to breath, though that was normal. He almost always had a little more trouble breathing after a few minutes of conversation with me. After a time he said what he always said when he felt absolutely helpless against the anger that was building within him, "Oh yeah? Oh yeah?"

I told about grandfather and the woman, the seaplane that he had hired, the house that he had bought. Father said in a very mild voice, for he was torn between the desire to hear no more and the desire to let me ramble on and give him the words that he could store up to later throw back in my face, "I know you want to be a writer and that it takes imagination, but you shouldn't invent crazy stuff about the family."

"But I'm not inventing," I said. "It's all true. If you don't believe me here's another story that you can check out." I told him about his sister listening in on the phone to grandfather's last conversation with that other woman. When I was through and the youthful laughter had died down, my father in a weak, mild voice said, "Oh yeah? Oh yeah?"

Soon afterwards the three of us went back to the campus, and I didn't see my father for many months. But a few days after he had left I got his letter. Two pages, single-spaced. It was incoherent with rage and because it was written out of red-hot fury that made his hands tremble, the typing was almost illegible. If I couldn't quite make it out, I was to understand it later for I heard the same thing repeated many many times and through all the years until his death received a small trunk load of almost identical letters.

Those goddam Commie college professors had sucked out my brains and they ought to take that whole bunch of red agitators out and shoot them. What in Christ's name were they doing corrupting the young and being paid by the taxpayers to do it? It was that Jew president Rosenfeld and he's no president of mine. I was a Commie. I was sick, sick, sick. I had no respect for the best system of government in the world. If it wasn't capital that created jobs, what was it? I had worms in my brain that made me hate people who had made a success of their lives and who had worked hard to better themselves. By God, those men on the breadlines – they could find work if they wanted to, but no, it's all gimme, gimme, gimme. I read books, Commie books written by spiteful, jealous men about the robber barons. I mocked the great Americans who with their intelligence had amassed great fortunes. Out of spite and jealousy I spit on the names of our greatest men, men like Henry Ford and Rockefeller. But I wasn't satisfied with that, no. *In front of perfect strangers* I had shamed my own grandfather, pissed on the memory of a great man. No doubt your grandfather was a robber baron, too, wasn't he? It was pure spite. I was a liar, a fucking Commie radical, a little rich-boy pip-squeak who had never done a day's work in his life, who thought money grew on trees, who could only say, Gimme, gimme, gimme. Mark my words and mark them well: Herbert Hoover will go down in history as the greatest president we ever had. Just give me the word, anytime you want, and I'll buy you a fucking one-way ticket to Russia. You make me *sick*. Your loving Father.

The man who lay in bed that night and wheezed as I opened up an area of his father's life that he could hardly bear to face was going through the most terrible period of his life. I realized this without having the wisdom or the sympathy or the inclination to support him, though I think now that no one could have supported him for his needs were insatiable. Within a year both his father and his mother had died. Without a doubt he had had very mixed and complicated feelings about them, but he had never grown up enough to free himself from their domination, one as tough as a steel fist, the other as soft and comforting as the special socks she kept knitting him. He was not ready, but he had tried to take his father's place in the business and keep it together, but the Depression had become terrible by now and the assets melted away and company after company became moribund or went into bankruptcy. He had gone into a little partnership and financed his best friend. It turned out that the books were not in order; one night mysteriously the establishment burned down. My father staggered under this blow; it wasn't just his best friend, it was almost his only friend. He had bought large amounts of National Biscuit stock on margin and hardly a week passed that he wasn't forced to put up more cash as the stock steadily dropped in value. Out of panic and an innate egoism he had engaged in some shuffling of the family assets to protect his own interests. His sisters called a secret meeting and threw him out of the company. (I never had the courage to investigate one of my aunt's accusations that he had even trans-ferred half of my inheritance to try and save himself.) One day in a rage he struck my stepmother in the face, and she proceeded to divorce him. All of this within three years. He was about forty-five years old and except for the house and an insurance policy that paid him something for being sick, he had lost everything — his family, his wife, his money, and his reputation. Of course, in a way he still had his children, but I imagine he would have howled with hysterical laughter had anyone suggested that we were assets. It was his money that he mourned; it was his money that had given him his self-respect.

He had cracked up without a sense of grace; he had gone down howling and throwing things like a child in a tantrum, like a man in a poker game who, having lost ten hands in a row, begins breaking up the furniture and slugging the other players. I had watched him through those years as he disintegrated, secretly terrified, but in his presence showing him a smile of cool contempt that drove him into even more extreme behavior. I wasn't the only one. I think everyone who knew him was appalled by his lack of style, by the way he had come crashing down, screaming with self-pity, as though he were the only one being ground fine by the best little old economic system in the world.

All of these things happened to him within three years. When his wife left him he had a nervous breakdown and disappeared into a rest home for some months. I used to visit him at infrequent intervals and finally stopped, relieved, when his psychiatrist said that my visits were deeply upsetting. Yes, indeed, so they were. In 1935 the psychiatrist suggested that my father take a long trip on a tramp steamer, preferably to a hot country. He was to lie on deck under a tropical sun, eat plainly, sleep twelve hours a day – and try to put some kind of a life together again. He took a trip to someplace, and he was coming back from that same trip when he stopped off to see me in Eugene.

And it was that night in Rio when I had dreamed of my father as Pizarro riding through a plaza, riding down Indians, that I had put forgotten things together and had awakened with a connection made. It was to Rio de Janeiro that my father had gone in 1935. He had walked these same streets, lingered before these same bronze monuments, wasted his afternoons beneath the big trees in these same parks. His life had been as empty as mine was now. How strange and almost frightening, for I thought that I had completely rejected him, that out of some impulse that I would never understand, I had been impelled to come to the same place and with the same goal.

Sitting naked on the bed and gazing out over the pink roofs of Rio, the figure of Pizarro riding across a plaza, riding down Indians, slowly fades away. For the first time in years, perhaps for the first time in my life, I begin to remember that whole evening in Eugene. That final hour as we sat around my father's bed had been only the last half of a strange visit. There are other connections to be made; they lie out there just past the tips of my fingers that are straining to grasp them. There is a plain and simple logic in that dream that has turned my father into a conquistador complete with sword, armor, implacable horse.

.   .   .

My father was waiting for me in the lobby of the hotel. He looked fine, much younger, tighter, more compact, and with a new feistiness to his walk. His face was tanned. Most important, he was smiling. If, as the evening progressed, he didn't laugh at my jokes, at least he laughed at his own. He had begun to wear his hair like my grandfather, in a short, brisk pompadour. We kissed each other, I told him he looked fine, and we went into the dining room.

I had dreaded this meeting a little. He had loaned me his car while he was gone, I had taken it skiing one weekend to Mount Baker, and the motor block had frozen and cracked. I had replaced the cracked block with a new one, but there was a ninety dollar bill for the work waiting for him in Seattle. One of my father's illusions about me was that I didn't lie to him; still, I was nervous about his reactions, which were always unpredictable. I had put antifreeze in the radiator before that trip to the mountains, but obviously I hadn't put in enough. I was afraid he wouldn't believe this excuse, which smacked of falsity. As we ordered dinner, wanting to get it out of the way and feeling that he would hesitate to spoil a whole evening's reunion with his anger, I told him what had happened and told him the garage where he might pick up his car. His face paled a little, but he only said, "Well, these things happen." He gave a little cough, a little wheeze, and an abstracted look passed over his face as though he were looking into himself, alerted to vague symptoms.

"You're sure looking good," I said. "Like a million dollars." This was his expression, and perhaps I used it with a touch of malice. A million dollars, he claimed, was what he had just lost, and perhaps the words touched a raw nerve. He said that he was feeling pretty good except for his bowels. He was developing, he thought, a tendency toward constipation and found himself depending more and more on a daily enema. We talked at some length about my father's shit as we had our soup. Enema bags and flushing out those old poisons seemed to be a subject that he found totally engrossing. Although I tried to conceal my distaste he probably caught in my tight, closed face a reflection of my feelings. If he did he would see it as a rejection. He wheezed a little and said with surprise, "I think I'm coming down with a cold."

What I wanted to tell him then but didn't, deciding to save the information for another time when I would be more justified in wounding him, was that I had just been reading Freud about anal-repressives, about constipated people who were reluctant to let go of their bodily wastes since they had made a connection between gold and their painfully accumulated creations. (My God, I was a smart little bastard at twenty, and smart enough this time, for once, not to tell him what I knew. He hated Freud — called him Frood — and was terrified and outraged by his sexual theories. He hated Picasso, too — Pisscaso — who was the final proof when we mentioned him that we were being taught subversive stuff, godless degeneracy. Pisscaso was a charlatan, my father would cry, his face flushing. How, I used to wonder, could I have been so smart at twenty, my father so stupid. How, I wonder now, could I have been so smart at twenty, so stupid at sixty. Was Picasso occasionally a charlatan? I used to know the answer to that one.)

Dishes of ham covered with raisin sauce were placed before us, and as we ate my father pulled some snapshots from a breast pocket and shoved them across the table to me one by one. This is Sparks, the radio operator a great guy. Here's a long shot of tilted water from a tilted camera with a town riding on it — Guayaquil. Yours truly getting his hair cut on the deck. Yours truly crossing the equator and having a pail of water thrown on him. The crew was all great guys. That guy dressed up like Neptune, that's Shorty the cook. Waves breaking over the bow — a storm coming through the Straits. Here we are in front of Bolivar; there's a statue of Bolivar in every town in South America, their George Washington. This is Rio, the Rio Bolivar. Jim, the engineer on one side, yours truly in the middle, Mike, the first mate. Great guys. A little bar with girls where they took our picture; we're feeling no pain. Another shot of Rio; let me see. Well, I don't remember, but I think it's Rio. Yeah, see the sidewalks with the patterns.

"It's a great city," my father said, putting the pictures away. "Full of niggers, of course, but there's nothing wrong with a nigger who knows its place. If I were a younger man that's where I'd go. No fooling; that town is crying for a little know-how. There's a million dollars waiting there for a guy with a little savvy."

"Like what?" I asked.

"Well, here's just one idea I had. Look, that place is *backward*. They don't know beans about merchandising, and this idea you could do it without capital. I mean it, a gold mine. If I were twenty years younger I'd take a million dollars out of that place in three, four years. Four years at the most; I'd come out smelling like roses."

"Come on, don't keep me in suspenders."

"Look, there's no milk in South America," my father said. "You can't buy a glass of milk in that whole continent. No soft drinks, no sandwiches. I swear they don't know what a hamburger is. It's a question of education and merchandising. You go down and start small. You buy one of these new machines that are just coming on the market. It makes a product like ice cream. Better than ice cream."

"But if there's no milk in South America . . . "

"Shit," my father said, "there's no milk in this new product either. It's a formula; you ship it down there in packages. Soybean oil, kelp, sugar, some flavoring, a little coloring. You mix it up with water; a pound of that stuff will make a gallon of product." He laughed. "Hells bells, put the machine on high speed and it's all air. It's all profit – air, water, and half a penny worth of formula. You sell it in a paper dish for a nickel; the people down there would go crazy for it." My father got a dreamy look on his face. "A million dollars, I swear to God."

"Sounds like a good idea," I said without enthusiasm.

"Even you could do it," my father said off the top of his head. "If you weren't such a dreamer, if you could just get things together." He stopped eating and looked at me for a long time, and though it didn't seem that he much liked what he was looking at, I had an idea of what was coming. Oh shit, I thought, why doesn't he get off my back? "I might even help you get started," he said cautiously. "You could get down there for a couple hundred dollars, the machine costs about six hundred . . . "

"You mean quit school and go to Brazil to sell ice-cream cones?" I asked sarcastically. "How much would the little white cap cost?"

My father bristled. "It makes more sense than this scribbling business, this newspaper reporter nonsense."

"Well, as a matter of fact," I said, "I think I'll get out of journalism. I think I'd like to try writing for the movies."

"You're like a fart in a skillet," my father said, his voice rising. "You don't know what you want to do; one day it's this, the other day it's that."

"Maybe," I said, "but I know I don't want to peddle fake ice cream in Rio de Janeiro. How do you do it, pushing a wheelbarrow?"

"You do it like a *man*," my father said, beginning to shout. "You start small and you build a business. You learn to crawl and then you learn to walk and then you learn to run. But you're too good for that, aren't you? That getting your hands dirty, that's beneath you. You want to start at the top."

"Yeah," I said. "Like you. I want to do it like my daddy."

We stared at each other, angry but half-smiling, amazed that our relationship after so many months of separation was getting back to normal so quickly. My father's face was helpless with frustration and distaste. "Oh shit, do what you want," he said. "You've never listened to me. According to you I don't know shit from tar."

"Daddy, it's a good idea; it's a great idea. But you know it's not for me. I'm not like you; you could sell iceboxes to the Esquimaux. That kind of stuff makes me embarrassed."

We ate in silence. The ice cream came. I tasted it with suspicion, wondering if it was real. My father, taking deep breaths like sighs, stared into his coffee and stirred it roughly and interminably. "Is there an awful lot of coffee in Brazil?" I asked, humming the tune and smiling brightly. And got no answer.

My father paid the check and we went out into the lobby. "I'm going right up to bed," he said. "I can feel a cold coming on; I can hardly breathe."

"I'll come up for a while," I said. "Some friends are coming by who want to meet you."

"Yeah," my father said. "I can imagine what you've told them." We stood waiting by the elevator, and just before it came he turned to me, shaking his head in dismay and puffing for breath. "Goddamit, I'm good enough to loan you my car, and what do you do? You don't have it ten days 'til it's wrecked. I don't understand. I don't understand. I don't understand such carelessness. It's criminal. You're a man now, you're twenty years old, you've got to start putting your head on straight. Jesus Christ, what kind of a damn fool goes into the mountains without antifreeze?"

In Rio I was preoccupied with the memory of my father's enthusiastic but short-lived conviction that he could take a million dollars out of Brazil. "Like taking candy away from a baby." Though it would not have been as simple as he imagined, the plan was probably sound, and if he had attacked the challenge and reinvested his profits in expansion – there would now be a chain of "Big Charlie's" dotting the continent and delighting the Latin public with American junk food. But, my God, how blatantly and tastelessly he would have done it. I sit in Rio shaking my head and sadly smiling at the vision of my father making his million and dressed up like Colonel

Sanders. He would have come up with something exactly like that or worse. He had the soul of a salesman and would have done something outrageous – and he would have walked out with his goddam million.

And Pizarro? The connection is all but made.

Since coming to Ecuador in 1965 I had developed a loathing for that man, a loathing that may seem extreme and psychotic considering that the son of a bitch has been dead for five hundred years. For me he symbolized the destruction of a continent, the ruthless murder of whole nations, the introducer of those Spanish traits – avarice, nepotism, cruelty, political corruption, and a contempt for work, that have become fully absorbed into the South American psyche. He had conquered and enslaved under the banner of the Catholic Church, the biggest landowner in history. The continent had lain raped and bleeding under that bastard and his bastard sons too long. Too long. Too long. South America is Humpty Dumpty, that broken egg that will never be put together again. There are no solutions anymore; the continent will never recover.

·　　　·　　　·

At midnight on another trip I had come to Peru and had driven in a taxi through the Plaza de las Armas looking for a hotel. And seen just off the plaza, Pizarro, looming out of the night. He was in full armor, his sword swung out, charging ahead – an enormous bronze statue three stories high, an incredibly cruel figure mounted on the cruelest looking horse. It was the first public monument that had gripped me in South America. Seen at midnight, dimly lit and half-hidden between buildings, but ready to burst out into the plaza, it was doubly stunning, actually quite terrifying. "Pizarro," said the taxi driver, "the richest man in the world," and as we passed him I looked avidly, feeling contempt and anger.

Waiting for a restaurant to open six hours later I had come back to stand beneath that statue in the early morning. It was cold under Lima's overcast. I drank coffee and went out and walked around Pizarro again trying to study that sadistic and arrogant face hidden beneath a helmet. I was choked with a disgust that gave me pleasure. You bastard. You bastard. When the cathedral across the plaza opened its doors I rushed across to it and searched out the corpse where it lay in its own chapel, Pizarro in a cheap, glass casket like an aquarium. Skull, naked bones, dried skin the color of a roasted chicken, boney fingers and the arms crossed above a caved-in chest. I had lived for years in a country shattered to its foundations by the corruptions of the conquistadores' legacies, a country where half the population

lived outside the economy and enslaved by the *hacendados* – Indians, clinging to an ancient culture that aroused contempt among the masters or feelings of sentimental quaintness among the tourists. Indians, an invisible
presence in the country. Stinking, lice-ridden, as human as dogs. "If we had
only shot them like you did," an engineer had told me once. "How can any
government integrate these people into a nation that lusts to embrace Western technology?"

It was early, and I was the only one in the chapel. I looked around, not
wanting to be caught, and spit a nice gob on the floor at the head of the casket. Feeling better and thinking of an epitaph that I had read recently, I
went back out into the main cathedral.

> *Beneath these stones lies Theophilus Macguire,*
> *Stop, traveler, and piss.*

A Peruvian with the face of an Indian but wearing a dark suit stood just inside the main door of the church; I had just paid him seventy-five cents for
the pleasure of spitting at Pizarro. Now I went out and talked to him. "How
do the people of Lima feel about having this guy lying in your cathedral?
He's really the star of this place, isn't he?"

"We honor him as the founder of Lima, nothing more," the man said.
"We don't honor him for the destruction of our culture or for killing off our
poor Indians."

I looked at him in surprise, my mouth gaping. He had been corrupted
too, this Indian who denied his blood, and who, because he was wearing a
suit and a tie, would have been insulted had you called him what he was.
My look must have disturbed him for he rushed on. "It was his daughter
who built the cathedral; how could they refuse the man a chapel when his
daughter was paying – and when she begged?"

"He is a dishonor to your *pendejo* church," I said.

"That body in there isn't Pizarro," the Indian said. "Nor is the Catholic
Church my church."

Over a continent whose culture had been shattered by the Spanish and
the Portuguese was now laid a double curse. Over a continent still dazed
and that in four hundred years had never been able to absorb and live
decently with an imported European culture, a continent broken into sad
principalities and dominated by a few landowners and their *lambón* dic-
tators or their pet military mediocrities was now laid the unfathomable
confusions of Western technology. The new rulers of the earth, the masters
of technology, have come and they will throw down the old kings, the old

rulers, the old landowning classes; the new order is at hand. When I walked in Rio afraid to cross a street for the rush of traffic or watched the early morning buses taking a million people to the factories at the edge of the city (and bringing them back twelve hours later), or peered into a hundred different holes in the main streets where broken pipes discharged tons of water into the already overloaded drains, or walked sullenly past ten thousand cops and soldiers who had set up enclaves in every part of the city, wasn't I seeing that first wave of Western progress that was about to break over a people who were too human to handle the complications of a mechanized society? Their qualities, these earthy people who had a feeling for the soil and the sun – an inherent innocence, a wild individualism, a respect and delight in their sensuality, a sentimentality mixed with an irrational mysticism that ran deep beneath their incredible pragmatism, all these were about to be transformed into more passive traits. Brazil would be the first industrialized country in South America. Football, television, Carnival: how easy it had been to pacify a nation; how willingly people who considered it a privilege to eat had swarmed into the cities to overrun the slums and to seek out factory jobs. God's face now takes on the form of a time clock, and a hundred million people will now dedicate themselves to the production of a mountain of products all skillfully designed to wear out in three years – cars, radios, tv sets, and tape decks, outboard motors and pocket calculators, hoola-hoops and little plastic dolls that when you squeeze them make wee-wee in their plastic panties. How incredible that we have come so far that we can stamp out a pissing doll from a nickel's worth of plastic and never wonder if the girl at the machine who stamps them out for eight hours a day year after year is living a life that gives her satisfaction. "And what did you do with your life, my child?" God asks at the gates of paradise. "I stamped out pissing dolls, Lord." "And are you happy with the life you've had, my pet?" "I ate, Lord."

Pizarro can no longer symbolize for me the simple destruction of the continent in the middle 1500s. He is the greatest capitalist the world has ever known, and his figure, the eyes still flashing with avarice, still strides across the continent, across the world. The consequences of his ignorance have been catastrophic, and even his most benign efforts changed the world in ways that he could never have foreseen. If it was Pizarro who sent the first potatoes to Europe, it was he who set things up for that explosion of population that would follow the discoveries of Pasteur and the saving of babies. Thirty tons of potatoes to the acre, cheap and abundant food for horny peasants, babies who no longer die of tetanus. The stage is set for some final drama that a few of us may even live to see, and who in thirty years will be soft-headed enough to claim that life is sacred?

The manipulators of technology are the new Pizarros; the directors of the multinationals are the new rulers of the world – nice men with gentle manners some of them, connoisseurs of wine, modern art, beautiful women, the latest jet-set hideaway. They are the most honored men, sharing the admiration of the world with the politicians whom they have bought off and who serve them. They live straight, hardworking, fanatically focused lives and for the most part operate squarely within the morality that we have constructed to control them. There is no law that says it is immoral to overwhelm an agrarian culture with a technological one; to trade with Brazilian Indians, cut roads through their jungles, teach them about sin and guilt. The cutting down of the Amazon forest will be conducted in a most legal manner (the bastards will change the laws if necessary to make it legal), and the people who do it will be honest, dedicated to progress, in love with the idea of a modern world. These guys may own the world, but they don't control it: they are puppets caught up and driven ahead by the cresting wave of an incredible science that is way past their power to control: they are puppets blind to the consequences of their actions, alive only to the big chance. They are the bastards, these sober-suited Pizarros, who are going to kill us all.

One of my grandfather's favorite sayings: "You can't walk through shit without getting shit on you." He was a most honorable man, honest to a fault, and I never heard a word directed against his integrity. It is easy now, eighty years after the fact, to say that when my grandfather sat down with Diaz and came out of the palace with a contract to bring modern technology to a primitive society, that he walked away from that appointment with shit on his shoes. But who could have dreamed of saying that in 1900? It is easy to mock my father now because forty-five years ago if he had had the guts he would have come back to Rio and twenty years before it finally happened, crammed junk food down the throats of a lot of innocent and eager Cariocas. Pizarro sleeps in a great cathedral, but we've got Acapulco for *our* monument. Maybe someday I will sit down and try to figure out just what the hell I'm doing in South America. But not now. It is still not eight a.m., and I have already had a rough day.

Depressed, I face another morning and prepare to go down into the streets. And suddenly I begin laughing. I have just taken a big bite out of gringo Charlie's bun.

Rio II

When it came time for the young composer Villa-Lobos to write his first orchestral piece, he chose to do it on a large scale and to compete with his French masters. He wanted to out-dazzle the dazzling Debussy and out-orchestrate Ravel. He almost did. He expanded the normal orchestra and then added a dozen native Brazilian Indian percussion instruments. The legend of *Uirapurú*. It is pure early-twentieth-century Parisian music that deals in a most authentic way with the Brazilian rain forest and its people. Toward the end of this tone poem in some of the most amazingly explicit music ever written, his hero, a legendary Indian, is shot with an arrow and transformed into a swan who soars away into the sky. It is music as ornithologically precise as an Audubon engraving, as truly observed – vision turned into sound – as the night music of Bartók.

It is my eighth or ninth night in Rio. Walking down the hallway to my room after an extraordinary meal in which out of some malignant confusion on the waiter's part I have been served both spaghetti *and* potato salad, I pass a closed doorway. From behind it the last five minutes of Villa-Lobos's *Uirapurú* is pouring out. I stop and listen until it ends, stunned by this music that I haven't heard for a quarter of a century but which is immediately recognizable, stunned to be in Brazil and listening to Villa-Lobos on his own turf. It resembles the same awe I had felt at listening to Rachmaninoff himself as he played his concertos in New York one year, but this time the emotion is stronger for I have come upon the music suddenly and without anticipation. The music is tight, constricted, full of menace, and then the chords suddenly open up, swelling, the man's arms stretched out and the feathers growing, and the arms turning into great wings. The bird soaring away over the black water of a jungle lake, over the great jungle trees. Jesus.

The overwhelming and mysterious power of music. The consolations of art. How strange that I have forgotten these things and, knowing that something was missing but not knowing what, have wandered so emptily through the streets of Rio feeling hungry for almost everything except food. After twelve years in the jungle almost without hearing music I have lost the habit.

The first thing next morning I go out and buy a radio. Later I stop at a drugstore and through some horrible misunderstanding am given an injection of tetracycline; I had wanted pills not injections. I am coming down with a hacking cough and a fever and my skin is peeling off my body as though I had been flayed. In the long run the radio will prove to be more therapeutic than the antibiotics.

Now after breakfast at a long community table on the first floor where I amaze the Brazilians by drinking cup after cup of incredibly strong coffee, I go back to my room instead of roaming in the streets. Scarlatti, Ravel, Bach, and Berg, they are all up there waiting for me. I doze through whole mornings with the music forming designs against my eyelids. These forms and colors, these moving, glowing lines or expanding constructions have more reality than anything outside. Listening to Villa-Lobos every day I feel that I am more truly experiencing the soul of Brazil than by observing a city that has given up its humanity to the pressures of progress and industry. For almost a week, coughing and sweating, I stay in my room, except for feeling pretty awful, I feel pretty good. The kid, Luis, knocks on my door. "I'm here to clean your room, *senhor.*" "No, no, some other day. Don't bother me; I'm nesting." For too long I had been playing with my own emotions; I had exhausted them. Now I lie alone and fill again with the emotions of other men: Wagner, D'Indy, Chausson, Stravinsky, Debussy. How Brazilians love the French Impressionists.

And now I begin to read again. In a most immoderate way I gulp down books in one hundred and fifty page gulps. Burgess's *Enderby* again, Conrad's short novels — *Youth, The Shadow-Line, The Nigger of the Narcissus, The End of the Tether.* My concentration is complete, and my admiration for Conrad reaches staggering heights. When he is at his best no one comes near him. After a week of this I am half-cured and ready to leave the city — and am held up for three more days because the long May First weekend has arrived and the tourist places that sell bus tickets are closed until Tuesday. The streets are empty, the restaurants closed, there is scarcely a car on the streets. I take *The End of the Tether* down into the almost-deserted plaza and read it through a long, quiet afternoon. I like the title, which seems to be revelatory of my own condition. Or so I thought for a time.

When I lift my eyes from the book I idly watch a little group of sad drunks who stand at the corner of a hole-in-the-wall bar across the street. They are trying to celebrate but the quietness of the city oppresses them. About four o'clock the group breaks up and one of them comes across the street. She is a girl in her twenties dressed in rather dirty slacks and a dun-colored shirt; she wears a turban on her head, and she is barefoot. Over one shoulder is a leather purse as large as a knapsack. As I watch her I suddenly realize that she is not drunk but heavily drugged. She walks not staggering but in a dreamlike way as though her feet were not quite touching the ground. For a long time she stands and stares at a tree quietly talking to it and tossing little bits of balled-up newspaper at its base, miming the few children behind her who are tossing crusts of bread to the pigeons. Then she sits down on the curb and sinks into a profound and motionless meditation as if experiencing an overpowering dejection of the spirit, though every twenty minutes or so she will address a question to the tree, which does not, I believe, give her the answer she is looking for. Here is a woman at the end of her tether, whether she knows it or not, and I want to imagine that she is facing her situation and looking into the near future and her own death. When I leave the park at six-thirty to look for an open restaurant she is still sitting on the curb; her shoulders have begun to twitch and jerk in a frightening, spastic way.

Now it seems that these final glimpses of dying people come in pairs, for up the first block I pass an old woman who is curled up and sleeping in the entranceway of a boarded-up building. She has crawled into an open-bottomed corrugated paper box but her head and feet are unprotected. I have seen her there many times before in the day without realizing that she sleeps here, too. She sells packages of crackers or a half-dozen oranges laid out in two rows on a piece of rag. At times I had seen her in little fits of mad-ness yelling bad words at the passing cars or, grinding her teeth, giving the people on the sidewalk terrible piercing looks as though she had seen through to the horrors that they were plotting against her. Her front room, the sidewalk, was littered with scraps of paper, mandarin peels, and hack-ings of mucus, and now I notice that before going to bed she has crouched in the gutter to relieve herself—making a little pool at the foot of a little hill roughly shaped like Sugar Loaf (and as black) — a pinched, inadequate turd as hard as a rock that hints at starvation or a human mechanism that is run-ning down.

These two women are powerful images to set against my insomnia. They have reached the end of the tether as truly as Conrad's blind captain, caught up and destroyed by life's treacheries. Giving myself godlike powers to simply observe them coolly, I find a kind of dismal grandeur in the inevitability of their deaths, which seemed but a few days off. How can I think of their endings as anything but a glad release from the brutal and meaningless chaos of their existences?

Another thing: I feel a kind of pride in being able to stand aside and see the figure of death looming up just behind them. I feel this is another of my talents — an ability to nose out death's intentions on the faces of people. At times death takes up residence in a body months before it makes its final, obliterating move. No wonder we honor and fear the doctor's sharp eye, which can recognize the fatal symptoms in a trembling hand or a flushed cheek or the shrinking skin that reveals death's symbol, the skull. After a week of coughing and sweating, I could more clearly see my own death peeking back at me out of sunken and heavy-lidded eyes. Still, she didn't seem in any particular hurry to claim me; I found a dim satisfaction in recognizing this old friend hidden in a stranger's face, as though engaged with other things, she would let me be for a time. Death is working the Rio district, and Tuesday I will be leaving for Bahia.

But is it stupid or wise to think of this presence, for whom I have no particularly friendly feelings, as a friend? The consolations of art for all their power to hint at design and grandeur in life don't offer much solace in the presence of that face that stares back from the six-foot mirror. Here is what is horrible about dying, I decide: not that you are obliterated by death but that everything you love is also obliterated. The eyes close for the last time, the brain deprived of oxygen comes unplugged, and everything, everything is destroyed, the world disintegrates — trees, lakes, mountains, children, wind and sunshine, the sea, canoes floating across tranquil rivers, ponds full of frogs, night and the stars, music and the music of silence. It is all destroyed, it all fades away as though it had never existed. This trip, which has opened me up to the uselessness of my own existence, has also helped me to see that my own face has been completed for years and must now disintegrate with time. I have been brainwashed enough to realize that my thoughts are morbid and that it is un-American to think about dying except as a hypothetical event in a constantly receding future, and so, trying to be upbeat in the face of these disloyal preoccupations, I resolve to consider at the earliest possible moment the positive features of dying. Immediately, without even trying I am given an answer: death destroys not only everything we love, but everything we hate as well. Our rages, our betrayals, our failures, our capacity for evil. It is all destroyed. How can death, then, be anything but a friend since so much more pain than joy is obliterated. Poor death, that ambiguous friend who is never invited to our parties. Well, uninvited or not I feel her presence; she is out there casing the streets and collecting women. I am wandering around looking for reasons to spurn her kiss. I have not yet found a clue to death's alternative, a final time span that would hold a meaning for me, a weapon to flourish in death's face. I can think of no reason for not saying, "O.K., I'm done here now; come and get me, I'm ready, I've had enough."

But how wrong I was this time about those two sad wrecks; how foolishly I had loaned them some of my own desperations. On Monday morning, the last day of this long quiet weekend, once more sitting in the empty plaza, once more I see the young woman. It is about ten o'clock and the same sad little party across the street is still just barely in progress. The girl is leaning into the arms of a large black who is dressed in the modest clothes of a workman; she is gazing into his eyes with admiration, and her movements are quick, nervous, and intense. I think of a Royal Coachman being manipulated above a fat and sleepy trout who has not quite made up its mind. Later when the two of them cross the street and pass close to me, I see for the first time that the young woman is actually a young man. Beneath the lightly powdered face a black stubble has sprouted during the night. Celebrating life not death they wander away toward those low buildings with the round beds.

And as for the old woman who slept in a paper box — I am wrong about her, too.

I must shatter the chronology for a moment to report on her ambiguous ending for she disappeared one day, suddenly, leaving a strange emptiness on the steps of that deserted building. But it was a year later and almost to the day. I had come back to Rio less burdened by illusions and wanting to confront a place where I had lost my identity. Walking up that old street a couple blocks from the same hotel I had met the old lady sitting in her spot. I was amazed for I had thought of her often but always as being dead. She was selling a strange, intensely colored fruit like a pomegranate, six of them spread out on a rag beside her. As I watched her she took one of the fruits, pierced it with a nail, and sucked out a little of the juice. Then she replaced it; it was still for sale.

I passed her almost every day. Sometimes she was selling peanuts, oranges, or soda crackers — sometimes nothing. She still pissed in the gutter, but she had cleaned up her act a little. In the early mornings she would take a whisk broom from the little bundle of her belongings and carefully sweep her area of sidewalk. From time to time she still shrieked and shook her fists at the passing cars and still glared at those of us who passed through her territory. That incredible woman had not changed at all, and I began to think of her as being immortal. Ignoring the styles and inventing her dresses from scraps of old material, she had a kind of dignity, an authenticity in the simplicity of her long skirt and in the two plastic cherries that she sometimes stuck into her hair. Her chicness was only slightly marred by a pair of enormous six-inch-high tennis shoes.

And then one day she was gone. Though I had never spoken with her or bought her crackers she was my oldest friend in Brazil; I had known her for a year. She was gone and there wasn't a trace of her, not even a stain on the marble steps of the old building with its high padlocked iron doors. (I think, because she had given a kind of life to that corner, that it was only after she had gone that I realized that the building was empty.) Now there was nothing in a two-block stretch except an enormous hole that bulged out into the street and from which water was continually pumped that interpreted the city to me. She was gone and I could hardly believe it. I had already talked about her with the owner of the hotel who said that she had been living in that doorway for years. Of course, I immediately suspected that she had been murdered, for part of Rio's fame has been built around a special squad of police who collect tramps, cripples, blind down-and-outers, kill them, and toss their bodies into the bay – a kind of "Keep Our City Clean" squad.

"That old woman in the next block," I said to the hotel owner one day. "She's gone."

"So you noticed," he said. "Yes, a neighborhood landmark, the old black gypsy. She's finally left us."

"Where did she go?"

"Ah, who knows?" he said shrugging "Perhaps she has found a better spot, some doorway with a little morning sun."

"Then she's not dead?"

"Oh, no, no, no. She's not dead; she's moved, that's all."

"How do you know?"

He shrugged, put on his glasses, and went back to his ledger.

"Killed maybe?" I insisted.

"Oh, no," he said, frowning and dismissing me. "They don't hardly do that anymore. No, no, no, no. Who would want to kill that poor old helpless creature?"

Yes, who indeed, I thought, the memory of her suspicious glances now taking on new meaning.

Going up in the elevator that night I corner Payaso. "That old lady that's been here for years, the old *gitana* that sells crackers, where has she gone?"

"Batatas fritas," Payaso says, very slowly, scarcely smiling, and drawing one hand across his throat.

On Tuesday morning after the long weekend, still coughing, still a little disoriented, I walk up Rio Branco to a tourist office and buy a ticket for Bahia. Twenty-eight dollars for a thirty-hour bus ride, almost a thousand miles along the Brazilian coast. The way I'm feeling, if that doesn't kill me, nothing will. At the counter of Cambios I check the rate of exchange; they are offering twenty-four fifty for traveler's checks today. But I am carrying Citibank checks and the Citibank headquarters is only one more block up the street. Surely they will treat me better.

Coming into that hushed marble mausoleum as silent, as dimly echoing as St. Peter's after the wild surging traffic on Rio Branco is a little like finding eternal peace after an awful life of struggle. I am suddenly standing in the presence of God. Falling to my knees and confessing everything seems like an appropriate response in this solemn place. Ah, Citibank, Citibank, you little breath of Wall Street. Everything is so serious, grandiose, reverent, and unearthly. People speak with muted voices and move on tiptoe. No one laughs in Citibank. I now have one of my last conversations in Rio; it is with a trim blonde goddess who sits in a shrine behind glass. She has puffy pink-rimmed eyes like a rabbit and the aloof cool manner of a bank employee, and her face is as blank as a blank tv screen with its promise of infinite banalities.

"I'd like to change two hundred dollars into cruzeiros, please."

"Passport," snaps Isis, the Delphic oracle.

"O.K., but first, what's the exchange?"

"Twenty-two," says Deirdre of the Sorrows, deeply engrossed in her nails. While I stand there speechless she whips out a small mirror from a top drawer and begins to practice smiling. She has incredibly white, intimidating teeth; in my anger I am beginning to find them fanglike. She looks closer and removes a fleck of carmined goo from a front tooth; perhaps it is a bit of gore from a previous customer.

"There's no black market for dollars in Brazil, is there?"

"Of course not. Passport."

"On the street the exchange is twenty-four fifty."

If I had not lived for years in a Latin country I would not even notice the almost imperceptible and subtle shrugging of her shoulders, the only reaction to my remark. She stares at me with a composure that robs her face of the little humanity that it had had; with an incredibly long red fingernail she picks delicately at a spot on her hairline.

"A block from here I can get twenty-four fifty," I insist. "Why are checks for fifty dollars worth five dollars less in an American bank?"

Lucrezia Borgia stares through me and runs her tongue over her teeth, first outside, then inside – very slowly. She studies her nails.

"But how can your bank do something like this?" I ask finally, beginning to lose my cool. "This is just plain *ladrâonismo;* first, I pay one percent for the checks; now the bank wants ten percent more. And the truth is you've already invested my money in municipal bonds that are paying another ten percent. What the hell. Does Citibank want it all?"

"You wantee changee checkee – pasaporte," the future manager of the Rio branch says. I have met my first completely hateful Brazilian; wouldn't you know she'd be a banker.

I storm out and stand for a moment at the edge of the traffic, coughing and trembling with outrage. Still, this is my last day, and I want one last look at this mysterious and vibrant city. I go back to Turismo, change my dollars, and then walk down toward the bay. Across the lawn in back of the Museum of Modern Art and hidden below the seawall there are a number of hovels thrown up among the granite rock chunks that have been hauled there against the sea's erosion. The huts are made of paper, driftwood, and pieces of corrugated iron. The people who live there tear bunches of mussels from the rocks, cook them in five-gallon tins of sea water, and sell these clusters, steel blue and as glistening as grapes, to the local public. Sitting on the grass and studying the landscape – the incredible skyline of high buildings, the rush of car traffic along the shore-front freeways, the languid sea, man-tamed, the great black granite upthrusts with their cable cars, the steady flow of planes turning inside Sugar Loaf to descend in identical flight paths to the city airport – it is startling to see the upper bodies of the fishermen suddenly appearing from behind the wall and putting themselves in the way of all this rich and luxurious grandeur. They are naked and scarred, their wild hair menacing. They are the other reality of Rio behind the postcard lies.

Enroute to Bahia

An hour out of Rio and the houses start moving back from along the edges of the highway to hide themselves in scattered groups in small tropical gardens of bamboo, bananas, bougainvillea, mangos. The countryside, exploding, opens up in its immensity. Behind us a hundred motels, walled off and ominous, a hundred little barrios of mean huts built around factories, a thousand vacant lots, new factory sites, empty of everything but high grass and expensively fenced off with brick, barbed wire, or Cyclone fencing. It is strange to move through a land with so few people in it. Another hour and even the houses disappear or have begun to collect themselves into little towns in the middle distance, or on the edges of some large hacienda form into unlikely rows of identical shacks, squeezed together wall to wall as though the land were too valuable to waste on living space for human beings. Looking at these rows one thinks: Jesus, a healthy fart at midnight in cabin A will wake the whole town to hysterical laughter, A through Q, the simple pleasures of the poor. Forty or fifty houses without breathing space on the steep slope of a hill and around them miles of pasture or, further north, enormous and undulating miles of oranges or, still farther north, miles of sugar cane. The houses are adobe or wattle and where the thin mudlike skin has fallen away from the walls in patches, the inner wall of sticks against which the mud has been plastered can be seen. The houses are small. Imagining families of six or seven enduring the confusions of those two small rooms is distressing. That enormous twenty-room house of my father's was scarcely big enough to contain our rages even though our rooms were so far away one from the other that I could hardly hear the words when my father and his wife screamed out their ritual hatreds. These huts are all painted in bright colors, the roofs are tile or tin, the windows small and usually closed, houses under siege. What prowls the Brazilian countryside after the sun goes down that has turned the houses into fortresses? Don't the people know that the devils that will destroy them are locked inside with them, that they are sleeping in the next hammock?

For over a hundred miles the land is incredibly dramatic and unlike any other place on earth that I have ever seen. The highway climbing and moving away from the coast enters narrowing valleys whose sides are formed by the same upthrusting black granite domes of Rio, their dark walls streaked with darker lines where small springs drip and stain. The domes are a thousand feet high, or higher, and on their tops or on the sides that more gently form these swellingly beautiful forms, heavy tropical forests grow. If I were only younger what challenges these soaring walls would offer; now I get scared just looking. It seems likely that some of these peaks have never been climbed and that their summits, heavy with great trees, are as empty of life as the day they came pushing up out of the earth's depths. Only birds, only the great birds can have explored these impregnable peaks – or those wild kids from the Sierra Club.

For a few hours I try to make sense of the landscape. I try to interpret the kind of life that country people might live here by studying their identical shacks or the grander but unimaginative houses of the *hacendados,* try to figure out who owns the rolling hills or the wide river bottoms by estimating the size of the farms, try to figure out by the dryness or greenness of the pastures what limitations the climate has laid over the land. Why are the shacks so small when the land is so rich? I am not smart enough to make sense of what I see; there is something else invisible laid over the land, and only hints of some sad truth can be seen in the general austere quality of the poverty and in the apparent hugeness of the individual land holdings.

The highway is superb and managed in an inhumanly precise way. Narrow steep dirt roads rutted by horse-drawn wagons connect the workers' huts to this elegant cement band. But the connection is merely symbolic and gratuitous. The highway is an intrusion of privacy as it curves and sweeps through another more tranquil, more feudal century. There is something shameful about its incongruity. Every hundred miles or so lounging police at checkpoints as spreading as the international border buildings between the United States and Canada stop and scrutinize the highway traffic (and collect a toll). Every two hours the bus arrives at other enormous installations where the passengers are allowed twenty minutes to pee and to drink coffee or eat something. Each of these places is built to one plan – a large shop full of incredibly boring tourist crap, a fancy restaurant with tablecloths and heavy-looking Spanish chairs (where no one ever ate); a fresh-juice store hung all around with sacks of oranges, papayas, avocados; and long counters manned by swift-moving youngsters. After stopping a few times to eat identical sandwiches from identical buildings, the trip begins to seem unreal. I don't know if I am hallucinating or if my cold has taken a turn for the worse.

Late in the afternoon we move away from the coast, or more precisely, since the coast has been invisible, away from the feeling of following a coastline. And to be even more precise or at least to indicate the limitations on my ability to be precise, I am not sure now that it was late or early in the afternoon. By this time I am running a fever and the view outside the bus window is turning into long stretches of blankness with here and there stopped-action scenes of meaningless but razor-sharp detail. To the west the wide river bottoms and the empty horizons of tide flats disappear and we skirt the edges of a hostile land as dry and forbidding as the most worthless parts of Texas or Mexico. Low blue mountains stand in the distance dimly seen through dusty air; arroyos cut across dry plains where nothing grows but cactus, spikey shrubs, and small frail trees with tiny dull green leaves. Very thinly scattered across this waste, low mean huts of wattle, some without walls, lean-tos of dry mud and straw, corrals of piled brush, a few goats, and a very few listless cattle, their lowered heads staring at the ground. Cow hides hang from sagging fences as raw and orange as flayed flesh, and whirlwinds, dust-devils of dirt, sticks and leaves move in the distance through the still air, whipping the earth.

We are crawling across the very edges of that awful land called the northeast, the *sertão* where years-long droughts have once again created a desert. Last year there were millions of people out there; they hung on and hung on until they were driven out by the realization that what they were contemplating in those dry clouds that passed over them month after month was the immediacy of their own deaths. The *sertão*, the very center of the world's poverty. The still seriously unpondered problems that it poses for Brazil and anyone else who thinks about such things are like great spreading, festering cancers. The land empties and fills with people as the rains either fall or fail to fall, but at its best it is a country of shamefully modest expectations. Is it love or desperation that drives the people back to the ruined farms after the first rains have started up the grass and the dead sticks of trees burst into life? Probably both. Man's deepest passions are centered on land and the water that brings it to life. And what suffering won't a man endure to live in his own hut on his own land, proud and half-mad with the delusion that to some extent he is in control of his own destiny.

Now the land is being emptied again; the cattle, covered with ticks and lice, are dying; the old people have died, the water holes are drying up; the springs no longer flow; the frogs no longer sing in the dry ponds behind the huts. The pretty young girls have wandered off to the cities to become whores; by the time they are fifteen they will be used up, their faces gray and lined. The men in orange jumpsuits sweep the parks or cut weeds along the highway with their machetes. There are supposed to be sixteen million homeless children in the country; most of them live in the big cities; you have seen pictures of them sleeping in doorways or curled up in little bunches like litters of wolf cubs, wrapped in old newspapers on the beach at Copacabana. In the poorer barrios they travel in packs like dogs, begging, stealing, whoring to stay alive. Some of them say they are going to be doctors when they grow up. Some of them are looking for a little length of rope that they can steal to hang themselves with. The northeast is a factory that mass produces these subhuman fucked-over creatures being driven to new lives of crime and squalor. Starved for protein, crippled by malnutrition, they have lost about twenty percent of their intelligence.

As the hours pass I become desperate and angry. In visualizing Bahia I had forgotten what had to be passed through to get there. I feel like a cheated tourist; like a traveler being taken to the temples of Nara, by way of Hiroshima, to Dresden with a tour of Auschwitz thrown in. For all the monotony of the land, it produces a choking intensity of emotion that cannot be discharged. It is only a little less distressing than driving past a rocky hill of no great splendor and learning that it is named Golgotha and that three crosses once stood upon its summit.

The sertão, while it has produced more morons than artists, boasts some of the great Brazilian writers. The rudeness of the life and the cruelty of the land, like the Israeli deserts, has been a breeding ground for men of intense, poetic, and fanatic emotions. A boyhood spent under that glare of sky, washed in the spaces of infinite distances, whipped to the bone by ruthless nature and by men made desperate and corrupt by hopelessness, and you can hardly ever write about anything else. Forty years later in Paris and the eyes still burn, and at night you groan. The desert has blasted open your soul. And if you have never learned to write, driven by luminous and inchoate feelings you turn into a religious prophet as cracked as some Spanish bishop in the Inquisition, or a Communist leader of people who smashes blindly at the corruptions of the ruling powers, or a bandit leader like Lampião whose head until very recently was exhibited in a medical museum in Salvador.

Lampião? That bad-ass Robin Hood of the northeast? Let me quote a few sentences from João Ubaldo's *Sergeant Getulio* about Lampião; it will give you a feel for the *ambiente*. "Often he would lose his temper over some little thing. He used to put a man's nuts in a drawer, lock it, throw the key out, and set fire to the house. Not without first leaving a knife within reach of the wretch. The way I see it, it's better to burn to death than to lose your nuts. Your voice gets thinner and thinner and so does your beard, you become pederastic, false to your body. But most people prefer to cut their balls off rather than turn into charcoal. Nowadays that kind of thing isn't done anymore. Would you put up with a thing like that? There was another time, when Lampião tied up a judge's wife, maybe it was in Divina Pastora or Rosario do Catete or Capela, he tied this wife of this judge to a tree and stripped her stark naked. Now whoever saw an old woman like that with so much hair on her parts? Have you ever seen such indecency? Not even the worst whores, how about that? And he peered over his glasses this way and that, and ended up pulling all the hairs off the woman's twat in front of everybody, everyone gathered there on Lampião's orders, because everything he did was always in front of everybody. There was great badness in him, he killed without ideas. So naturally he ended up with his head cut off in Bahia and put on exhibition like it was a wild bull's horns."

I have not read much of the Brazilian literature that has come out of the northeast. Very little of it has been translated into English, scarcely more than Graciliano Ramos, who grew up on a disintegrating cattle ranch with a family driven half-mad by defeat; Jose Americo de Almeida, who describes the endless lines of people staggering down the dusty roads away from a dead land to the slavery of the coastal *hacendados* with their empires of sugar cane; Jorge Amado, who writes about what happens to the girls who, having escaped the desert, end up in the coastal bordellos of Ilhéus or Salvador.

And João Ubaldo, the youngest and greatest of the regional writers and perhaps the strongest writer in Brazil today. His second novel, *Sergeant Getulio*, has been published in English. It is incredibly subtle, unbearably brutal, and while it has not made me want to see this land he writes about, it has made me want to see Ubaldo. I have made arrangements with his editor in Boston, and Ubaldo has sent back word that he will see me in Bahia. Meeting him will be the high point of my trip to Brazil.

The afternoon wears on, it is really quite endless. The mountains fade away in the distance behind us. Over on the left above the bushes something has died or is dying and where a moment before there was one black pair of circling wings, suddenly there are dozens of *gallinazos* settling lower, moving around and around like something dirty being slowly stirred in the sky. They look like the same vultures who always gathered on the farm when I was disking. They hopped behind the tractor with their ragged half-opened wings, snuffling in the sod for dead snakes. They are nature's garbage collecting squads, but I dislike them; they make me think of the many unpleasant ways that one may die. And speaking of *that,* it has been a long time since I have felt so clearly that some final struggle is about to take place in my lungs. As the day has passed I have felt a growing fever and that dry, naked tenderness in my nose and throat that means that all my defenses have been routed and that my poor membranes scraped clean are now being overwhelmed by bugs. Again. In the middle of one cold I am now coming down with another. Tomorrow, if I last that long, is going to be a bitch. Defiantly, as though I were committing suicide, I sit by the window staring out at the desert and smoking cigarettes. They are tasteless, hateful, painful, burning, my head aches and my throat is raw, but I sit there smoking two or three an hour, smoking them down to their nasty little filtered butts as though they are the only thing that can dull the tedium of this encircling desolation. My thoughts begin to tend toward incoherency.

From time to time we pass through little collections of buildings disguised as towns: a gas station, next to it an awful square closed-in building as dark as a grave that advertises food — roast or skewered chunks of beef, an adobe lean-to with a sign "Borracharia" that in Spanish has something to do with drunkenness but in Portuguese has something to do with flat tires. What is being suggested: that we get drunk while our tires are being repaired? A sign: "Tears of the Blessed Mary. Population, 32." The people in these places standing in shadow are dimly seen, diminished in the landscape to spots of dull color; they are swallowed up and transformed by the *sertão* into undifferentiated figures upon whose almost identical faces the land has stained a kind of vacant mediocrity. They frighten me. It is not the land but the people who frighten me. I look at the few passing faces with suspicion, lowering my eyes, menaced, thankful for the thick blue-tinted windows that separate us; for once I am unashamed to be a tourist, isolated in my privileged place, just passing through.

I have absorbed that little bit of Brazilian literature that defines these people and that has defined them as cruel, desperate, and casually murderous. The villains of the books I have read embrace all classes of the population: cops, priests, politicians, cowboys, storekeepers, the parents of small children with their knotted ropes, and grandparents with whips of leather, even the bored adolescents. It is the land itself, of course, that is the villain and that has brutalized the people. I see them as a threat to my sense of my-self as a man. That guy over there with the curling mop of hair and the thick black moustache—he looks like someone who, for a snap of the fingers, would nail my nuts in a drawer for the sheer joy of lifting for a few minutes the heavy boredom that deadens his face. I don't want my nuts nailed in a drawer and the house on fire and the knife in my hand. Decisions like this I can do without; fuck these macho exercises. I don't even want to walk down one of these dusty streets to confront and test myself against the lazy insolence of the men's stares. I am no Norman Mailer who staggers around on the ledges of high buildings testing the authenticity of his vibes. These Brazilian tests are too macho, the failure to pass, too permanent. Let Mr. Mailer get his nuts nailed in a drawer, not this kid. Would his next book af-ter that experience take on a kind of high-pitched whining? The way I see it is this: in 1943 I flew twenty-seven combat missions over Europe in a B-17; I am a goddam hero and have the papers to prove it; I believe they are signed by Franklin D. Roosevelt. No more tests. I can be a self-respecting coward for the rest of my life. Drive on, driver; let's get the hell out of here.

By some miracle I am now given a little hint of another truer reality. Ahead of us something has caved in or broken; a bridge is out or a stretch of highway is being resurfaced. The bus stops behind a couple of cars and we wait. There is nothing to look at but brown earth, a dry, gravel-covered stream bed, and low hills. From out of the bushes, from out of a little hovel made of piled weeds, two young men carrying baskets, their contents cov-ered with brilliantly white napkins, climb up a little incline and knock on the door of the bus. They walk down the aisle with the napkins folded back above the baskets, saying in low voices (Is it a holy word?) the same word to each of us. The napkins are the color of the cloth that a priest uses to wipe the Communion chalice. The word they murmur is not *humitas* and not *tamales*, but that or something very like it is what they are selling—corn-meal ground from ear corn that is not quite hard and cooked within rolled husks. One of the men is a mulatto, the other is white with dark but sun-streaked hair. The skin on his face and arms is spotted with the enflamed sores of skin cancer. It is impossible to guess even vaguely at their ages; the country has marked them and burned something from their faces. Is it anticipation that they have lost? The expectation of something exciting ever happening? Perhaps they are about eighteen with the faces of thirty-year-olds, teen-agers moving directly from childhood to middle age. They have the thin, spare bodies of acolytes.

They move up and down the aisle and at first no one will buy. We turn our faces from them and stare out the window, embarrassed to be refusing this food that has been prepared for us and is being offered so humbly. But there is a powerful magic in those baskets; a steamy incense, a primitive Stone Age perfume is filling the bus. There is a growing sense that we are being invited to participate in a primitive religious rite for it is an absolutely fundamental smell that rises in that steam, the musty smell of damp earth, goat sperm, rocky soil, blast of sun. Concentrated in the corn is the essence of this land.

For almost the first time in fifteen years, against all my prejudices, I feel impelled to buy food from the street, food that has been prepared under suspicious circumstances. One of the more blatant manifestations of my cowardice in South America has always been a shuddering reluctance to put into my mouth much of the food that has been offered to me in the houses of very poor people. I have never bought food prepared in a roadside kiosk. Often it is worse than a reluctance, it is a physiological impossibility. Sensitive to the risk of offending and driven by the laws of courtesy, I have had to test my courage past its limits. Pushed into the last corner, smiling, saying, "Oh, this looks GOOD," I take something gruesome from the plate and force it into my mouth. The food lies there heavy, like something dead, the muscles of my throat are paralyzed, I sweat, my stomach knots in repudiation. I have gone miles out of my way to avoid these confrontations and when caught have invented horrible sicknesses like cancer of the liver to explain why, lamentably, my doctor has forbidden me to eat iguana, sloth, armadillo, the little ratlike jungle *juanta,* the tiny nocturnal possums with their enormous wondering eyes, or the cunning, masturbating *cuzumbís,* those awful things cooked in their own black juices and centered on the best plate above a little pile of rice. (When Ramón was suffering from asthma in the peanut harvests he made a broth from the larva of the *jualpa,* those great, pale, fat, wormlike blobs with horny red heads that were killing our coconuts. When Ramón's father has a peaked kidney he will drink for a few mornings a glass of his own urine.) There is nothing that separates me more from poor people than the food they eat. How many nights have I gone hungry, miles out on some muddy trail, unable to do more than nibble at the food that has been placed before me by people who wish to honor me with the best they have. Thank you, you are very kind, but no, I couldn't, no more snake. But thank you, thank you. I draw my hand across my throat to indicate that I am full right up to here; it is the same motion I would use if I had a knife in my hand.

Those goddam anthropologists. How I envy and hate them when they come back from the villages along the Napo or the Marañón, pink-cheeked and bouncing. They have feasted on the fermented juices of masticated yucca, roast howler monkey, *jualpa* larva, guinea pigs, and alligators. How they underline my timid cowardice or, as I prefer to call it, my sense of decency or as Ubaldo would put it, my sense of not being false to my body. Or vice versa since it is my body who takes control and makes me say, thank you, thank you, but no more.

But now I am being tempted; it is like an unfulfilled obligation. Eating this strange and basic food that has been cooked in a battered pot over wood of mesquite or sticks of acacia, eating this food that has been pounded on a slab of wood by unparticular hands becomes a kind of test that I have seldom passed before. I buy two *humitas* and hold them in my lap. It is like a signal to the other passengers who now begin to call to the youths waving paper cruzeiros.

The road is open now and the soldiers are motioning us ahead, but the bus driver and his *ayudante* wait patiently until all the passengers have made their purchases and as the young men leave, accept with smiles their gift of food. Once more we move across the desert, the *humitas* cooling in my lap. They are still hot to the touch, hot against my leg, and they lie there cooling – damp, heavy, and limp, as mysterious as the bandaged phalluses of Quechua gods. I unwrap the *humitas* and eat. The flavor of the corn is strong and innocent; it has the seminal taste of reproduction, of musk, the Aztec taste of fertility. The goat taste of the cheese is as sharp and brutal as a blow; a rushing stream of saliva fills my mouth. Bowing my head over the food is like bowing down to the land and eating its food. I feel vaguely that I am being exorcised of its curse. Seen now in the light of early evening it is stark and bone-pure, a twisted land that suffers with the twisted people it has made.

.   .   .

I go to sleep in a desert and wake up a few seconds later just as it is getting dark in another country that looks as though I have died and gone to heaven. In the blinking of an eye hell has been replaced by paradise. At the time I accept this miracle without question; later studying maps I will be unable to retrace the journey or identify the spot. From some unidentifiable point until morning when we reach the outskirts of Ilhéus I move through country that seems to be constructed out of hallucinations. We have entered a land made beautiful by the loving hands of men. It is the only time on this trip, almost the only time in South America, when there is a blending of my perception of how life is with my feelings of how life should be. I am flooded with joy to see this place, its slight imperfections (if there are any) masked by the dim light of approaching night. Through the years it has become increasingly difficult to imagine a world that is fit for more than just a few to live in. But here it is, a testament to my sanity. The kind of world I thought the world might make, here it is—so easy to do, so logical, so inevitable.

An immense country of gently rolling hills, all of it intensely cultivated and planted into neat square patches. The plants are a brilliant green, proud and healthy in straight and measured rows. There are no weeds. Each patch proclaims its own pure glowing essence—half-acre squares of vegetables and flowers, enough to feed a million people—tomatoes, carrots, spinach, marigolds and zinnias, Swiss chard, peas and bush beans, sweet corn and *caraota*, sweet potatoes and yucca, mile after mile. Small brightly painted houses stand at the edges of these fields; there is about one house to every ten acres. There are soft lights in the windows, small cultivating tractors in the yards, children running, women standing in doorways silhouetted against candlelight, and men, slow and tired, walking down lanes with hoes or machetes laid across their shoulders. What is heaven for most of us if it is not the satisfaction of having worked hard for yourself, and of knowing that after you have eaten well that you will lie down, make love, and fall into the deep eight-hour sleep of total obliteration that you have earned?

The highway follows a curving stream around the bases of the hills; between the stream and the road at intervals of a mile or so groups of stores form miniature towns—a drugstore, a grocer's, a dentist's office, a bicycle-repair shop, a couple of places with tables under large trees where men sit drinking beer. It is all made perfect by the failing light and the soft glow of lamps and candles; it is pure nostalgia. But its true beauty lies in its meaning, this tremendous landscape that has been shaped by men. Under their care, which is like passion, they have created a world that pours out an incredible flood of richness. The beauty is in the grandeur of the conception, and the miracle is in seeing good land being worked by the men who own it. It is almost the only place in South America I have ever seen where an immense piece of good land has not been turned into the private fiefdom of a single man. If it is not heaven, it is as close, no doubt, as I will ever get. I sit at the window blowing my nose and harshly coughing and staring out the window until it is completely dark. Once again I fall asleep, but I am beginning to feel like hell. Beginning to sweat I float away from time to time in a mild delirium; it is as though I am taking a trip in two dimensions, in two directions at the same time, and I have the interesting presentiment that I am going backwards in time to observe my own death.

.   .   .

One morning in October of 1969 I got into my father's car and slammed the door. Though I didn't know it at the time this sound, so expensively orchestrated by the Ford Motor Company to give the impression of richness and stability to their product, was a symbol of the strange and powerful coincidences that erupt out of our lives from time to time and give us the feeling that underneath all the chaos there is possibly some design that we ought to be considering. Is it true that in the moment of Jung's death a bolt of lightning split in two the great oak tree outside his window? Was there a connection between that car door and my father's death?

After five years of the most intense involvement with the Peace Corps I was finally leaving it, and the portentous sound of that slamming door had its own sad and final meaning for me. I had been four years in Ecuador as a volunteer; after that I had worked for a while as a recruiter and for the last three months I had been in Montana helping to train a new group of volunteers who were going to Ecuador. That morning in 1969 was an ordinary morning in Montana. We had been training on a dude ranch, a small oasis of fir trees set in the middle of great pastures, and now the training was over. The new volunteers were packed into a bus and whisked away to new South American adventures. A great calm fell over the countryside as the bus disappeared, and the dude ranch suddenly seemed as dead as some animal with its throat cut. Those of us who still remained—a dozen or so staff members—had a short final meeting and discussed each volunteer (we had promised not to do this), said good-bye to one another, and parted. I had stolen my father's car to come to this place and must now take it back to him, though I suspected that he would never drive again. Four days later in Seattle I learned that at ten thirty in the morning, in that same minute that I had slammed the car door and driven away from the Peace Corps across the cattle guard, my father had died.

Simultaneously I had lost those two figures who in some degree represented the authority around which I had tried to build my life: my father, who had made me into his opposite (I hoped) and had forced me to play the role of a hypocrite, and his substitute, the Peace Corps, which in a more benign way had offered me another more satisfying role that ultimately I had had to disown.

My father, when he heard that I was going into the Peace Corps, had dis-owned me as a Communist radical. He felt that by involving myself with a project dreamed up by the young playboy Communist John Kennedy, that I was doing it solely as an insult to my father's more decent and traditional conservatism. I was doing it simply to break his heart. For three years he refused to write me. He had cut me out of his life. He did finally what his psychiatrist had recommended thirty years before. I hope it was as happy for him as it was for me. But it probably wasn't, for during my last year in Ecuador as a volunteer I began once more to get his strange and menacing letters. Some of them I opened and read. They had taken months to reach me. In refusing to recognize the actuality of the Peace Corps institution or my physical presence in a particular country, out of contempt and illusion he would address my mail to Venezuela, Uganda, or Guatemala. After my name, to which once again he had begun to affix my rank from the Second World War, Captain, he would write "Piece Corpse." These letters, arriving in inappropriate countries, would be sent to the Washington, D.C., office and eventually forwarded to me.

About once a month I would leave Rioverde, the village on the ocean where I worked, and take a truck or a canoe into Esmeraldas, the provincial capital. I would pick up my mail, buy up old *Time* magazines, eat smoked pork chops at the German restaurant in Las Palmas, and talk English while drinking beer with the Americans in town who shipped bananas or ran the shrimp boats. At night I went to the movies or sat at outside tables on the main street watching the parade of pretty girls. The next morning I would do my business – pick up boxes of day-old chicks or sacks of feed or leave an outboard motor to be repaired or buy a pot or medicine or a pound or two of seed for someone out there on the beach. Late in the afternoon if the tides were right and the beach was free I would take the truck back up the coast. Sometimes instead of staying in Esmeraldas I would grab the afternoon bus and go up to Quito because at times the village became a very depressing place and after a few weeks with no news of the outside world, or worse, having been too deeply involved in the irrationalities of Rioverde and be-ginning to suspect that nothing else was real, I would feel apprehensive and unhinged. Atomic bombs could have been popping over the cities of Europe and America for a month and none of us in Rioverde would have known it. I don't know why it was so important to know that the bombs hadn't fallen yet, but it was. More important than atomic war, I had to get away from Rioverde and eat a few decent meals to keep from starving to death.

·   ·   ·

I went in early one morning to Esmeraldas in the canoe with the intention of continuing on up to Quito. Thought of meat, green vegetables, and milk shakes had taken possession of my imagination. I had never had any big thing going with a hamburger, especially with the Ecuadorian hamburger, but now I had reached the point of feeling that if I didn't get a hamburger within the next few hours that I was in danger of losing my mind and of breaking down into protracted fits of uncontrollable weeping. Literally. I could get an erection thinking of hamburgers, though unlike Portnoy I had no unnatural designs on them. I was eating pretty much like a poor man eats, or trying to – or forced to – and it had begun to affect my emotional stability.

There was mail for me at the post office, letters from a girl in San Francisco and Stan Arnold of the *San Francisco Chronicle*, who enclosed a letter from a New York editor. The editor wrote to say that the articles I had been sending to the newspaper would make a book but he hoped I would put in some black teats and some juicy screw scenes on the beach if I wanted *his* company to publish it. And the first of my father's letters arrived. It had been forwarded from Washington via Costa Rica and had taken four months to reach me.

It was an amazing letter and I read it with a sinking heart; he had begun again to communicate with me as casually as though his last letter had been written the week before. Casual but threatening, he spoke of his desire for a reconciliation but realistically, knowing there was no other way, he hinted that I would be rewarded with the only thing he had that made me salivate and tremble, that made my ears stand straight up – his money.

For twenty years I had kissed that man's ass for his money. He had a lot of it, including some of mine if the rumors were true, and since the war, lacking the character to make a break with him, to make an independent gesture that would free me from his shadow, I had created a kind of semi-satisfying life for myself that would be semisatisfactory to both of us. He had wanted me to run errands for him in Seattle, but I had bought a farm in California; it was something that he could just barely forgive. He had helped me with loans of money from time to time but had always insisted on being repaid when I was least able to do it. As he moved into his seventies one of my most powerful and enduring fantasies was built around my father's death and the money he would leave me.

When I finally went broke, five thousand dollars would have saved me. My father waited for me to come to him and beg for it as I had been in the habit of doing for the previous twenty years. But this time I couldn't do it. For twenty years he had been telling me how stupid I was, that I had no head for business, that he was disgusted to see me walk into his house tieless and wearing Levis. I had finally come to believe that I was as stupid as he said I was. He was dumbfounded when he learned that I had sent in an application to the Peace Corps and he wrote me a furious letter. If I persisted in bringing chaos to the tranquility of his "sunset years" he would sure as shit "cut me off at the pockets." For almost the first time in my life I stood up to him; I told him where he could stick his money. It would not be true to say that I had never regretted this show of independence though I had certainly gotten a lot of pleasure out of it at the time. Now over three years later he had begun to write me again, holding out the same promise again. I read the letter feeling sick to my stomach for I knew immediately that I had been instantly seduced, that I would go back, that I would sit by his sick bed and kiss his ass until my lips fell off.

I took my mail down into the main part of town where the restaurants were and on the way bought some of the recently old *Time* magazines. While I ate ham sandwiches and dishes of ice cream I began to read the news. On the cover of one magazine was a group of photographs—the burning of Watts. I read the article sinking into a despair that I hadn't felt since Kennedy was murdered. I was already undermined with hunger and that letter from my father, who was half-promising me a half a million dollars if I would only come back and go through the motions of making peace with him.

Instead of continuing on to Quito, instead even of buying supplies of food to take back to the village, I rushed down to the *malecon* and caught a returning canoe. If I had any family at all now it was out there in Rioverde, and I felt a terrible need to be there. At six o'clock that evening, ten hours after I had left, I was sitting in my house eating rice and tuna fish; at six thirty alerted by the candle burning in my room, the Rioverde gang had gathered—the young Rioverde fishermen: Ramón, Orestes, Rufo, Wai, Pancho, Ramón Arcos. What was wrong? Why was I back so soon? Why had I not gone on to Quito? Here is why, I said. I opened the *Time* magazine and tried to translate the article and burst into tears. The young blacks stared at one another, uncomfortable and embarrassed. I had never broken down publicly before; something awful must have happened someplace that would make a white man weep. "Ah, those dirty black savages, those sons of bitches," Ramón said, trying to comfort me. "No, no," I cried, "you don't understand. What they did had to be done, and someday you will have to do it, too. That's why I'm crying; someday you will have to do it, too."

But why, really, had I wept that night? A half hour before I had read about Watts, I had felt the beginnings of a despair that would culminate in those tears. I think it was this: that in reacting so immediately and so basely to the simple trap my father had set, I had been confronted with the in-authenticity of my presence in that black town. I realized that I was like an actor who, caught up in his role, suddenly forgets his lines with the aware-ness that the swords that will pierce him are made of wood, that in another hour he will be strolling down the boulevard with friends, looking for that special little place that will serve him oysters and champagne. And he will sit there talking about the nuances of his performance.

If in some degree we are all actors and are playing the part that we feel best expresses our essence, still most of us engaged in an action where swords will be waved about do their best acting when they are under the impression that the swords are real. In the war being shot at with real bul-lets or watching my friends, their parachutes ablaze, falling slowly through the spaces of high altitude, I had never felt so authentic. I was real right down to my quivering asshole, my shrieking testicles. Now, after three years in the Peace Corps, my father's letter had illuminated my real position in Ecuador; I was engaged in the ultimate bourgeois gesture. I had come to live for a time in a poor village where, in spite of being the most minor of the minor characters, the most irrelevant person there, still I was the only one who would be shot at with toy guns, slashed at with wooden swords, the only one who would bleed catsup. When things got too rough: if I got sick or the food became unbearable or if the town for some reason or another should erupt into drunken violence or if, even, the *ambiente* of the town be-came too boring, I could simply jump in a canoe for Esmeraldas and catch a bus for Quito. I was the only one in town who could solve his problems by simply going to Quito. In another year I would be leaving Ecuador for good. If I played my cards right and put kisses in the right places, most probably I could arrange to be undisinherited and would end up being well paid for that lifetime's kissing, which, being only half-hearted, had not pleased my father and had humiliated me, had in fact corrupted my life.

I didn't understand all these things at the time as clearly as I understand them now. Mostly I was just confused, feeling that great contradictions were testing my sanity. I wasn't ready to realize that in filling an emptiness that had appeared with my father's rejection that I had used the Peace Corps as a surrogate family and had thrown myself into a sentimental relationship with it, offering it a fanaticism that it didn't need and demanding from it a dependence that it couldn't fulfill. But from that time when I read about Watts I began very tentatively to plan another kind of life. What I wanted was a life that was absolutely permanent and stable. I needed to lock myself into a situation, to be so deeply committed that I could not escape from it and that I could define as safe because no one would have the power to eject me out of it. What could be more final than to take the last of my money and buy a jungle farm with it? I would trap myself into living a real life and by staking everything I had would lock myself into an honest situation at last. My situation would be as authentic as an astronaut's, bolted into a capsule and whirling out past the Van Allen belt. It is easy twelve years later to construct a logical philosophical framework to explain this decision, which was so eccentric compared to the possibilities that might reasonably have been projected for me. Now I perceive inevitability, but who could have imagined a few months before Watts, least of all myself, that I would plan on spending the rest of my life as a tropical farmer? All this rationalization however, was nothing beside the stronger pull of my inclinations, which were purely emotional. I didn't want to go back to the United States where for most of my life, it now seemed apparent, I had been only half-alive.

Just before I left the Peace Corps, Ramón's wife, Ester, had her first child, Martita. Ramón said, "If you come back to Ecuador Ester and I want to have another child; the second one will be yours." I had fallen into another deeper trap; looking into Martita's face I knew instantly that I had put down new roots and that at last I had a family. How nice it was to be able to choose my own.

·　　　　·　　　　·

My aunt, the youngest of my father's sisters, and I were the only members of his family who were at his funeral. Everyone else was already dead or permanently estranged from him. The two of us sat together in a chapel just behind a woman whom we didn't immediately recognize – an old woman with badly dyed blonde hair and wearing a dirty tan-colored polo coat. The coat looked familiar. "Who is that woman in front of us?" my aunt, who was quite deaf, whispered to me in a voice that echoed up and down the aisles. I shook my head and studied this half-familiar, half-pathetic woman and after a minute realized with a shock that it was my father's wife, my stepmother. How casual and dirty she looked; as though she had momentarily interrupted her work in the garden to pop in to the chapel and bury her husband. She would no longer speak to me, and we did not speak that day. A very few very old business associates tottered up the aisle to stand a moment before the open casket and appraise the quality of the embalmer's work. "Do you want to look at your father?" my aunt whispered. "No," I said. "Nor do I," said my aunt, to whom my father had not spoken for years until a few months before he died, when, his brains wandering away on ancient paths, he became convinced that he still loved her.

As the minister recited his eulogy my stepmother began to tremble. It was not grief that shook her, it was rage. That same minister had once publicly referred to her as a Fascist, had come to the house to apologize for his imprudence, but upon leaving had gotten up and said, "But Mrs. Thomsen, you are still a Fascist."

We drove out to the cemetery behind the hearse and behind the car that carried my stepmother. The undertaker's assistant was an old skiing friend of mine, he said. He sat beside the driver in the front seat and we talked about skiing at Mount Rainier when we were young. I didn't remember the undertaker's assistant nor having skied with him. He was bald and it shocked me to think that I had once known someone who had ended up in such a weird and distasteful profession or that I had known someone my own age who was now so old and spent. Was this the guy who had painted my father's lips with rouge and had sniffed among the banked flowers for the signs of corruption as the highway patrols of three states searched for me? We gathered around the grave standing on yards of plastic grass that had been unrolled to hide the piles of honest earth. The casket was lowered into the ground; the last words said. As we waited for the limousine to take us back into town, an hysterically weeping woman came up and embraced me. "I'm so *sorry*," she kept repeating over and over, "I'm so *sorry*." I was embarrassed because I didn't quite recognize her, and because I had no idea what she was so sorry about. Had some terrible inappropriate something happened at this final rite that I hadn't seen? Had the casket dropped? Had the minister been drunk? If she was mourning my father's death, as a little later I had to assume she was, I found the intensity of her emotion to be highly suspicious and inappropriate. My father had been in a hospital for months and much of the time completely out of his head. Under restraint was what they called it when they had had to rope him to the bed. Why was this woman weeping for the end, finally, of so much suffering? "Who is this woman?" my aunt asked with a stern and outraged face, affronted by this lack of decorum.

Back in the car the undertaker asked me where I wished to be taken. "You will come for lunch," my aunt said, saving me from having to admit that I had no place I wished to be taken and that this visit to Seattle, the last I would ever make in my life, made me feel like that moment when the last leaf falls from a naked tree. Now in every sense I was disconnected from a horrid past and hoped only to be blown to far places where even the memories of this town would fade. There were two things I had to do: talk to my father's lawyers and buy a ticket back to Ecuador. No, three things. While I waited a scarcely decent two days to see the will, I borrowed ten thousand dollars from a bank and put up as security against this loan some shares of stock I owned. It was the last of my assets. On the third morning I went to see the lawyers and they gave me a copy of the will. "We did the best we could for you, but as you know he wasn't easy to work with." I glanced through the intricate provisions; I had kissed and kissed but he had fooled me again. Most of his money went to my stepmother, a lot of it to the Spastic Society, great gobs of it to the Humane Society and to some perhaps still unborn genius who would invent a contraceptive for cats. "He's left his money to the fucking *cats*?" I asked incredulously. "But can't this will be broken?" The lawyers laughed. "We wouldn't be very good lawyers if we had made a will that we thought could be broken," one of them said. "It's not as bad as it sounds," said the other. "My, how we fought for you. The principal will remain in the trust, but you will draw interest on your share until you die; after that it goes to the cats." He looked at me and sniggered. A few minutes later I stood outside their offices chewing on my tongue, which felt swollen in my mouth; after a time I went back into the office. "You can give me the contraceptive money," I said. "I've just invented a fool-proof system." "Oh?" one of the lawyers said, smiling. "And what is that?" "Stick a fucking cork up their asses," I said. I marched out slamming the door, and a couple of days later I was back in Quito. All in all my father's death had been a kind of gruesome slapstick comedy in which his madness had finally made itself publicly manifest. His fortune to a bunch of yowling pregnant pussy cats, for Christ's sake? Ah, there's many a slip twixt the cup and the lip.

·   ·   ·

A terrible paroxysm of coughing awakens me. God knows what time it is but it feels like after midnight. What blackness. The bus is traveling fast and straight along what seems to be a miles-long beach front. The highway is lit with a row of tall, cement streetlamps; they give off a cold blue light that stretches away to the horizon. On the left, thinly spread at intervals of a thousand yards, deserted parking lots and glass-fronted stores lit from within but locked and deserted; on the right a tremendous blankness that suggests the sea. There are no cars and no people and the long row of street-lamps illuminates nothing and makes of the night a surrealism that has never been painted—a nighttime study of perspective and abandoned desolation. Another terrible fit of coughing; I am, in my desperation, the perfect figure for this empty landscape. My lungs feel as though while I slept someone had filled them with cement that is now setting up and hardening into a solid concrete chunk. I am turning into a figure by Magritte, half-stone, half-suffering flesh, the perfect monument to tourism. They will have to blast me out of this bus with charges of dynamite. I feel too rotten to be frightened, like a seasick sailor, death and an end to suffering would be a welcome diversion. I am filled with despair knowing that we are still four-teen hours from Bahia and a hot bath and a week in bed. Sweating and shivering, coughing and gasping for air, I move interminably across that in-sanely lit stretch of emptiness. Six distant lights off to the left suggest a sleeping village; miles away on the right a single light becomes a boat or a lighthouse or an airplane warning on the top of an oil rig. I populate this landscape, which is nothing but lights and sand dunes.

We approach a gas station that is brightly lit, and the bus slows down. The inside of the bus is briefly illuminated, and in this moment, beginning to cough again, I glance into the window beside me and am struck dumb.

·   ·   ·

At lunch that day my aunt had led the conversation in curious directions. I was uncomfortable and repelled by her talk but felt that I understood her preoccupations. She was almost ninety years old, and my father's death and the funeral that morning had excited her imagination. It had been years since I had seen her; I had never known her well for she lived in Europe much of her life, but I had never seen her do a vulgar thing, never heard her speak in an offensive way. (This is another more civilized aunt and not her older sister, the amazing and formidable aunt who would take her teeth out and wash them at the luncheon table.) And so today I was unprepared and startled when she began to speak of death in a most earthy way. I suppose for years being very old she had been contemplating death and had come to terms with it; I suppose like those shambling old men who had been drawn to contemplate my father's corpse, she was fascinated with the mechanics of dying, the sight and the touch and the smell of it, of the way life rushed away from a body. Old age's pornography.

She had called the hospital where my father had died and done her research. Now as we ate and drank a glass of wine she told me what she thought I ought to know. A final and necessary part of intimate family history was being passed on to me.

"I talked to the nurse who was on duty. At ten thirty she came into Charlie's room; it was time for some of the medicine he had to take. When she came in he was sitting propped up against the pillows. His radio was off, but he was awake. He had taken his dentures out and held them in one hand. She took the glass of water and the pills and offered them to him. He began to reach out and then stopped with a look of amazement on his face. He coughed once. Hard. And then he couldn't breathe; he couldn't get air into his lungs. He looked at the nurse with an imploring look and began to beat at his chest with one fist; he let his false teeth drop onto the bed. His face turned red, his eyes opened very wide, and then he lay back slowly and closed his eyes. It took less than a minute. . . . It was a nice way to go; Charlie had an easy death."

As soon as my aunt had begun to speak of this final minute I had closed my ears, or rather, I had begun to think my own thoughts and allowed her words to run through me, in and out again. I did not need a graphic description of this intensely private moment to make me know that he was dead any more than I had needed to see him laid out in his old blue double-breasted suit. I had never felt the need to share his death. I truly believed that I had never really heard my aunt's words, those words, which coming from her lips, are doubly obscene, until that moment in the bus when the lights in the gas station throw my reflection against the window—and I see my father, his face red and his eyes starting out of him as he tries to fill his lungs with air. My aunt's words rush through my head. Looking at myself I watch my father die. The lights faded away behind us, and we moved once more, fast and straight, across that empty black midnight beach. I lay back exhausted and shaken, waiting for the trip to end.

Salvador, Bahia de Todos os Santos

From the window of my room at the back of the hotel where I lie in bed for almost a week, I can look down into the lower, older part of the city: to the sixteenth-century harbor, the great bay that turns gold and bronze in the late afternoons, and across the water to the island of Itaparica. The town belongs to Jorge Amado, that romantic who has made truth out of a lying vision, who has superimposed over the squalor of an incredible poverty the soul of a new race. Everything is buoyant, mildly glittering, strangely silenced and distanced, suspended in the sea air of the deep tropics; everything floats, matching my own delirium. Although I have scarcely stepped into its streets and have already seen terrible signs of decay, overcrowding, widespread poverty, and public corruption, I have been seduced by this city. I gaze down into the tiny harbor with its star-shaped stone fort or sit in the meltingly beautiful evening light thinking with amazement, "It's the most beautiful city in the world, the realest city in the world, the only city I could learn to love." Later when I have seen its narrow back streets blocked with garbage; walked through the barrios where the prostitutes call to you out of dark doorways – sections of town so collapsed and stinking that only Amado with his obsessions could have reinvented them into places of passion and the possibility of finding love; talked to some of its hordes of little shoe-shine boys who are twisted with hunger – after all this and more, Bahia will still remain that magic city, that mysterious, throbbing, and sensual place for which, against all common sense, one feels a kind of tragic urban passion.

At first I go out of the hotel only to eat. Breakfast is free, and I drink coffee on the second floor where I am waited on by a tall dour mulatto who never speaks and seems to resent being interrupted in his reading of scriptural material. He is that almost typical fanatic who loves God but can't bear to look into the faces of human beings. Faced with this gent each morning, I add an extra sugar to my coffee to cancel out his bleak vision of sinful man. It is usually the middle of the afternoon before I am driven out by hunger to stagger down the street. I eat a plate of rice and shrimp with a large beer almost every day, going to the same place because the food is close, good, cheap, and because the helpings are so purely Portuguese, so gigantic that I can give three quarters of it to the small children who cluster in the doorway waiting for a signal. They come to the table holding out scraps of cardboard that they have torn from the piles of garbage in the alley and onto which I shovel piles of beans, rice, and shrimp, and over which they empty that staple of the rural tropics, *manioc,* a yellow meal made of yucca. They seem to like its tasty tastelessness. Then I go back to bed and lie there coughing, sad and passive, with Conrad stretching his open pages across my chest. I am not making a trip now so much as simply trying to stay alive.

The woman who comes in each morning to clean my room is strong and beautiful—a young mulatto mother with a radiant smile and lovely dark skin. I appreciate the concern on her face when she hears me coughing, and when she is late I go out looking for her in the hall pretending to need a shirt or a pair of pants washed. We talk about her children who are, she says, incredibly beautiful. Toward the end of my stay she promises to bring them in so I may meet them. But she never does, and now, undisillusioned, I hold the memory of them in my head: a little boy and girl with the angelic faces of my own Moncho and Martita.

One afternoon I feel strong enough to go out and I walk down five blocks toward a plaza shaped like the deck of a ship where a statue of Pedro Alves, the poet of the city, stands with his back to the sea. In Amado's novel *Tereza Batista* it is this poet already dead and immortalized in bronze who comes down from his pedestal to fight beside the prostitutes against the brutality of the police. The barrio of the whores on the narrow sloping streets below the park is still there; the ghost of the poet had saved them from being driven out to a shoddier part of town. If there is a shoddier part of town.

Walking back to the hotel I pass a large church set back from the street and secured behind a high steel picket fence. It is built at the very edge of the cliff that plunges through the whore's quarters. The main doors are closed, but a small gate swings open as I pass, and an old woman moves out and puts herself before me on the sidewalk. She is black, erect, and her hair is cut short like a man's—gray-white ringlets shaped to her head. She is saying something that I don't understand, but smiling and saying it over and over as though it were a special message meant just for me. She points to the church and to a basket that she carries, a basket full of balls of yarn. Where she is pointing at one side of the church is another small open door and behind it a long, dark tunnel-like passageway with a curved roof. In the doorway another old black woman stands gesticulating, and at the far end of the passage, silhouetted against the bright light from the sea, standing black before the golden glitter of the bay, is still another woman. They are both looking toward me and waving as I lean toward the first old lady, scowling, and trying to understand what she is saying. I will remember this encounter and try to find a meaning in it, for in some profound way, it closely resembles a dream that I had in Quito shortly before leaving on this trip. It had been so strong and clear that I had tried to draw it: the long, dark passageway, the two women in the shadows, the intensely bright light at the end of the tunnel. I listen to the woman for a time and shake my head and explain about this little problem I am having with the language. *Yo no falo Português.* The old woman seems to understand, she smiles, and I pass on.

João Ubaldo is the editor of a newspaper. Off the street I buy copies of every paper but the right one and study the editorial pages looking for his name. I go into a dozen bookstores on *Sete de Setembre,* but no one has heard of Ubaldo, the greatest of Brazil's young writers. The stores are stocked mostly with American authors in paperback. Hot off the press: Steinbeck's *In Dubious Battle, Of Mice and Men,* Thomas Wolfe's *Of Time and the River.* All of Hemingway, Sinclair Lewis, Edna Ferber. It is like going into a bookstore of fifty years ago. Brazil is represented by Amado. Like doing everything in South America, getting hold of Ubaldo becomes complicated, and at the end of the first week, feeling better but still not well enough to meet him, I take a small boat from the quay at the *mercado modelo* and go across to Itaparica for a few days. I have read in my traveler's guidebook that on one tip of the island is a hotel run by an Englishman, so after the boat I head across country by taxi and end up in a ghost town; there is nothing more symbolic of passing time than a resort in the off-season with leaves blowing through the streets and the houses nailed shut and deserted. The owner of the hotel, an old man dying of boredom, welcomes me. As well he might. I am his only guest, and he offers me my choice of a hundred rooms. He is a nice but unenthusiastic old geezer, and in the evenings I am invited to eat at his table, but my passion to hear English is quickly satisfied. He is a man stuck with a large hotel that he'd like to sell and since I don't appear to be a buyer he confesses over and over that with nigger help it is impossible to run a decent establishment. I am amazed at his passion; the boys and girls who run the place are the only graceful touch in this silent mausoleum.

"I've been looking for João Ubaldo all over Bahia," I say finally, trying to change the subject. "Tell me how I can find him."

"Never heard of him," the owner says. "What's his game?"

"He's a writer. He's written *Sergeant Getulio,* one of the great Brazilian novels. And he's a newspaper editor."

"His name again, please."

"João Ubaldo Ribeiro."

"Ah, yes. I did hear that little João wrote a book. Certainly, I know him. He's a Ribeiro. Know his mother well. Her family practically owned this island at one time. His mother lives here in town, but I think she's over in the city now."

"Can you call him for me?"

"Nothing easier, old man."

But it is not that easy. Two days go by. The lines are out or nobody answers or Ubaldo's mother is out for a while. To pass the time I walk along the edge of the water looking for shells. The beach of this resort has long since disappeared and now lies under six inches of mud, industrial waste, and plastic garbage. I have been told that there are no shells here, but in two mornings I collect fifty small conches with slick insides as passionately colored, as pink and throbbing as great erotic art. I pile them on the dresser, and at night the hermit crabs within the shells tumble onto the floor and scuttle across it making weird and awful noises in that deserted place.

In the afternoon there are other noises. A couple of hundred feet out in the water directly in front of the hotel a couple of sunken and rusting ships are being dynamited by the Brazilian navy. Piles of iron scrap lie on the beach. From three to five p.m. tremendous explosions shake the beach and geysers of boiling water erupt around the wrecks, first one and then the other. Lying on my bed one afternoon shaken awake by the noise, the concussion, the trembling of the hotel walls and the rattling at the windows, I open my eyes just as a great crack opens on the ceiling above my head. It strikes me as miraculous as some camera trick in a De Mille spectacular and fits in perfectly with my perception of Brazil as a country that is shaking itself to pieces faster than it can build itself up. That evening the owner shows me a dozen other cracks, long ones underneath the windows on the outside portico and cracks that encircle the square cement posts that support the outside walls. The navy will pay him to repair the damage, he thinks. The hotel is built on leased land within that thirty-meter strip at the water's edge that the navy controls. He really can't raise too much hell or they'd tell him to move his hotel back twelve feet. As we sit in the portico talking about it and waiting for dinner there is a final explosion and bits of plaster fall from the outside walls outside the dining room. And a minute later, sitting down to eat, the owner calls into the kitchen and says something in impatient Portuguese. A waiter comes out and wipes a thin coating of plaster dust from the table. "These niggers just don't give a damn," the owner says. "We could be sitting here up to our asses in dust and they'd be out there in the kitchen humming and dancing."

During dinner I am called to the phone. "This is João. I got Kathy's letter a month ago. Where have you been? What in the *hell* are you doing on Itaparica?"

"Every time I open that damn traveler's guide I end up in some weird place. This time they sent me to a graveyard. When can I see you? I'm coming in tomorrow to Bahia with Sam."

"How about Friday? We'll have some dinner, and then I've got some music I want you to hear."

"Good. Real music from Bahia?"

"No, not exactly. A little *conjunto* that sounds exactly like Glenn Miller."

Ubaldo is speaking English in a lively way but treating the language as a joke. Tonight he sounds like an Iowa farmer; later I will listen to him as he mimics Southern redneck, Texas drawl, and Shakespearian rhetoric, mixing it all together, showing off.

"I wish I could invite you to stay with me, but I'm in the middle of a divorce and living in a very small cabin on the beach."

"No, no. No problem." I give him the name of my hotel. "I'll see you Friday."

But it is almost another later Friday in the next week before we meet. For no reason my cough has become much worse again, and I go back to bed. "João, I'm sorry. I have this damn cough that I can't shake; I think I'm dying, at least I hope I'm dying. But I'll call you in a few days if I don't, O.K.?"

"Yes, of course. I'm sorry. Call me when you feel better." He is polite but just a bit incredulous as though he couldn't quite believe that anybody would be too sick to celebrate life in Bahia. Thinking about it later I wish I had coughed some of those dry, hard, excruciating coughs into the receiver for him so that he would have had to believe me. They would have been authentic sounds of agony, impossible to fake.

I have come back to the hotel in the city and am treated like an old favorite. At no extra cost I am moved out of a nice back room and put into a front room with a twelve-foot-high closet and hung with heavy purple drapes. The sounds from the street are persistent and shattering, but loving Bahia I embrace her imperfections. In the afternoons I sit in the window watching the people on the sidewalk. Almost everyone is young, poor, colored, and beautiful. Everyone moves at a pace that is decent and without that panic that makes Rio seem hysterical. There is an openness in the faces that is like a kind of secret joy, and there are no lines of discontent or frustration around the eyes of the girls. What mankind wants more than anything is to be beautiful, sexually irresistible, capable of attracting love and giving pleasure. Here is a city that openly acknowledges this secret. It is a city where, underneath the normal pursuits, the people in it seem to be thinking of nothing else but their power to attract and of the great psychic charges that are going off between people in their most casual encounters. Connections are being made; people are looking at one another and with innocent delight.

In the botanical gardens in Rio, sitting with a mob of people waiting to hear a concert, I had begun talking to a Brazilian fellow with a German name. His heritage consisted of a single word, "Schiesse." When I told him I was about to head for Bahia his face lit up and he whispered something to a woman sitting on the grass just in front of him. She turned, smiling. "This is my wife," he said. "I was lucky and got me a Bahiana." She was not really beautiful, but there was a tremendous calm power that radiated from behind her pleasant but ordinary features. It was an absence of hang-ups, a sense of joyful acceptance, a glow of pleasure at the miracle of being alive. In one second she communicated to me that rare and beautiful sense of being completely human. No wonder I loved Bahia; I loved it before I ever saw it.

·   ·   ·

I lie in bed reading the last chapters of Amado's *Tereza Batista.* That poor raped and tortured girl comes to a happy ending, and at her wedding party in Bahia everyone is there, even the cynical young intellectuals who tip up the bottles of whiskey, checking out the prices printed on the bottoms. How smart I feel at this inside joke; Amado lists the intellectuals by name and João Ubaldo, his godson, is one of them.

·   ·   ·

One afternoon I begin to read Conrad's *Heart of Darkness* for the tenth time. I walk up the street and find a little opening between the buildings where the sun above the bay shines down on a single tree, a single bench, a little stretch of iron railing. I move into the center of this stage set and look across to Itaparica and the fishing boats scratching slow lines across the water, and, directly below me, gaze into the back patio of a small house with a small swimming pool and in it a little black kid playing by himself with a big ball. Bahia is very African, and especially now with Conrad in my lap. By this time I know that Conrad's story is almost literally true. It is no melodrama, no story invented to horrify, and now I read it as reporting, trying to move beneath the noble writing to the rage and disgust, to the acute observations. And come to that part. A French warship anchored off a jungle coast lobbing shells into a solid wall of trees, firing into a silent and unmoving continent. I have been reading *Heart of Darkness* for forty years but today it is not literature. Here in the bulge of South America the African coast lies just over there, a stone's throw on my left. Dakar is a couple hours away on almost daily flights. Bahia is Africa, and that warship firing into the trees no longer strikes me as a half-comic illustration of European stupidity. That gunboat is no longer Conrad's symbolic introduction to the rape of Africa that he is about to unfold. I read it as something absolutely real. It happened a hundred years ago, but I can almost hear the branches breaking as the shells crash into the trees. The echoes of those explosions are still rolling out over the Congo, over the Amazon, over all the continents of the world where people of color have suffered and wastefully died under the domination of Western ideology. Reading *Heart of Darkness* in Brazil gives to the story a special urgency; it is, or would be if it were allowed, like a headline in the newspaper. Driven out of Africa finally the same people who raped Africa have now discovered South America. They have left a ruined continent that quite possibly will never recover from their presence – and their plans for this continent are identical.

Until 1763 Bahia was the capital of Brazil; until almost a hundred years later it was still the capital of the slave trade. Bahia is a monument to the extermination of the Brazilian Indians, the enslavement of the African continent, the dominance of the Catholic Church, the institutionalization of the large *fazendas* along with the poverty that would make them pay. Bahia is a living museum to this past; it is all still quite real. The old things are still here to ponder: the slave market, the old slave quarters, the slave church, the feudal embankments, the walled fortress city more or less impregnable behind its cliffs and battlements and guarded by ancient cannons. Bahia

was the center of an odious culture, the focal point for a civilization that enslaved and murdered millions.

But sitting here in this golden light how can one believe it? How can this
beautiful and tender city have grown out of such sadism, such avarice, such
monumental criminality? How could the white seed of the rapists have produced such a race of people? For this is the miracle of Bahia: its people. Out
of a mixing of blood—white, black, Indian—a new race has been created.
These people are not like the uncertain, questing, still unformed zambos of
coastal Ecuador with their self-loathings and their amorphous and un-
constructed sense of their own identities. In Bahia, out of crushing poverty
and oppression, a new race has been born that knows itself; somehow out
of the filth that has been imposed upon them they have discovered the
secret of being human. How impossible to explain such things—or talk
about them. This perception contradicts and confuses my conviction that
the world is lost and that man is about to destroy himself in stupid madnesses. I sit in the sun not thinking clearly, but thinking of this hybrid
people, neither black nor white and burdened with a double prejudice, a
double vision. Is it possible that this people will someday overcome and
gain the power to make a new world?

Young Conrad, out of a job in a strange northern town where he knows
no one, waits for a berth in a ship that will take him away. He eats daily in a
restaurant where "the waiter who brought me my cup of coffee bore, by
comparison with my utter desolation, the dear aspect of an intimate
friend."

Reading this one afternoon, another afternoon in another park, still almost too weak to walk but driven by a desperate boredom to leave my hotel
room and the contemplation of its purple funereal drapes, I begin to shake
with a weird combination of emotions. I am weeping for Conrad and
laughing at myself, for I recognize in the utter loneliness of the young sailor
my own capacity to form passionate friendships with perfect strangers. One
morning as I sit on the toilet reading, my glasses slip from my nose and one
lens shatters on the cement floor. In the *Otica* where I go to have the lens replaced I become intensely involved with the girl behind the counter. Her
name is Maria de Lourdes, she is from the country, she has never talked to
an American. My God, what foolish questions I answer and how I prate and
babble to this sweet girl. She has never heard of D. W. Griffith but when I tell
her that I was born in Hollywood and lived for a time not more than a block
away from the lot where he was shooting his Civil War epic, her eyes widen
and she touches my arm as though I were some holy relic who could offer

her salvation. My God, Hollywood, she whispers. Yes, yes, I tell her. I have seen Charlie Chaplin, Lupe Velez, John Barrymore. In an elevator one day with Joan Crawford I very softly put my hand out and caressed her. I don't say where, but it was true—my hottest teen-age encounter. My God, she whispers again, Hollywood. Travolta.

For the last week I have been eating in a new place, a little upstairs restaurant beneath a bar with outside tables where students drink beer in the early evenings. I have this friendship with Fausto, the waiter, in a place where the food is neither especially good nor cheap, where I went at first because it was so close to the hotel, but where I go now simply for the delight of receiving Fausto's smile, of calling him by his name when I enter and hearing him call me by mine. Like Maria, he is from the country, too, and his Portuguese is impossibly rural, like the suckings and gushings of water swirling into a drain. *"Otra vez,"* I beg in Spanish, *"pero mas claro, mas despacio."* No way. He talks away making sounds like a flushing toilet, like the twitterings of sleepy birds, like an old black woman crooning, like an old fighter with his teeth knocked out. I make him talk by pointing to something on the menu and asking how it is made, but apparently everything in Bahia is made of the same ingredients. I learn the words for tomatoes, onions, garlic, salted codfish. When the restaurant is empty, and it usually is for I eat very early, Fausto sits down across the table from me, and we make unfathomable but friendly noises at each other. Some evenings he lets me buy him a beer, and we sit at the table without speaking, like old friends who communicate without words. Toward the end of my stay when he pours beer into my glass he will lay one hand on my shoulder as though coming in to work from out of the countryside. He too is lonely in this large city where he knows no one.

One evening I am eating at a table by the window when a customer climbs the steep stairs and sits down near me. Even before I notice that he is carrying an English translation of *Crime and Punishment* I identify him as an American. Is he a Peace Corps volunteer? Who else would be reading Dostoevski so late in life? He is the right age to be newly graduated with a B.A. in history, and he displays cultural scars that look familiar. Certain volunteers seem to go to extreme lengths to prove Conrad's thesis that a white man's soul is corrupted by the tropics. They arrive in an exotic culture having read Maugham and Conrad and act as though they had been programed to disintegrate. I have seen a few volunteers shortly before they resign from the organization with that same muddy complexion as the fellow who sits at the next table, those same dazed, sunken, and inward-looking eyes, that same careless and rather disgraceful way of dressing. There is a certain disconnection between the clothes and the shrunken man within them who has lost forty pounds since the day six months before when he bought the Levis and pasted the flowered decals across the back pockets. In a sense this guy is a cliché, or so I see him: that type who has been tossed and twisted in another culture that he can't make sense of, a man at that certain point in his cultural confrontation just before he throws up his hands in surrender and flees. Well, volunteer or not he looks like a man with the kind of problems that I would just as soon not hear about again. He reminds me of an old volunteer from Santo Domingo who, in order to externalize his horrors, would go each morning at three a.m. to the slaughterhouse and stand there shaking and drunken while the fat hogs had their throats cut. Listening to the shrieking of pigs, he said, helped him understand the deep despairing emotions of poor people.

I reach across my plate of Shrimp à la Bahiana and flip over my copy of Conrad so that its English title cannot be read.

When he turns to me ten minutes later and asks what time it is in a Portuguese that is mostly Spanish, I am reading again and taken by surprise and without thinking, without even looking up, I answer him in English.

"Well, holy midnight blooming cereus," he cries, lifting his eyes to the ceiling and making the sign of the cross, "interesting, interesting. The gentleman speaks English." He moves his chair around so that we face each other and looks at me with anticipation.

And so we talk across the tables as we eat. For a while Fausto stands behind this newcomer who has interrupted our intimate babblings. He smiles at me behind his back and wrinkles up his nose with a kind of mild and comic distaste. He is not going to hold anything against me.

Like strange dogs smelling at each other's rear ends we go through the usual tourist preliminaries. I'm so and so, a farmer from Ecuador, on ex-PCV. Used to have a farm in California but went broke. *His* name is Lewis, with a W, grew up in Indiana. He's not a volunteer but his brother is. In Bolivia. When I tell him something about myself he says, "interesting, interesting," but he would rather talk than listen. I sit back and try to put him together from the pieces that he offers me, but there are gaps in his life that seem to be as puzzling to him as to me. Precise details about British Columbia fade into a gray obscurity and suddenly we are jolting down some dusty back road in New Mexico trying to sneak past an agricultural inspection station.

His business is cactus; he is an international cactus smuggler. It's an interesting business; it really is. Interesting, interesting. National borders mean nothing, agricultural restrictions are a farce. A few dollars in the right hands, that's what this business is all about. In New Mexico the inspectors had even helped him go international; before that he was just shipping cactus out of Texas and like that there. He had his own truck and friends in Mexico. Borders didn't mean nothing. And man, there is something sweet about one of those mothers sitting out in front of a motel and lit up at night, sticking up there like you know what and softly glowing under colored spots. He took out beautiful specimens worth thousands, knew his business, sold all over the states as far as New York.

"What percentage died?" I ask him.

"Hardly none," he says. "Cactus I understand. It's all in how you take them out, wrap the roots. Maybe, no, less than 10 percent. Cactus travel well." There is a big gap now, a silence as his face goes vague and he tries to figure out what happened. "They took the truck away from me. How can you sell cactus without a truck? I had a dandy. Flatbed, a big tarp, a bed in the cab. I cooked out there alone under those big sunsets. Good vegetarian stuff."

"Who took your truck away from you?"

No answer; his eyes go unfocused and he looks at me as though I might know. "I'll bet there's *fantastic* cactus in Ecuador," he says finally.

"You'd clean up on the Galápagos," I tell him. "Those islands are pure cactus. Of course you'd have to dynamite them out of the lava rock, but that wouldn't be a problem to someone on his toes. Then there's the tortoises, those big ones, you could smuggle them out, too. There's not too many left, we killed them all off, but that makes it better, no? Now they're rare and worth lots of money."

"No shit?" Lewis says. "Interesting, interesting. Tortoises would be easy to handle. I read they live a year without eating; just throw them down in the hold like stick wood. The transportation is the problem. I can handle the cops. What does an Ecuadorian cop make, a hundred dollars? I was buying Mexican cops for pennies."

"Here's a million-dollar idea, Lewis. I've thought of doing it myself. Stuffed finches. Think of it, stuffed Darwin finches from the Galápagos. They'd sell like hotcakes. Here's the beauty of it, Lewis: they're so goddam tame they light on your hands. You go out in the morning and sit in the sun and the goddam finches arrive and land on your head and eat out of your hands. Shit, you could catch a hundred an hour. When they light on your hands you just close your fist and squash them. You could ship out finches by the ton."

"I think you're kidding," Lewis says, "but as a matter of fact I'm into stuffed birds."

I sit in a kind of speechless sadness now and listen to him. If I had not heard so many just like him I would have had to think him mad. But there are so many gringos down here with schemes and I have had the luck to meet them all—the guys who are smuggling orchids, birds both live and stuffed, tigers both live and skinned, the smugglers of marijuana, cocaine, gold, pre-Incan artifacts both real and false, boa constrictors, iguanas, and dried human heads, some of them real, some made out of baby sloth heads.

Lewis takes me to Puerto Rico and we dig up cactus; between a vague time and another we are doing something exciting and unscrupulous in Canada. Rhododendrons, I believe, in West Virginia, and a split-second later we are roaming around Argentina and Paraguay. He has a brother in Bolivia, Peace Corps. Would you believe it, after two weeks his brother refused to have him in his house, told him to get out of the country or he'd turn him over to immigration. "My own brother." Asunción is his headquarters now. Paraguay has some fantastic plant life. But transportation is a real problem. He's having a rough time in Paraguay. At the moment he's smuggling electrical equipment into the country from São Paulo, things like electric showerheads and fuse boxes. But that thirty-hour bus trip from São Paulo to Asunción is a killer. Every week, man; thirty hours going, thirty hours coming back, the passport so stamped and torn you can't read it. But he's making a couple hundred dollars a week and there's no trouble with the cops. Paraguay lives by smuggling and Stroessner is in charge of it all, gets a cut on every hank of hair. "Jesus," Lewis says, "I'm a thousand miles from Paraguay but I want to lower my voice when I talk about that son of a bitch. You can't fart in that country but Stroessner knows it. That guy is *spooky*.

"I was broke in Asunción, I mean right down to empty pockets, living with this whore; and this American, Mac, says doughnuts. Doughnuts is the thing, Mac says. Well, why not? I got my whore to making doughnuts and I'm out there on the street with a big basket. We didn't do bad, actually. Then, Mac says, don't you feel degraded peddling doughnuts on the street? And I hadn't 'til he asked me. Every time I'd see him he'd say, isn't it degrading work? don't you feel degraded? Finally, I felt degraded and quit and went back to smuggling. Had to break up with my whore, too."

"And don't you still feel degraded?" I ask.

Lewis looks at me with frightened eyes and his lips begin to tremble. "Well, shit, man," he says, "this electrical bit is just temporary. I want to get back to my plant life."

"Well, that's not exactly what I meant," I say. And then, after a long pause, "So. You're a long way from Asunción. Is this a good place for showerheads?"

"No, I'm on to something new. I met this Jap in São Paulo, well, actually he's a Korean. Jesus, those bastards come in here dressed in coolie hats and grass slippers and six months later they're millionaires. He's the cigarette-lighter king of Brazil, smuggled in a boatload. He put me on to something and it's almost absolutely legal—Amazonian Indian handicrafts—blow-guns, spears, masks, feathered headdresses, those necklaces made out of birds strung together, shit like that there. You ever seen one of those necklaces? Fifty yellow birds strung on a string. They're fantastic."

"Lewis, I was kidding about the stuffed Galápagos finches. That kind of shit's not legal. You ever hear about parrot fever?"

"Yeah, the bird part, the part with the feathers, that might be kind of problem making. But there's other possibilities with the plant life—orchids, ferns, the parasites like the Bromelius. Hey, you know what a parrot's worth? *Thousands, man.*"

"I heard about a guy who spent months down in the Orient collecting boas," I say. "He caught about a hundred and had cages built and brought them up to Quito. He wrote to all the zoos and found only one buyer. I think it was San Diego. They offered him three dollars a snake."

"Well, of course, you've got to research your markets. I'm not going up to the Amazon to ship out water hyacinth, you know."

"Too bad the Amazon isn't all cactus," I say.

"Ah, cactus," Lewis says. "That's my baby. That's what I love. I've taken out cactus so big you have to winch it into the truck."

"I don't know much about your racket except what I've read," I say. "You're the first cactus thief I ever met, but I have the idea that the Sierra Club regards people like you as real first-class sons of bitches."

"Oh man," Lewis cries, "don't do me that way. You sound just like my brother. I'm not bad, I'm not bad."

We look at each other across the table, both of us trembling and half-smiling.

"I'm good," Lewis says. "I'm a vegetarian. Look, I left Puerto Rico. Puerto Rico was a place I could of extincted. I don't want to extinct no place. I don't believe in violence; I don't believe in killing. I can't even stand the sight of blood. I'm *vegetarian*."

Maybe he is. He is eating a nice salad of lettuce, sliced onions, tomatoes, palm hearts, and squared potatoes. Fausto, pretending not to be alarmed by the passion in our voices, is standing by the window looking down into the patio where the students are drinking beer. Through another corner window the bay is disappearing into night and a thin row of lights shines along the Itaparica shoreline. My throat is raw from talking, and I begin to cough. This goddam conversation has set me back a week. I look at Lewis, feeling sad and guilty. If he is not a mental case, he is at the very least operating with some missing cogs, and in his desperation it is difficult to justify my condemnation. There is a long silence between us that has to be broken, but neither of us quite knows how. Contemplating each other, two wanderers in a strange world where we have been so long isolated from human communication, we are both stunned into depression by the simultaneous realization of a common dislike. We are like sex-starved men who, after months of fantasizing, suddenly find themselves in possession of a woman who is impossibly repulsive. I think about the bird stuffers, the butterfly collectors, the gringos, some of them missionaries who have moved into the Ecuadorian countryside and seduced the Indians into friendships simply to buy their woven or knitted tapestries and sweaters for export, paying shameless prices that ensure nothing but the continued enslavement of the indigenous people. And suddenly I think of the Panamanian frogs. Before I know what I am doing, I have begun to fill this awkward silence with a ridiculous story.

"Lewis, I just thought of something. There was this Peace Corps director in Panama. He worked there about ten years ago, before the Peace Corps was asked to leave. I didn't know him but hear he was weird—a Baptist minister with some very naive ideas about development. The Peace Corps should have known better. Well, he was walking down the street one day in Panama City and saw some tremendous stuffed frogs in the window of a tourist store. They weren't as big as those three-pounders from Colombia, the *Bufo blombergi*, but they were big enough to make you shudder. He went into the store and talked to the owner, who told him that stuffed frogs were a very popular curiosity and that he could sell ten times more frogs than the people were bringing him.

"The director was having a hard time thinking up projects that would help stimulate the economy at the rural level, and, while he was ordinarily not an impulsive type, he was suddenly struck with an idea that almost dropped him to his knees. He was the kind of man who tended to feel that sudden illuminating ideas that flashed into his brain were personal messages from God. Maybe it was the first personal message he had gotten for a long time. At any rate he got sort of super-enthusiastic. What had flashed into his mind was this cottage industry that would transform the lives of a desperate people; under Peace Corps direction they would make something of value out of nothing.

"So he rushes back to the office and has his secretary prepare a Flash Bulletin to all in-country volunteers, and that afternoon his message goes out to every corner of the country: "Flash. It is strongly recommended that all volunteers immediately investigate possibilities of stuffing frogs."

"Is this a true story?" Lewis asks, looking at me suspiciously, as though I were inventing something that would end up being directed against him. "I just happen to know a little something about Panamanian frogs; not just that they're awful big, but that they're awful poisonous."

"Goddamit, Lewis," I say, "don't spoil my story – and incidentally, it *is* true. The director is a thorough man and so he goes that evening to the library or someplace and starts reading up on frogs. He wants to know all about them, and what he found out is what you just said: the only poisonous frogs in the world come from Panama and Colombia.

"It was the end of the project, of course – and probably the end of his credibility as a man with most of his marbles. Can you imagine the headlines that *he* might have imagined? '123 Peace Corps Volunteers Struck Down by Killer Frogs: Cuban Involvement Suspected,' or 'Frog Spit Wipes out Peace Corps in Panama.' The first thing next morning he goes tearing down to the office and sends out another message all over the country. "Flash. Under no circumstances will volunteers stuff frogs."

"Is that the end of the story?" Lewis asks, smiling bleakly and observing me with amazement as I sit there laughing wildly with tears streaming out of my eyes.

"Yeah, that's it," I say. "God, I can't get a laugh out of anybody in this country."

"Are you really against stuffing frogs?" Lewis asks after a long time. "I mean *really,* are you a pro-frog man? Because frankly, I think the director had a good idea. Maybe not for everybody in the Peace Corps, but as a small rural project. Does that strike you as immoral?"

"Now, shit, Lewis, I am not a fanatic antifrog-stuffer but isn't it a frivolous occupation? Isn't it spooky to be putting dollar values on every little something that hops or flits or skitters in South America? Isn't it spooky that there is a market for such things and that such things sit on mantels in American living rooms?"

"Tell me the truth," Lewis says. "How many stuffed frogs have you seen on American mantels?"

We confront each other across the tables, and I think to myself, Jesus, this is getting incredible, this has gone too far, it is time to change the subject. "As far as I know this is not a reciprocal madness. I think the only stuffed animal in South America from the Northern Hemisphere is a stuffed elk shot by the king of Sweden and presented to the museum in Popayán, Colombia."

"Interesting," Lewis says. He sits and stares at me as though I were completely mad.

"O.K.," I say finally, "you are asking me to take a position. So, O.K., yes. I guess somebody has to stick up for frogs. Yes, you can put me down as a pro-frogger."

"Jesus," Lewis says, "this is the weirdest conversation I've had since my brother kicked me out of Bolivia."

"Yeah," I say, "and it's the weirdest I've had since my partner kicked me off my own farm. Well, have you read any good books lately? What do you think of the Dostoevski?"

"The *what?*"

"That book you're reading."

"Interesting, interesting," Lewis says. "I spend so much time alone; a book is a lifesaver on a long bus trip. This one is a nice tale, sort of slow moving but – interesting. What are you reading?"

"About another kind of crime. It's murder, but another kind. Elephants and black people. This guy is into ivory; he's trying to extinct elephants."

Fausto brings me coffee, I give him some money, and he goes downstairs to make change. I am going to have to leave him an enormous tip tonight for having so thoroughly ignored him. "Did you notice that gook," Lewis says. "He's been laughing at us."

"Maybe he thinks we're funny. *I* think we're funny. Maybe it's your imagination. I know him and he has no malice."

"No malice, no malice. How can you know these people? One second it's big black smiles, and you turn around and got a knife in your back."

"Why don't you go home, Lewis? There's lots more cactus in Arizona than Belém."

"It's cause I like the South American whores; I like these little dollar hotels where you can take anyone you want up to your room and no hassle."

"Oh, come on; a vegetarian sex maniac. I don't believe it."

"O.K., then I'll tell you. I can't go home. There was this little thing, maybe you heard about it, this little thing called Vietnam. Look, frogs I can kill. Not people. I'm on the loose, buddy, I'm on the loose."

"That can all be straightened out now, Lewis. Go on back."

"I go where the winds blow me," Lewis says. He looks sad and thoughtful and then his face brightens. "Hey, frog-lover, you want to buy a good cigarette lighter?" He takes four or five gold-plated butane-operated lighters from his pocket, lays them on the table, and begins to demonstrate their qualities. He finally gets a flame out of the third one. "Let's face it," he says, "Korean shit. I won't sell to you. These are for domestic consumption."

· · ·

A half-hour late João Ubaldo bursts into the hotel lobby where I sit waiting for him. He is short, strongly built, vibrating with energy, and his black curly hair is as alive as snakes. We recognize each other immediately: I, from the picture of him on the back of his book; he, I would guess, from my dark E.B. White sports jacket that I am wearing for the first time in Brazil and which immediately identifies me as a gringo who does not know how to dress when invited out to dinner in Bahia.

"Well, at last," he says, grinning. He grabs my arm and hustles me outside to his car. "I'm glad we connected; this is my last chance to see you. I have to go to Natal Sunday to a writers' conference; it's going to be a drag. How's your cough? You're going to be hot with that coat on. Look, let me apologize. Before we eat, before we hear the music, I've got to appear at this opening at the museum. A friend of mine has blown up some photos and is having an exhibition. We'll pop in for just a minute."

"The museum down on the water?"

"Yes, you know it? Beautiful, isn't it. Slavery wasn't all bad, eh? It was a sugar refinery in the old days. The owner had his own chapel, his private docks, his own slave quarters, his own private whipping block—a real spread. They knew how to live, those old bastards. Here, climb in back. This beautiful creature on the front seat is Lilian."

Beautiful Lilian, a student at the university, greets me in English, and we head downhill for the museum on the water. Ubaldo holds one of Lilian's hands as he drives. "Oh, my God," I can hear him say, "Lilian, sister, daughter, lover." He addresses me through the mirror. "Everything I make goes for alimony; now I'm going through another divorce. Where will it end? I am struck dumb before the beauty of women. I have sacrificed my life for love and beauty; I am helpless before this passion." He draws Lilian to him and caresses her hair, whispering. It is pretty to watch, but I feel as though I had stumbled into the middle of a movie with an intricate plot.

We go rushing up and down hills, most of the time in the wrong direction. I have been to the museum on foot and realize that we are lost, but how we get there is none of my business; it would be presumptuous to know more about Bahia than one of its most eminent inhabitants. We circle once again through the whores' quarters, and Lilian finally points the way. "I don't go out anymore," Ubaldo says. "It has been months since I've gone to one of these parties. I'm caught up in another book and completely out of the scene."

"How is *Getulio* doing in America?"

"Who knows?" Ubaldo says. "The publishers never tell you anything. At least directly. If a book isn't doing well, they move away from it as though its failure to sell had nothing to do with their failure to push it. Did you read the reviews?"

"No, but I hear they were excellent. Didn't *Newsweek* or *Atlantic* compare you to Homer?"

"Yeah," Ubaldo says without enthusiasm.

"It's a fierce book, about the roughest book I ever read, as intense as Gabriel García Márquez's *Otoño del Patriarca*.

"I'm pleased you think so," Ubaldo says. "As a matter of fact Gabo wrote me a beautiful letter about the book."

"What I don't understand is how you could publish it in Brazil."

"That's simple," Ubaldo says. "Nobody reads books in Brazil and nobody knows this better than the military. You can say what you want in a book because nobody's going to buy it. Newspapers, television, that's something else. As a newspaper editor I'm perfecting my skills in irony. In my editorials I insist that everything the generals say is absolutely true, and it's driving them right up the wall. General X in charge of the state puts out an announcement, and I run it on the front page as an editorial. 'There is no police brutality, no torturing of prisoners; there are no political prisoners in the jails.' I write it straight. 'The general says there is no police brutality, no torturing of prisoners. We know that the general as a man of honor would not lie, and we congratulate the military for this enlightened regime where

Ubaldo's friend, who has put this show of photographs together, is a professor of architecture at the university. The pictures are grainy super-posters printed on paper that accentuates blacks and whites and turns his scenes into either bright sun or deep shadow. It is as though he were saying, This is not art, this is reporting. The professor has an interesting comment to make; it is perfectly in tune with Bahia's racial obsessions and the lip service that intellectual Bahians pay to the overwhelming black presence. What the professor has done is this: he has mixed up thirty photographs without identifying them as to place. Half of them have been taken in Bahia, the other half in Dakar—pictures of markets, beaches, fishermen, native sail-boats, people strolling beneath cocoa palms. A real puzzle, a real revelation. There is no way to separate South America from Africa; they are identical.

As we enter the hall Ubaldo is greeted with cries of astonishment and en-thusiasm, and in honor of his linguistic talents most of the friends who gather around him speak English. He has come back from teaching a course in creative writing at the University of Iowa. How nice it is to stand in a room by the sea, drinking Scotch whiskey, listening to familiar words, and watching the clowning of friends who love one another. It is like a reunion of combat soldiers. "João, for God's sake, where have you been? Haven't seen you for months." Someone from across the room calling in delight pushes through the crowd; he embraces Ubaldo; they hug and wrestle, laughing. The black waiter with a tray of Scotch and sodas stands at our end of the room, and like some magic trick empty glasses replace full ones; watching the whiskey disappear is like watching a film strip speeded up. The waiter is the only black man in the room. In thirty minutes we are drunk, and when I leave Ubaldo's side to make a tour of the gallery he has begun to recite Shakespeare in a deep rolling parody of Olivier. "This is the winter of our discontent . . . " Having come from Quito, where everything is quite different I am delighted by this performance and by the feeling of being in a roomful of people who have grown up together and have tri-umphed over the constricting intimacies of their somewhat provincial iso-lation. In a country where, because of political repression, the artist is either more or less irrelevant or in exile, this group of people who cares for each other strikes me as poignant and noble. Unlike Quito also they have not downright rejected me; by being an American I am not automatically ex-cluded as though I were some kind of a leprous monster who has sneaked into the hall to rape their women or hand out bags of poisoned chocolates to their children. People are smiling at me. *Que raro.* I want to affirm my brotherhood, be clasped to their bosoms; I drain my glass and shudder, and toy momentarily with the idea of climbing on a chair and reciting something from Robert Frost.

The professor of architecture comes up to welcome me. "We've met, I think. I've seen you. Do you like the pictures?"

"Yes, very much, and especially the idea of mixing them up. I was down here a couple days ago to see the drawings in the chapel and wandered over here and watched you hanging yours."

"But, of course. Let me apologize. Yes, I saw you standing in the doorway; I should have invited you in, but I was so busy, and of course, I didn't know you were a friend of João."

"No, I should apologize for butting in that way. But now I've seen them. They make me want to go to Dakar. But isn't the point of the pictures – that I *am* in Dakar?"

"And how do you like the place?"

"Bahia? It's incredible. It's not quite real, more like a dream of how the world could be."

"Yes, yes," the architect says. "You feel it, don't you? You feel it. But of course you would. You are _____." (He mentions a name that I don't catch) "_____, the old white-haired god from the sea."

"I *am*?"

"Hasn't everyone told you? The feeling is very strong. You are absolutely _____. We all pretend to be Christians here, but there's not one of us who doesn't believe in the Candomblé and in the old African gods. That is what will save us – this religion where there is no guilt, these gods who take you as you are."

Now another man approaches us; he is quite drunk but handles it carefully. The architect excuses himself. "I must shake your hand," the new man says. "It is a great honor to meet you."

"Well, thank you," I say, "And it's a great honor to meet *you*."

"No, no, I am nothing, but I understand you are a famous writer."

"You are absolutely wrong. I'm a farmer from Ecuador, a farmer who has written a book. I'd like to be famous, of course, but it hasn't turned out that way."

"You are too modest," the man says, looking at me with a kind of veneration. "I have not had the pleasure of reading your book, but I know your name, and I am deeply, deeply honored. I want to invite you to my house. I want to present you to my mother, to my wife, to my children. I want to show you my engravings."

"You're an artist then?"

"Yes, but not famous like you."

For about two seconds I glow like a heat lamp, a writer with an international reputation. How incredible to be known in Brazil. But the illusion will not bear consideration. My fame is purely local and has never spread out past the Peace Corps family where for a time my book was required reading. "You are making a terrible mistake," I say finally in a grumpy voice and feeling that I am being trapped into a very false position. "Nevertheless I will come and see your pictures with much pleasure."

"You are not famous? You are sure? Are you not a doctor who has written a great novel about practicing medicine?"

Oh shit.

"Perhaps you are thinking of Morton Thompson," I say coldly. "He is dead, I believe; I can understand your confusion, but I am not a doctor, not a writer. I'm a farmer; I raise cows and bananas, oranges, things like that. I apologize. I'm sorry I'm not famous."

He looks at me for a long time and decides to believe me. "Well," he says, "I have invited you to my house and that still stands."

We arrange to meet at ten o'clock the next morning; he will pick me up at the hotel. I don't know which of us is more dismayed to have found himself locked into this unfortunate obligation. His English is awful, and I imagine with a sinking heart the sheer protracted horror of having to grin and grunt for an hour with his wife and mother, who, of course, won't know a word of English. I visualize his engravings – hopelessly black, and abstract, fifty, a hundred, all of them practically identical. He will ask me which I find the most striking and will present it to me.

Over at Ubaldo's end of the gallery four men with their arms around one another's shoulders are singing a mournful song from the *sertão*. It is about Lampião, the famous murdering bandit, but the music has turned him into a folk hero. I am just drunk enough to find it extremely beautiful, and my eyes are misty.

> *Acorda Maria Bonita*
> *Levanta vai fazer café*
> *Que o dia ja vem raiando*
> *E a policia já está de pé.*

Ubaldo is standing by an open window that looks out onto a graveled patio with a large, mysteriously lit mango in its center. He has buried his face in the breasts of a tall, good-looking woman who is looking above the heads of the guests at one of the photographs apparently unaware of what is going on down below. The scene has a joyful cartoon quality because both of them are standing erect and Ubaldo's head is exactly level with the breasts of the very tall blonde. Lilian wanders by, smiling. "Ubaldo is a very romantic type," I say.

"Yes, isn't he? Poor João, he is a wonderful man, a truly fine friend, but he wants to love all the women in the world. If anyone can do it, he can."

The architect wanders by, smiling. "Who was that fellow I was talking to a few minutes ago, the artist?"

"I never saw him before in my life," the architect says. "He was not invited to *this* party."

"He invited me up to see his etchings," I say.

"Oh *dear*," the architect says.

As the drunkenness becomes more general the talk gradually reverts back to Portuguese, but from time to time Ubaldo will bring me one of his friends who speaks English or Spanish: a beautiful girl from Argentina, a political exile; an American widow who is confused about her attitude since her husband died in the middle of a divorce; a pretty girl who teaches English in a language school. In general this is what we talk about:

1. Jorge Amado. What a shame that he is in Europe and that I won't get to meet him. Amado is the absolute star of Bahia; every conversation includes references to this man who has interpreted Bahia to the world.

2. Bahia. The most civilized city in the world.

3. The blacks. The glory of the city and the owners of the spiritual glue that will cement the races and make of Bahia a paradise on earth, if it isn't already.

It is strange that everyone talks so much about a race of people that is so little in evidence in this gathering of painters, writers, teachers, and poets. I am thinking about this when three black youngsters, two girls and a boy, enter the gallery through the open window where Ubaldo still stands with yet another handsome woman. The newcomers are the dancers from the restaurant next door, and they have come in to see the photographs during an intermission. They are dressed in Bahian costumes, the girls in long full skirts and tight white bodices, the boy naked to the waist. They are all highly made up, their cheeks rouged, their eyes purpled and sequined. It is stunning to see such young kids so made up that they look like dolls and to watch them move through the crowd of people with the practiced grace of professional performers. Their presence in the room is electrifying, as though Fonteyn, Nazimova, and Nijinksy have suddenly strolled in to grace this place with an illumination of perfect, controlled beauty. And yet as we watch, what is more stunning than the beauty of these youngsters is the way the two girls walk through the room. They have perfected the ballerina's curious and theatrical way of moving – the feet slightly turned out, the toes coming down first, the hips swinging sinuously – that walk that takes absolute possession of the dancer's space. And they have not just perfected these classical motions, they have transcended them and made them their own: something black, profound, and natural. Smiling, the three black children stand before the photographs and study them intently; they create their own tension, a kind of pride among the white Bahians. Now, not counting the waiter there are three black people in the room. Maybe someday the honkies are going to be fully accepted.

That minute that Ubaldo had planned to spend at the opening stretches away into the drunken mists. Time rushes by without moving; one moment it is ten o'clock, in another minute it is almost midnight. Many people have come and gone, but the little nucleus of insiders with Ubaldo and the architect at its center has taken possession of one end of the now almost-empty room. I am feeling very good, for right underneath Ubaldo's nose I have made a date with one of his girls. We are going one evening to the American cultural center to see the first part of *Roots* and then have dinner. Ubaldo is slowing down now; he has joined the singing.

> *Cabelos pretos, anelados*
> *Olhos castanhos, delicados*
> *Quem nao ama uma morena*
> *Morre cego e nao ve nada.*

Between the cigarettes, the whiskey, and trying to talk above the babble of the party, my throat has once again become a stripped and naked membrane, and I have retired to the patio to hack away my life. In between these painful spasms I watch the party in a bemused and drunken daze. The alcohol is making me melancholy and portentous. I feel that there is something that I am missing beneath what at first had seemed childish and innocent play; drunk, I now require darker explanations. What I think I am watching now becomes quite quickly a kind of poignant Cheeverlike drama with its sad, barely concealed implications: artists of that certain age, neither young nor old now, but straddling that awful time between their youthful ambitions and the growing awareness of the forces outside their talents that will cut them down. I am in a room with artists who live in a country where people do not read books or buy paintings, a country where certain truths cannot be expressed and where, because of this, the power of the artist as commentator or prophet is reduced toward that point where he becomes as important to his society as an interior decorator.

In Quito I have stood on the fringes of similar gatherings and watched the local intellectuals, the young Marxists with their beards, black turtle-neck sweaters, and leather jackets, the old conservatives in their blue serge suits. What a difference between these friends in Bahia who seem to be supporting one another and the cold, dour formalism of Quito where the same people keep meeting at identical gallery openings in a strange psychotic mood of repressed resentment. Quito perhaps is a place of more modest talents, and the success of one artist is a threat to everyone else in the room.

Sometime after midnight finally and sadly we confront the realities. Almost everyone has gone, the party is over. "We might as well eat here," Ubaldo says. "I had no idea it was so late." He seems to be mildly depressed.

I have been standing in the patio watching the young dancers through an open door. They have been performing a version of the *Capoeira*, a dance of incredible gymnastic fireworks, all cartwheels, walking on the hands, nip-ups, flashings and brilliance, a dance that originally was a form of foot-fighting in Angola but was transformed in Bahia with drums, tambourines, jungle stringed instruments, and smiles into a fake dance that would fool the slave masters who didn't approve of fighting. How creative of the blacks to have turned boxing into ballet; how funny to think of two furious blacks fighting each other to the death in the very presence of the man who owns them and who, having forbidden brawling, is cheering them on with olés and bravos.

"Will the dancers dance for us?" I ask Ubaldo.

"Don't look at that trashy performance," Ubaldo says. "Don't look, don't look; this is just a hash dreamed up for the tourists."

"But I don't care. How can I not look at something so beautiful? It's beautiful, beautiful."

"Perhaps. But the authentic *Capoeira* is electrifying. You must see it before it disappears from the world, before it gets Walt Disneyized."

"Like the bongo and marimba music from coastal Ecuador," I say. "That's almost all that's left of Africa. Now all the kids have transistor radios, and they're ashamed of the more subtle beat of the old-time country music that their parents danced to. They prefer the disco music, that cheap shit that sells Cokes."

We go into the dining room; it is almost empty, but they are keeping it open for us. One of the waiters, an old man, lets out a cry when he sees Ubaldo. He comes over and they embrace each other, and later when we are sitting at the table Ubaldo says, "That is Sergeant Getulio."

I study this harmless, tired-looking man in a black jacket and a black leather bow tie who has been turned into a murderous monster in the book, and Ubaldo, noticing my disbelief, says, "Well, of course, Getulio is many men; I've taken something from all those tough old men who served me or my father. They've all taught me something."

"Quick, then, without thinking: tell me one thing this man has taught you."

Immediately, laughing, Ubaldo says, "Don't trust *anybody*. The real Getulio worked for my father. Remember where he is waiting to gun down the men who want to kidnap the boy? I was the boy, but my father was a rigidly honest man, not like Getulio's *patrón*. Getulio had a high, effeminate voice, a lisp. He used to paint his fingernails bright red; he was very vain, very prissy, but in spite of his mannerisms no one for a second ever doubted his manliness. He was too tough to kid. His eyes . . . "

Before leaving for Brazil I had written to Ubaldo's editor at Houghton Mifflin and said that if I could meet him and talk to him that I would like to write a long review of his book for the local Quito magazine that covers cultural events. I was sure (though this proved to be absolutely wrong) that Ecuadorians would be interested in learning something about a great Brazilian writer and of reading about a police brutality in the state of Bahia that so closely resembled the local horrendous police lawlessness of Manabí province. But now as we sit down to what I imagine, and what I have imagined for a couple of months, is going to be a serious talk where I will be presented finally with the inside scoop, a couple of things happen: first, as though a curtain had been rung down between the world and me, I am abruptly isolated in the profoundest kind of drunkenness, and second, that woman with the lovely, milky-colored breasts has come to eat dinner with us, and Ubaldo, sitting between Lilian and Beatrice and looking like a younger, fitter Henry the Eighth than the one we know as interpreted by Laughton, is carried away by delight. He has more interesting things to do than talk bookish things with a drunken old man. Screwed again.

The dancers have gone, there is no music, the tables are empty. Through the open windows an exhausted sea breeze, that little wind of one a.m., stirs the curtains. It is one a.m. in Salvador, Brazil, and I am sitting at a table talking English and eating curried chicken with two beautiful women and a great writer. There is nothing else for the rest of this trip that will prove to be quite so dramatic – or so it seems to me in my drunken state. But it is certainly not the drama that I had imagined or a drama that I can use. I had come five thousand miles to see Ubaldo out of an invented need because it had seemed somehow shameful to make so long a journey without some kind of object. I am like someone driven from San Francisco by desperation who will fly to Madrid to stand before some single Bosch that is hanging in the Prado. More precisely, I am that traveler who arrives to learn that the Bosch that he had centered his hopes on has been sent for six months on loan to some museum in Oslo. Talking to Ubaldo and making an article about him had been, aside from my conviction that if anything were going to happen to me it would happen on the Amazon river, my only excuse for making a senseless trip that so far had proved to be about as pleasant and revealing as falling through space from the observation deck of the Chrysler building. Into that imaginary notebook, though the project is already faded from my mind, and into which so far I have written no more than two imaginary sentences – "I have seen the future and it made my asshole pucker" and "'The overpowering importance of one's emotions to oneself,' Joseph Conrad" – I now decide to carefully concentrate on Ubaldo's words, no matter how drunkenly lugubrious they seem, for some future inclusion.

But it is hard to hear the words; Ubaldo's head is turned away and he seems to be directing his speech toward Beatrice's breasts; he puts his mouth down quite close to them as though he suspected that a microphone were concealed in that voluptuous cleavage. When he is not gazing at those lovely globes, which threaten at any moment to burst into the room and overwhelm us all, he is making the most intense kind of eye contact with both Beatrice and Lilian; it is like watching a John Gilbert – Gloria Swanson silent movie, circa 1927. No one, not even _____, the old white-haired god from the sea, can compete in a situation like this.

From time to time while Ubaldo is fixing his gaze on those things that have so intensely captured his imagination, Lilian will turn and ask me about Norman Mailer, one of whose books she is studying in her English class. Almost unable to speak I answer as best I can. Later, in trying to reconstruct the end of this evening, I seem to remember having said the same thing over and over again, something about the incredible footwork of Mailer and his skill in making brilliant connections between disparate facts. It was a nice comment, but did I make it *fifteen* times? Or was I falling through a momentary White Horse time warp like Castaneda with Don Juan as they watched the same leaf from a tree fall over and over?

With a little stab of disappointment I realize that I have been talking to Ubaldo for the last few minutes, and I make a tremendous effort to concentrate for that article that I know now I will never write.

•   •   •

Unknown to the general public, at least never appearing in the newspapers, a hundred civil wars are erupting all over the country. Especially in the Mato Grosso and the Amazon—land wars, men with power and money using the politicians and the police or their own private gunmen to drive small farmers from their farmlands. Ubaldo is writing a novel about a family who is driven back farther and farther into the jungle by groups of more powerful and ruthless men.

"Oh Jesus," I say, "that kind of a book has to have a happy ending."

"Yeah," Ubaldo says, "I'm thinking of giving it a happy ending. Those who remain, those who aren't murdered, finally find a piece of ground."

"Have you read _____?" I ask, mentioning some book whose title I can no longer remember—and I hope to God now that it wasn't *Grapes of Wrath*, though in my condition it might have been something even more inappropriate—*Lost in the Woods*? For Christ's sake.

"I don't read books," Ubaldo says. "Only Rabelais."

I sit there staring at him, dully trying to imagine a man reading the same book over and over for thirty years. I realize I am being fooled with, but I am too drunk to be able to figure out why he would say something so ridiculous. He does not know that I had wanted to write about his book for the Quito intellectuals, is under no pressure to make eccentric statements. Is it possible that in a country where people do not read books that even writers do not read books? If so, the situation is sadder than I had imagined.

"And the Bible, of course," Ubaldo says. "I believe in God and in Jesus Christ. But I also believe in the African gods, and don't tell me that you aren't _____, the old white-haired god from the sea. Lilian, isn't he _____?"

It is later now. We have left the restaurant and Lilian and I are sitting in Ubaldo's VW waiting for him to say goodnight to Beatrice and talking about Norman Mailer. From the seawall and from behind Beatrice's car we hear a rather splendid rendition of the Macbeth soliloquy, "Tomorrow and tomorrow and tomorrow." The clipped English phrases roll out over the sea. Later still, just before I am dropped off at the hotel, I mention to Ubaldo how cleverly I thought he had rewritten Hamlet's soliloquy and put it into the uneducated mind of Getulio. "That's marvelous of you to have noticed," Ubaldo says. "I think you're one of the few who did. . . . But what an evening. We haven't had a chance to talk. We've got to get together again before I go to Natal. Look, I'll call you at the hotel."

"Yes, we really haven't talked. That's great, I'll wait for your call."

For three days, coughing steadily, I wait in the hotel. Anticipation and apprehension cancel themselves out; how awful if I should be out looking at etchings when Ubaldo calls. I needn't have worried. Neither Ubaldo nor the drunken artist is heard from again. On Tuesday, the day before I leave Bahia, I have dinner with the American widow, Barbara, and her friend, Dagmar. We eat pizzas near the beach at Barra and talk about the childish and irresponsible charm of Brazilian men, about machismo, about death. I listen to myself talking like a jilted woman but without bitterness. If I have correctly understood the underlying meaning of our conversation and the classical inevitability of its flow, it was this: a great many women, after close and varied contacts with Brazilian men, find that death has lost its terror. It is a consummation devoutly to be wished, or, as Sergeant Getulio has put it, "It's better to die, because there are no dreams when you turn your soul loose and everything ends. Because life is too long and has disasters. Why endure old age coming slowly, tyrannies and false orders, the pain of cuckoldry, the slowness of things, the things that can't be understood, and the ungratefulness that's undeserved, if you can dispatch yourself with a plain knife? Who can carry this weight, in this life that brings only sweat and fights?"

Recife – Natal – Fortaleza

O ut on the northern edges of towns, lying along the coast, massive, miles-long sand dunes rolled down toward the sea. Some of them seemed to be hundreds of feet high; at times they looked as though they were trying to crawl back into the ocean, at other times, as though they were trying to overwhelm the continent. In the distance, across bays or rivers or glimpsed in the spaces between groves of trees, they shone in the sun as white and sterile as clouds, but changed by their nearness to the ocean and its heavy air, through which one saw as though through water into the soft and insubstantial shapes of low-lying fog.

Where were those sand dunes? Outside of Recife, Natal, Fortaleza? I can't pin them down, the trip has been shattered out of its continuity. I felt like a man riding on a train to no particular destination, riding through a tunnel where I am only occasionally given a glimpse of a landscape through a rift in the rock walls. Many of these glimpses were insane repetitions, like living yesterdays over again. The land was still immense but undistinguished, the kind of nonlandscape that is impossible to describe and which, ten minutes after you have left it, has faded from your mind. Big, crude, made yesterday out of snippety leftovers: sand, clay, scroungy looking palms with sloppy dead leaves at their crowns like the crazy rumpled feathers on Daffy Duck's head. God, six hundred miles, interminable armies of Daffy Ducks; they cluster on the low ground and around swampy bogs and pools. But though I am hundreds of miles north of Bahia, there is still enough of me back there to diminish the present. How can I be seduced by these northern Brazilian cities that strain to ape the brilliance of Bahia but are only pale copies that repeat themselves in an increasing mediocrity?

Recife, Natal, Fortaleza; they are just stops now, places to sleep on that

long trip north to what is now the destination: the Amazon river. If anything is going to happen to me on this trip, it is going to happen there. For
ten days I move between that Bahia that I can't let go of and Belém, a river
city that I can't begin to imagine. The cities become smaller, the buildings
one-storied, I dream that they are built on sand, Dutch faces replace the
blacks: small-headed women, men with vacant faces and square haircuts.
They look like models for Diane Arbus, mildly grotesque, waiting to be cat-
egorized. Even the litter in the streets makes me sniff disdainfully.

.   .   .

There was a monumentality about the garbage-choked streets that plunged
down hillsides in the poorer parts of Bahia that could never be equaled anywhere else. These stinking, stunning mountains of filth, which made it impossible to move through certain areas, had in their grandiose excess a
shameless logic that prophesied the drowning of the world in its own shit.
Outside of huts where the garbage was piled to the windows, on awful
streets, in doorways cut out of flat, white plastered walls, in barrios without
lights or water, beautiful children played in the refuse; beautiful mothers
watched them. Out of this excess—an excess of filth and squalor, poverty
and Negroes—has grown an exuberant culture, a superrace that strives to
triumph over the awfulness of life by the purity of its perceptions, its openness to experience, and its freedom from guilt. And beneath all this there
was a deeper secret, one I had tried to pierce for years, the ultimate secret of
the black soul. What was it? I had lived for a dozen years with black people
trying to identify and put into words that quality of vulnerability, of inner
radiance that broke my heart with pride for them, that made me admire in
some degree even the most disgraceful rascals.

Now I sat on a bus one day traveling between Bahia and Recife or Recife
and Natal or Natal and Fortaleza looking out dumbly at the sand dunes
shimmering on the horizon with their unseen promise of the sea behind
them, and suddenly out of nothing a definition began to form—this thing
that was unique to blacks. I sat there tense with excitement making a
sentence out of a new illumination that held, I felt, a great truth. How
strange that living with blacks for so many years I had never pinned it down
and that this truth had come to me not from thinking about black people
but from contemplating that hybrid cross of blacks with Portuguese and Indians (and that it had come to me as I moved away from the intenseness of
Bahia, that overwhelming place that was like a "climax" forest where a

greater quantity of organic dissolution had created the most beautifully radiant trees and flowers): blacks are a people who have been unable to build defenses against evil.

Recife, the reef. The bus arrives at night, not late, not early. Tired, I submit to the taxi driver who takes me to a hotel that I cannot afford, or don't want to. I am afraid to ask for a really cheap place. What may be cheap to him might strike me as disgraceful, or vice versa. True communication between cultures is a chancy thing especially where money is involved. I am spending almost a thousand dollars a month on this trip, the taxi driver is making something less than a tenth of that. What *is* a cheap hotel? (Later, directed to "the best restaurant in town" by the desk clerk I will be unable to hack that dish of brine-flavored salt cod that I have ordered thinking I have asked for *pargo.*) The hotel is plain and clean with a plastic brightness; perhaps it is even a middle-class brothel, for in the morning, following instructions, when I ring for breakfast three women wander in with the maid and twitter and joke with me like geisha girls. Though they may be women in their late twenties, they have the heavy bodies of much older women and their faces are puffy and ravaged. I feel like a young boy surrounded by loving but slightly disreputable aunts, and in the heady stimulation of beginning a day in such a fervor of emotion I stand in the middle of the room and thoughtfully allow my glasses to slip slowly, slowly down my nose and fall to the tile floor where one lens shatters. Again.

Should I look for another, cheaper place? I feel a compelling but slightly irrational urge to move a little closer into the city's center and its restaurants, but it is only later in the day when the move I finally make takes on strange overtones. Walking for twenty minutes as though directed, I immediately find a little hotel in the very heart of things. It is cheap, clean, crowded, and, with its cages of birds, its pools of fish, its hordes of tiny monkeys hanging from tiled eaves or making faces at me of loathing and extreme terror from the railings along the outside staircase as they slide and caper and swing, is like something out of a Graham Greene novel. The inside rooms are full and I am put on a balcony overlooking the patio. It is a little jungle of ferns, fish, monkeys, and parrots. Over the tops of tile roofs, a view of a row of buildings along a riverfront. It all looks as though it had been planned by English – rows of sedate, gray buildings, a dirty, low, slow river spanned by English bridges built of English steel. From the room, from a distance, Recife is as serious and commercial as Shanghai as seen from a ship anchored in the river.

In the *Otica* where I leave my glasses I have a stupefying conversation with a girl behind the counter. Her name is Maria, and we repeat almost word for word that conversation of ten days before when I had repaired the same lens in Bahia. It occurs to me that I have discovered a technique if I should ever find myself strolling through other foreign cities, raw and bleeding with loneliness: break something that I can take to a pretty girl to be repaired. We make a nice connection that leaves me lightheaded, and when she accepts my invitation to step next door for a glass of orange juice and a piece of chocolate cake I feel as smart and foolish as a teen-ager who, when he invents a racier version of what happened, will emphasize how close he came to a seduction.

From the street, the hotel that I have chosen is only a door. To reach the lobby and the patio, situated in the middle of the block, you have to walk through a long, dark passageway. At the end of this tunnel, far away, the light burns and flashes in the garden and in the fountain's splashing. It reminds me of—what? In the very instant that I identify this dark passageway with the church in Bahia where the three old ladies beckoned, I walk into the lobby. Sitting against the wall in wicker chairs across from the reception desk, three old black ladies sit knitting, large rattan baskets full of balled thread at their feet. I walk in upon them, into the light, and immediately recognize one of them, the woman with the graying hair cut short to the shape of her man's head. Our eyes meet for a millionth of a second; I pass on into the sunshine and walk around the pool with its black water and its golden carp—and turn and slyly try to identify the other two women. In the end I am not more than 99 percent sure that these are the same ladies who beckoned to me from that tunnel in Bahia.

.   .   .

Recife. O.K. I will walk across town and look for the reef.

The town's harbor, lined with rusty freighters and incredibly old coastal steamers, is like a wide river with the reef, now covered in a long, thin line with huge rock chunks, forming the river's far bank. The ocean breakers crashing against this long stone wall throw up spray that shines in the sun where isolated figures of boys in swimming trunks with long cane poles throw lines into the surf. Their poses as they wait are as languorous and studied as Whistler drawings. Everything, even the distant boys, the boats, the docks, the street deep in the shade of mangos, the piled rocks at the reef, has a timeless, frozen look. Something planned by Englishmen, something built to last, a memorial to a decent past, that old vanished world of my grandfather's "where a man's word is his bond."

This section of town where the sailors hang out is a barrio of neglected and seedy one-storied buildings, narrow streets, and old trees. In a way it reminds one of Haight-Ashbury, a place that reflects the passions and vices of another time. The bars are as menacing as opium dens; no screen set could capture the sense of danger and violence that these facades suggest. Looking into their dark entranceways one is surprised at the quiet (it is early afternoon) when one is straining to hear the shrieks of drunken syphilitics in various stages of delirium tremens or the whistle of knives being thrown into careless backs. The skid-row section of Recife, what a setting for the last chapter of a sordid novel about moral disintegration. In the last century. Conrad's bars, by comparison, are as classy as the Raffles Hotel; not even Jim in his moments of most intense self-loathing would have pushed against these swinging doors (were there really swinging doors?) from which the paint has peeled off in blisters as though boiled away by the heat of the passions and vices inside. Trying to imagine what kind of unspeakable conduct could peel the paint from the doors and walls of these joints, I scour the world and my memory of horror stories and put them here where they seem more appropriate: the old drunk woman in London's Limehouse who, standing at a bar, suddenly spread her legs a bit and, still croaking out some dirty Cockney limerick, pissed onto the sawdust-covered floor; the old waitress in Tehama, California, who hauled out one breast and squirted a stream of milk into the coffee cup of a customer who had complained that the cream was sour; the entertainers of Manila who lie beneath dogs or donkeys; the whores of Cairo who, when you are asked by the waiter "with or without" will, if you have said "with," crawl under the table and perform fellatio on you as you dawdle over your Chinese noodles, your bulgar with sheep's eyes; the sodomites of Istanbul who, to convince you of their cleanliness, will pull silk handkerchiefs from their assholes and offer them for your inspection. If these things don't happen in Recife they should; they would fit in with this ruined background, this sailor's hell invented by Hogarth or Gissing where, if these smells exist or not, the imagination fills the air with the odor of excrement and sperm, the sour smell of loneliness, the bitter salt smell of the open sea where deprived men will reinvent love from twisted desperations.

Close to the river some parallel streets have been closed to car traffic. All day and at night until midnight people stroll along these malls or sit on benches enjoying the coolness. There is a flower market at one end of one street, great piles of fruit massed at the other end; when seen from a block away even at night the pure glowing colors—orange, scarlet, apple red, the yellow of marigolds or daisies – are celebrations, great shouts of joy. Hucksters, magicians, kids or older men or women with trays of cheap jewelery or razor blades, or Japanese cassette tapes wander back and forth with small expectations. At ten o'clock at night comes a religious procession of priests and acolytes, and behind them heavy, soberly dressed women all with candles that illuminate the tragic faces they have assumed for the occasion, and behind them people off the street who fall in at the rear until the street is more procession than onlookers. Everyone is singing; everyone is solemn. It is sixteenth century; very heavy-duty stuff. It is intensely moving to be in a city where *everyone* believes in God, and I consider joining them, not because I believe in God, but because, though the spectacle is depressing for its ritual, I believe in the emotion that has joined them together.

One night, bored with sitting in the park just outside the hotel and bored with establishing half-comical, half-grotesque father-daughter relationships with the whores, I wander into the mall, drawn there by the sound of music. On one corner at the center of a small crowd two men are singing songs of their own invention: a highly stylized dialogue between friends, a friendly argument, the purest, most authentic music I have ever heard. The singers are two brothers in their late twenties. The older, one leg shorter than the other, walks with a terrible swooping stagger. They are poorly dressed in stained T-shirts and stiff, cheap trousers. An older man is working with them, an old confidence man in a double-breasted coat, spotty and rumpled, that is many sizes too large for him. His face has the blank corrupted look of a man who has fooled too many people with cheap tricks. His younger companions also have a blankness growing in their faces, a pitilessness as though they have begun to withdraw from a life that has lost its promise and its challenge. The three of them hold tambourines, and at the end of each verse they tap and shake them in a most subtle and controlled way, drawing from these simple clown's instruments the most precise and delicate sounds.

Each brother sings one verse to the other. I cannot understand the words except for the first sentence of each verse, *"Hermano, tu no sabes nada."* Each one emphasizes the last word, *nada,* in a way that is strong, innocent, and loving and then goes on to comment, correct, expand, or digress. "Brother, you don't understand how things are." The crowd is controlled absolutely by the singers, even the cops, who are mentioned from time to time in satiric ways. The people laugh, sigh, nod their heads wisely, or look vaguely at the ground as though great truths were being revealed to them by this simple and profound music that is coming to them from out of the heart of a great country. This is music out of the *sertão*, music made of dust, sticks, rocks, fickle women, mean storekeepers, fate, death, sun.

I listen for twenty minutes, for half an hour, keeping tight control of myself to not break into tears, to keep from dancing, embracing the singers, taking out all my money and laying it at their feet. In some sense that I don't understand, it is the most overpowering music I have ever heard; I want to sob, laugh, clap, and jump around; I want to shake one of the listeners, an old man, who seems unaffected and yell at him, "But listen, listen, this is incredible."

As they sing, as they lose themselves in the music, their faces become transfigured. They are radiant with a pleasure that comes from doing something with flawless skill. It is possibly, though I don't notice, that our own faces have changed and now reflect a profound delight, one of the best pleasures in the world: the joy in watching men who are doing something at which they excel.

If there is sadness in watching the singers it is one that is grounded in my American sense of values. It is sad to watch great artists wasting their sweetness. They are too great for the streets of Recife; there is an incongruity in their rags and in this little crowd of twenty that is gathered around them rather than at the amphitheater that would hold the thousands they deserve. I would not travel to Madrid to stand before some single Bosch in the Prado, but perhaps one day I will go back to Recife and wander the malls listening for the tapping sound of those tambourines, the glittering sound of those tambourines like a gush of water and those pure, plain voices revealing something profound and true about Brazil.

When the concert is over I give the older man a one hundred cruzeiro bill; he accepts it nicely, modestly proud that someone has recognized the true power of their art. And every night for the four nights more that I stay in Recife, I go out into the mall after dinner and stand in the crowd, stunned by the emotion that the three men create in those country songs that transform their faces and that opens up life to those of us who listen.

·   ·   ·

For those four years that we farmed together and before I moved across the river to live alone, Ramón and I would have a party about every six months for our workers and for all the people up and down the river. At first we hired orchestras from Esmeraldas, trios or quartets, old country people who with marimbas and bongos played the vanishing, traditional black music of the coast, that music out of Africa. Our workers were young, the music bored and somehow humiliated them, reminding them that they were black and poor and isolated from the smart world of jazzy dance bands. They wanted to belong to what their little radios had taught them to believe was the twentieth century: the cool hip world of Marlboro country, of Revlon, White Horse Scotch, and Tampax. Giving in to their pleas finally – after all, the parties were for them – instead of hiring orchestras we would rent tremendously powerful sound equipment and the latest popular Colombian dance music that came with the machines. It was awful music, badly performed, but there was something in its beat and in its volume that answered a need at a profound rhythmic and emotional level. These parties were big events for the country people where over a hundred of them would gather to eat, drink, and dance without having to pay. Perhaps in the long run these parties, which to poor people seemed unimaginably lavish, separated us from them as much as anything. It confused their perceptions of us because of the incredible amounts of money that they imagined we were willing to invest in their pleasure. What other proof did they need that our resources were unlimited, that we were desperately in need of their good will?

We danced in a big shed with a cement floor from which for a couple of days the pigs were fenced out. Under a big moon or dimly lit by a couple of hundred-watt bulbs the pigs would gather and lie in piles just behind the phonograph and the overturned canoe that served as a bar, sitting up from time to time to study with tranquil and interested eyes the ritual movements of the dancers. They seemed to be fascinated by the noise and a little sad at being excluded from the general gaiety. By midnight, their senses poleaxed, one by one they would stagger to their feet and slowly walk away. Shortly afterwards, my ears ringing, if I could do it inconspicuously, I would follow suit and lie all night never more than half-asleep, shaken and battered by this music that echoed out for miles over the river and the moon-drenched hills. Not so our guests, who at midnight were just beginning to loosen up.

For a couple of years, entranced as I was by the beauty of the dancing and the display of inexhaustible energy, I did not understand that it was more than sexual courtship, that in fact the people young and old were engaged in serious business. They were striving for something as mystical and ephemeral as a state of grace, a condition religious in every sense of the word and as charged with the search for union with God and its achievement as excessive fasting, peyote, or the use of the iron-tipped thongs of the flagellant's whip. They looked for and found God in the transfiguration of their sexual energy into a divine radiance; they dissolved themselves into the world. The stiffly starched dresses and trousers, the crowding of bodies, the dim light, the bottles of *aguardiente,* and this deafening repetitious beat were only elements that helped the dancers toward the transfiguration they sought. It was a condition that was achieved so rarely and so unpredictably that in a dozen years and a couple dozen dances I saw it happen only twice – this fantastic something that, being white, repressed, and locked into other cultural preoccupations, I find almost impossible to describe, much less understand.

Remember that moment in *Star Wars* where the spaceship shifts into overdrive, and suddenly we are hurtling through time, having broken through that final barrier, the speed of light? The dancing was like that. Into this space crowded with dancing figures, this little space in the middle of the jungle overwhelmed with moonlight, the black shadows of great trees, the frenzy of a cheap, loud music – suddenly – there is a *click,* a meshing of psychic gears, a hurtling into another dimension. It is though we are all suddenly drenched in a flood of tribal energy. The sound of the music fades away to a background noise, the night draws away and disappears, that area beneath the shed, now illuminated with an inner light, begins to pulse and glow. In an instant the souls of the dancers, deeply hidden within their egos, are drawn out of their bodies. Everyone is simultaneously aware of what has happened, this synchronization of individuals into a single, tremendous, and mysterious entity. The faces become intense, thoughtful, profound, the bodies become spiritual. (If I were to walk into this and take Ester or Ramón by the shoulders and shake them would they recognize me?) By surrendering himself each individual has become something much more powerful than himself; by giving himself to the group, to the tribal imperative, he takes on and shares the power of all. If death is the scattering and sharing of one's atoms, then this little death among the dancers would seem to prove that death is a joyful thing. Or could it prove even more? That the whole point of life is in dying? That God is no more than that rhythm that has dissolved and freed this yearning group of dancers?

·   ·   ·

The young German traveler, Martin Velbinger, has written a guidebook directed toward tourists in South America with modest budgets, long hair, and stout constitutions who wish to travel almost without money. Much of the book is concerned with how to hitchhike, with descriptions of beaches or parks to where one may safely camp. Fortunately, being unable to read

German, I have not been tempted to savor the fifty cent hotels that he rec-
ommends. Until Natal I had only half believed the rumors that all over
South America one might find in those hotels and *pensiones* rooms without
windows where the paper is peeling from the walls, where the plugged-up
toilets are full of slowly swirling, oddly shaped, and weirdly colored turds,
where at times you hang your own hammock in a community dormitory,
the walls are scrawled with passionate messages: "Velbinger, you son of a
bitch." "Fuck you, Velbinger." "Oh, Velbinger, you sad bastard."

In *my* guidebook, which is decently English (and almost always wrong),
in Natal I am directed to a two-dollar hotel – "Easy to find, it is on the plaza
by the bus station. A real bargain; the owners are friendly." The taxi driver
has never heard of it and, in fact, denies that there is a plaza anywhere near
the bus station; I tend to believe him. He is a friendly old man with an
honest face, and this time, trusting him, curious suddenly to see what a
really cheap hotel is like, I say it, *"Un hotel muito barato."* Holy God, he un-
derstands me and takes me to exactly what I have asked for.

It is a small three-room private house squeezed between two buildings
with a double row of criblike rooms at the back. The rooms are reached by
walking through the house and outside along a narrow corridor, stooping
under lines of drying laundry: sheets, diapers, patched Levis, incredible
quantities of pink nylon panties. To use the only bathroom one walks back
through the house and through the kitchen where an enormous family
doing homework sits incessantly at a long table smiling at you or rushing
over to help you tug open the sagging door to the toilet. My room is just big
enough for the cot; it costs eighty cents a night, and I feel grossly over-
charged. It is in this place where I am reminded of something real – that
many prostitutes have babies. The traveler has two choices in these rooms:
he can close the window and suffocate, or he can leave it open to the crying
babies, the swooping mosquitoes and the certainty of contracting malaria.
During the night I try both routes. Many times. And in the morning, checking out in the first light of dawn to look for another place, sure enough,
scratched across the door in fading crayon read, "Velbinger sucks. *Velbinger
du bist ein Schiessevogel."*

I find a new hotel and walk to it down two blocks with the blue bag,
which is apparently more at home in low places; it is speechless with rage,
fighting me all the way, banging against my leg and pushing people off the
sidewalk. The blue bag's last trip, it is not going gentle into that good night.
The three old black ladies seated in a row on the porch coolly watch me
above their knitting as I stagger, sweating, up the steps. Perhaps in their thin

smiles, their thin frowns there is a hint of recognition. Perhaps in my momentary look of terror they see a hint of the same thing. But on the whole, I
think, all of us, the pursuers and the pursued, prefer to pretend that we are
not participants in a charade and that there is not some little dump of a
town somewhere up the line, a dingy little place of hostile streets called
Samarra — where I have an appointment.

Natal. A sad town to walk in, but I walk. Stand by a sad sluggish river
and look across it to pale green clumps of trees that look like willows. Do I
remember sad sand dunes? Was there an ocean in Natal? An old jail turned
into a tourist center? I sit on a wall someplace and fill out postcards, sending
out sad and passionate cries for help to Ramoncito and Martita. It is almost
unbearable to watch the serious ten-year-olds with their bags of books
marching home from school through the tree-lined streets.

There is a sign above the lawyers club on a main street that is curiously
empty — "Restaurant. Open to the public." I climb up steep steps to the first
floor to see what lawyers eat, and, by chance before the meal is over, participate in a national tragedy. There is a big no-nonsense room with windows
on two sides and many small tables covered with beer bottles. (Brazilians,
like Ecuadorian machos, like to leave their empty bottles on display as
proof of their machismo.) The place is crowded with men; the drapes across
the windows have been drawn to darken the room, and a large color tv is
sitting on top of the bar. When I first glance at it the whole screen is green,
the violent pool-table green of something never seen in nature. A pea-sized
soccer ball rolls toward the camera, behind it, a horde of panting men. It is
one of the last days of the World Cup match, and Brazil is playing with —
Peru, Argentina, Chile? Brazil must win this game or be eliminated from
competition.

I sit over a plate of chicken and rice and drink two large bottles of ice-
cold beer, and gradually, against all my inclinations, I become caught up
and involved with these poor men who watch the screen with such pathetic
concentration. It is an absolutely terrible situation, the game coming to an
end, the score tied one to one, the other side playing in an obvious brutal
and illegal way, the referees refusing to notice disgraceful violences against
Brazil, and God, I love Brazil. I love the people and their innocent sweetness, their calmness before blatant evil. I love the modest huts, the lovely
gardens around houses, the breakers in the sun crashing along thousands of
miles of beaches. And we need to win; the military is taking us down the
road to destruction; there are terrible things ahead and we are in a country
where about fifteen percent of the people are winning everything.

And Christ, in the last minute we score a goal, we are one goal ahead, we have won, and everyone is screaming, we are all screaming, the chairs are flying over backwards and bottles and glasses shatter on the floor, and outside through the drawn curtains all over the city cracker bombs and firecrackers, horns and whistles are going off and thousands of people are screaming. Natal is losing its mind with joy.

And a minute later the goal is disallowed, the score is tied, the game comes to an end. Terribly let down, feeling as though I had been beaten on my kidneys with lengths of hose, I reach for my beer and note with astonishment that in the heat of the moment I had swept bottles and glass off the table along with everyone else. We finish this meal with calm, vacant faces. No one is talking. We are thinking deep things about defeat. Now that we have lost, it begins to seem that losing had always been inevitable, only one more thing that is lost and that is going to be lost.

Waiting in the bus station for a day's journey north to Fortaleza, I am sitting on one side of a double row of yellow plastic chairs and reading the morning newspaper. My lips are moving, my drip-dry shirt, though clean, is afflicted with tired blood; the blue bag, ripped and soiled, crouches, growling, at my feet. No one can take me for an American and I realize this when two people start to talk just behind my back. The old white-haired farmer, look at him, that disgraceful old fart, look at his lips, he can hardly read, could not possibly understand this intimate conversation.

"So I went to the doctor. They do it with vacuum cleaners here; I couldn't believe it. No thanks, I don't go for having a vacuum cleaner stuck up me. No thanks. It's not my first abortion, and I sure as shit don't want it to be my last." It is a girl's voice speaking in clear Western American accents.

"But Margie, what a waste," another woman's voice says. "To cut your trip off in the middle like this. It's not every day you're going to have the money to see Rio."

"Shirl, it's no big thing. Truly, I'm half-sick of this trip. I've had amoebas ever since Manaus; spend as much time in bed in some hotel wishing I was dead as I spend touring around."

"And what about Richard? I thought he was so cool. But I was wrong; he's *cold*. To let you go back alone, that's shitty. After all, you're traveling together."

"But Richard has nothing to do with this, and actually he offered to go back with me. You know, Richard is not the father. No way."

"Oh God, Marge, he's *not?*"

"I got knocked up in March, didn't see Richard for two months then. He was doing his final paper at Chico. Well, just for kicks I've tried to remember. It's weird to be packing a baby around in you and not know who the father is, a little bundle from heaven in my pootchie bag." There is a good minute now of shrieking laughter that gradually subsides to giggles. "Oh Shirl, I've got the coolest mother; that mother of mine is *cool*. I was feeling so blue. A month in Pomona without Richard. 'What's wrong, dear?' she asked me.' 'Oh, mother, I'm so *blue*,' I told her. 'Oh, honey,' she said, 'why don't you go out and get laid?'"

"Oh, Marge, what a cool mother you have. Jesus, that is *cool*."

"And now I can't remember if it was a Greek I met in the restaurant or a red-haired kid I met the next night. Or if those two exhaust the possibilities."

"Wasn't Richard pissed?"

"Oh, Richard, how could he be pissed? He was fucking one of his teachers. And you know what? She only gave him a C." A burst of laughter. "Well, that's just about how I'd grade him too, I think. That Richard, he gets so *excited*; he comes so *fast*."

The old Brazilian campesino, his eyes glazed, gets up slowly and moves away from a conversation that is giving him considerable pain. The tired old organs are retreating, there is a puckering, a puckering as I confront the future. I am intensely curious to see the faces of these girls, especially the one called Marge, the one with the cool mother. Listening to the voices I am unable to fit them with faces; my imagination has broken down. I walk thirty feet to the magazine rack and, pretending to study magazines, study my compatriots. I have met few women who have been so radically liberated. But expecting – what? – well, something sad and hard perhaps, something invulnerable and armored, I am brought down by their childish faces. Large clear blue eyes, a couple of perky turned-up noses, pink, radiant skin only slightly flawed with the hormonal eruptions of adolescence. Neither of them can be much older than eighteen. What immediately identifies them as Americans is the grossness of their asses, the straining heaviness of their haunches, a kind of Japanese horsiness. They have grown soft and flabby on milk shakes, pizzas, and plastic ice-cream sundaes. The carelessness with which they dress, the carelessness toward their bodies is almost a political statement about their contempt at being regarded as sex objects.

When they begin to speak again I saunter back to my chair to receive their knock-out blows. I have decided that the girl with the long straight

hair is the girl with the cool mother. She is speaking as I sit down just behind her.

"Shirl, there is nothing cooler than a victimless crime. God, that kind of
crime is *cool.*"

"But like what?"

"Like where nobody gets hurt. How else are you going to get your share
in this fucked-up world? Like these studs that figure out how to manipulate
a computer in a bank. They sit at home in a Pendleton shirt with the telephone and transfer like three million dollars to some account that they've
set up. Shirl, that is cool stuff. No guns, no violence, nobody gets hurt, it's all
done with the telephone, you plug in to the computer and send in your instructions. Like the studs that walk out of a supermarket with a hundred
and fifty dollars' worth of groceries hanging inside their coats. Like a friend
of mine, Bryan. He has a little uniform that looks official, and he'll just walk
into an office and start hauling out the chairs, the sofas, the pictures on the
walls. Bryan has the coolest pad I ever saw. Victimless crime. Nobody gets
hurt; those places are all insured. The insurance pays for it all."

"Well," the girl called Shirl says, "so they raise the insurance rates. In
every crime somebody pays, don't you think so?"

"Oh, Shirl, I could teach you so much," Marge says. "It's society that's
fucked up; let society pay. The system is so rotten, Shirl. We have to beat it if
we can. I wish you knew Larry, my history professor; he could explain it so
much better than I. You know what he does? He works as a waiter in the
evenings. Eight to midnight. Do you know how much he makes? I mean *extra.* I mean just by making out two checks — one for his boss and a special
one for the customer. Eighteen thousand dollars a year, Shirl. Any asshole
who is willing to pay a hundred dollars for a meal deserves to get ripped off.
Deserves to get charged for an extra bottle or two of wine. Larry drives a
Jaguar, goes to Europe every summer, stays at the Ritz. Now that is *cool,*
Shirl. A victimless crime and no taxes to pay either."

"Well, I don't know, honey. I don't know if I could live like that."

"Oh, baby, don't cut yourself off from life with phoney scruples," Marge
cries. "God, I almost wish I was staying; you *need* me. Let's face it; life at its
best is none too hot, you know that. It's more piss than kisses. Plato or
Dorothy Parker, somebody like that, said it: 'To live well is the best
revenge.' You want to end up canning peas in North Platte? You want to
end up in a log cabin like Joe and Ida worrying about if you can afford guitar lessons?"

Though the two clocks in the bus station do not quite agree, it is time to leave Natal. I am looking at the future and there is a puckering, a puckering. I get up and move away again, toward gate six, where the first passengers are having their travel documents checked. Like leaving the scene of a dandy auto crash, I have mixed emotions about leaving this conversation, which has given me such insight into a country that I haven't seen for ten years and that I now realize I scarcely understand. Listening to Marge and Shirl has been more educational than a year's subscription to *Time* magazine, which to an expatriate, though *Time* probably does not so intend it, clearly speaks of some final moral, social, and economic collapse that is lying just ahead over tomorrow's horizon.

But let me shift my characters around a bit and juxtapose the other four Americans that I saw in another place not far from here; looking backward into another time can be as illuminating as seeing the future. Instead of an airport restaurant where they more properly belong, let me put them in this bus station where they sit drinking orange juice and fearfully toying with plates of scrambled eggs. Four incredibly old American tourists – three white-haired ladies, one old white-haired gentleman in a scarlet baseball cap and clear cornflower blue eyes, dazed into vacancy by age and travel, but still reflecting a rural innocence. They are dressed plainly in decent cotton dresses and walking shoes; the old man in khakis, boots, and a short-sleeved Hawaiian shirt bright with flowers. They are farm folk from Iowa, Kansas, or the Dakotas, old people in their eighties driven finally into retirement and doing finally what they have talked about for fifty years – making a trip. If lately I have been telling myself that I am too old for the pains and disillusions of travel, what can one say about this quartet who are all at least twenty years older than me. And with my talent for nosing out death, how can I not be shaken by seeing so clearly the mark of death upon the trembling face of the old man whose eyes are senile and uncomprehending and the old woman across the table from him who looks as though she has just lost sixty pounds and from whose arms the flesh hangs in crepey folds? Either of them may well go home as cargo in the hold of a Braniff jet.

Though they display the stigmata, though they are archetypes, they are far past that age when one might be tempted to hold them up to ridicule as American tourists. Their extreme deterioration is humbling. In the way they huddle together, in the uncertain way they talk to the waiter, half-arrogant, half-apologetic, in the way they look around them, timid and blinking, what is most evident is that they are frightened and confused.

They are almost fatally disoriented. Yes indeed, here, if I am not, is the living proof: travel is the saddest of the pleasures.

They are thousands of miles separated from anything familiar – home's rolling hills of wheat or corn, the deep-rowed richness of soya, the big combines floating below their columns of dust, the safe intimacies of families or neighbors, the simple honesty of roast pork and mashed potatoes. Everything is strange, every minute is filled with a rushing strangeness, a vague menace, a jabbing reminder of estrangement, a hint of their own complete irrelevance. But behind their terror, for this strangeness and irrelevance cannot help but constantly remind them of their age and their vulnerability to age's last demand, they are displaying a magnificent courage. These four are a part of the real aristocracy of the aged; most of their friends who still live are rocking in the semiprivate rooms of rest homes. These four refuse to give in to their weariness; they will keep going until they drop. They have come to see new things in the world, and if the things they have seen are not exactly what they were promised by the travel agent or don't seem to have much connection with what they had imagined, they will conceal their disillusion, their awakening awareness of a banal world, and a general unfocused horror. They will totter along the esplanades by the ocean and pause, three of them facing into the sun, for the Kodachrome slides they dream of flashing on the wall of the Farm Bureau meeting hall. They will sit in buses with a guide whose English is thick and suspicious and whose knowledge is either pedantic or flawed, eat at that heavy food that is turning their bowels to water, and mourning something vague and awful, will nap, sweating through the long afternoons. Without wanting to, no, without even asking themselves if they want to or not, they will insist upon seeing everything that has been promised them in the tourist handouts. They are as ready, as unthinking as combat soldiers who storm some barricade.

What confounds them and turns the trip into a kind of dream so ephemeral and fading that it cannot be discussed is the identical nature of the hotels where they have stayed; the hotel in Manaus is an exact replica of the hotel in Miami, in Belém, Fortaleza, São Luís, and Teresina. My God, where are we now? What's the date? And of course they are protected. They will be protected by these cement hotels with the roof-top restaurants, the wall-to-wall carpeting, and the arctic chill of the air conditioning from whatever is real in South America; their reality is the gift shop in the hotel lobby that sells postcards of sunsets never seen, the identical airports, and that almost identical ride by taxi between airport and hotel. In almost every city in the world this strip of highway will be the best in the country and fringed and divided with statues, fountains, trees, and historical plaques – the whole project designed to detour away from the most authentic element of the world's malaise, the stench, the menace, the overwhelming symbol of a collapsing economic system – the urban slums. If these old folks have read someplace that 50 percent of Brazil's work force earns less than fifty dollars a month, they will find it impossible to believe in their fifty-dollar-a-day hotel room to which, isolated from the squalor, they have been carefully steered.

This is not the first time I have moved my characters around and put them beside someone else who will, perhaps, better illuminate their qualities or my feelings about them. But now I am very uncomfortable with this scene. It is too false to the probabilities, like putting the Shah of Iran in an Automat. No, these four travelers do not belong in a bus station. With a clever little swoop of the pen let me put them where they belong. A swoop that is doubly clever since it will spare you of 600 miles of landscape and land us in Fortaleza – for no more than 300 words.

Fortaleza. Larger than Natal, smaller than Recife, Low, spreading buildings and sand dunes to the north; there is not much more to say. Planning to stroll around it for three or four days I leave it in a kind of rout after less than twenty-four hours. There seems to be no center to this city, but I have not walked much more than five blocks on what may be a main street when just in front of me coming abruptly around a corner I am confronted with the three old black ladies. Holy shit. There has obviously been some awful screw-up in their plans for their faces are creased with new lines of nervous agitation. Only one thing can explain why when they see me their faces relax and brief, almost imperceptible smiles of recognition flit across their faces. They have come to Fortaleza on a mission, have checked into the right hotel and discovered with dismay that, evading my destiny, I have gone to another place. Is it possible the old white-haired gentleman has gotten away? For just a second we all stop walking and face each other on the sidewalk. Then, suppressing an impulse to groan in horror, I begin to cough instead and move around them and pass on. At an ever-accelerating pace, like a falling object, sixteen feet per second per second I rush away. Two blocks further on is the Cruzeiro office; looking behind me as I talk to the girl at the desk, I buy a ticket on the evening flight to Belém; it is a decision too sudden and irrational to have been punched into that itinerary that the three black fates have somehow gotten their hands on. And so that afternoon, hours before my flight is due, I am sitting in the Fortaleza airport carefully wading once more through the heavy German symbolism of *Death in Venice* when my attention, easily distracted, is directed toward the four old American tourists who are sitting isolated behind glass in the first-class airport restaurant. O.K., I have put them where they belong, and you have met them.

The River

In the airport in Fortaleza there was an old man checking the luggage in at the ticket counter, and because I had come out very early to hand in my bag and because the old man seemed to be bored, sullen, and even a little confused, I had my first presentiment of the trip that my bag was going to be hopelessly lost. It was a feeling so strong that if it had been concerned instead with the plane's crashing, I might very well have turned in my ticket and gone on by bus. Sure enough, in Belém I am reduced to the clothes on my back plus a briefcase that holds my passport, some traveler's checks, my camera, and a few books. Filling out the lost baggage forms takes half an hour, I have come in on the day's last flight, and gradually the lights begin to snap off, and the terminal becomes as unreal as any empty building without a purpose.

The clerk, held up by my bad taste in losing my luggage, goes down the list of the required information and then hands me the paper and asks me to check off the picture of a bag that looks most like mine. There are pictures of twenty different types of luggage, and they *all* look like mine. Trying honestly to reflect my confusion I check five of the pictures, and the airline attendant studies me suspiciously.

"It's canvas," I explain. "The zipper is torn almost the whole length on top; it's old and tired and doesn't have any shape. Or rather it takes on different shapes at different times depending on how I feel when I pack it."

"I see," he says, not seeing at all. "So what was its shape last time you saw it?"

"I don't remember, but that's not important. It's like an amoeba, you see; it changes. It's like a great blob; it has a life of its own. Speaking Portuguese now, or so I tell myself, I translate "blob" by putting an O on the end of it, and now because it is two o'clock in the morning and I am too sleepy to be angry or even very upset, I decide to make a little something of this depressing moment and give it some kind of life. "Look, it's a very special bag, a pet. I swear I've watched it move slowly across the floors of a dozen hotels absorbing everything in its path. A couple nights ago in Natal it sneaked into the bathroom while I was asleep and ate a towel, two small bars of soap, and a half a roll of toilet paper."

There is an awful silence after this speech that last about fifteen seconds as the airline fellow stares into my face. I have taken an awful chance at this awful hour, but once more I win; suddenly he begins to laugh. I have completely seduced this type whose moustache now begins to twitch wildly with glee as he reaches for me across the counter to pat my arm.

It took me an extremely lonesome two weeks in Rio to learn that to exist in someone else's mind an older person must learn to play this outrageous game, that he must break through a barrier that by being old has grown up around him and separates him from younger people as much as his white hair and his wrinkles. I have learned to love the power that this secret has given me. I have come, being alone in a strange land, to need the acknowledgment of strangers that I exist and to seek this acknowledgment in their admiring laughter or in the touch of their hands. Touching is a form of communication in Brazil, where everything is sensuous and where everyone wants to tend toward good feeling or delight, and I am not offended by this general intimacy. In fact I am much more comfortable being squeezed or patted by a stranger than by a friend. I have learned something beautiful and touching living with black people on the farm—that there are pure people so in tune with their senses, so suspicious of words that they can hardly understand you unless while you speak they can touch you. And that while touching you they will suddenly understand what before had been gibberish, the most complicated sentiments; why, for instance, in the tilting of the earth there will be seasons of summer and winter and at the equator, no change at all. Like a comedian who lives for the laughter he can charm out of that faceless mob behind the lights, translating their giggles into love, I think now of my trip through Brazil as having been a kind of minor triumph. Out of the most unlikely situations and with people that I will never see again, making at times a tremendous effort in the face of exhaustion or my natural reticences, I have made casual connections and have left behind me a score of people who have been hooked and landed by my outrageousness and impelled against their first intentions to like me, to pat and squeeze me, and to feel for just a split second as we prepare to part forever a stab of reluctance to let me go. Out of the desperation of loneliness how we will clown and whore to see ourselves reflected in another's eyes.

Still, there is a mystery here. Delighted by a vagrant smile or a casual pat, I will move away in terror at the hint of a deeper involvement. Like Milton Berle, I need quantity not quality.

"What color was this monstrous creature?" the airline guys asks me finally, smiling, and drawing excited little doodles on the margins of the paper he is filling out.

"Usually it is blue, I think. Dark blue with splotches. Then again after it has gorged itself it is a sort of dirty brown. When it is brown it throbs, and after it has eaten a small child it turns kind of purple and the zippers get rusty for a time."

"Perhaps you have mistreated the poor thing," he tells me, laughing. "Perhaps the poor thing has escaped and we will have to bill you for the parachute that has been stolen." We stand there in the empty airport and think of my bag safely landed and scuttling through the jungle and hiding underneath big leaves. Then he hands me some papers and says, "Well, my friend, don't worry; we hardly ever lose baggage. When it shows up I'll have it sent directly to the main office." We shake hands warmly and at the door I turn and we give each other that inevitable Brazilian thumbs-up farewell. I am, as we say in Ecuador, *"Jodido pero contento."* Screwed but happy.

·   ·   ·

Belém at two-thirty in the morning is sound asleep and my taxi, the last one at the airport, is almost the only moving thing on the deserted streets. We come into the city by a shortcut through a couple of miles of workers' houses, small, sad shacks of adobe with corrugated iron roofs set along the road in front of nondescript and third-class jungle. The land is flat and the air is warm and humid and a very light rain, what in Ecuador we would call a *garua*, is falling, though "falling" is not the right word either. We drive with the windows open and everything has to be half-imagined because it is intensely dark and the streets and the houses are unlighted. Having read Bates I fill the houses of the poor with Negroes, but will discover in the morning with disappointment that the good black blood of Africa has been overwhelmed here and that the people of Belém are a kind of mongrel race with — what — square-headed Dutch blood taking over. Dutch, Portuguese, Indian, a not entirely successful combination made apparent because I have come from Bahia, a black town with the most beautiful people in the world. Belémites, living on the river with a thousand kinds of fish to choose from, should be big and vigorous, but they are small and delicate and the pallor of their skins hints at a starchy diet, stomach worms, and the fevers endemic to the tropics. Their faces are passive, but there is a fierceness in the eyes; all that remains of the European violence is concentrated in their hair: long, oily, writhing, intricately curling, snakelike Portuguese locks.

We reach the city, and it is like diving under water; the streets are lined on both sides with enormous mangos, and the streetlights filter down through a wet greenness. We stop for a red light on the deserted malecon. On the right, blocks of stores, ship's chandlers that sell rope, canvas, nylon line, tar, paddles, fishnets, propellers; on our left, long, low warehouses behind which loom, dimly lit, the loading cranes of ships, and behind the ships an immense darkness and out of it now the low, nostalgic calling of a ship's whistle.

I have arrived at the Amazon river and am about to see it at last.

Up at seven for the free Brazilian hotel breakfast; bananas, papaya, coffee, and bread with a slice of cheese. Brazilian bananas compared with the noble and gigantic fruit from Ecuador (from the farm) are puny and contemptible, thin-skinned affairs. I eat four of them in four bites, four little fart-sized *animalitos.*

In bright sunshine to the main street. Down a little hill two blocks away between warehouses the river shows itself, and I rush down to it like a pilgrim to Lourdes and stand on a cement embankment looking out across a tremendous yellow flood that is slowly moving the wrong way with a rising tide. Tremendous, tremendous. Hypnotized, I stay there for a couple of hours in the shade of a giant mango, joined from time to time by what looks like visiting farmers fresh in from the country or country Negroes dressed with the plain and humble honesty that makes the city dudes in their platform shoes, their incredibly flairing hippie pants, and their bright nylon shirts snicker contemptuously. This is very strange, for the country youths are infinitely more stylish. And strange, too, this awe we share; it occurs to me that they have come from jungle plots hacked out of solid greenness and now for the first time have come to a place with a view, an opening where space stretches away for miles. We stand together (I, out of my need, imagining the togetherness) before this tranquil, sluggishly moving immensity, miles wide, and shiver under the implications of its majesty and its history. Seeing it now at last I can truly believe with the geographers that it holds twenty percent of all the world's fresh water. An island in the far distance lies just below the horizon shining in the sun: a low bank of trees as straight and thin as a pencil slash dividing river from the sky. Garbage, islands of water hyacinth, long, unidentifiable things that may be logs, move by with slow dignity, sliding upstream as though rejected by the sea.

A block from the river on the main street in a fine old Victorian building is the steamship office. Feeling very good, open, and feisty from contemplating the Amazon, I do everything but impersonations for the two young ladies in the office – including a proposal of marriage to one or both; this takes about five minutes. Afterward for something just under one hundred dollars I buy a first-class ticket, meals included, for the five-day trip to Manaus on the ship that will leave in two days. (I will interject here what I hope will be my only bit of tourist advice for gringos with delicate stomachs. The food on the boat was not quite totally awful, but awful enough; I suggest packing away a large jar of marmalade, some cheese and bread, and some tins of meat. A *large* jar of marmalade since out of human decency and lack of character you will offer to share it with your tablemates who, you will discover with mixed emotions, love sweet things. Tins of meat being small, expensive, and almost unsharable, I will leave it to you how or where you may hide yourself someplace and gorge alone on pâté without losing a little a sense of your own dignity.)

Drawn once more to the Amazon I stand beside it again and stare out across its vastness and try to fit myself into where I am, trying to be not so much in a place in space, as in time. The tide has turned, and the river has reversed itself. Pará. Belém. How can one not be enchanted with names so magic and accented in such a neat and clever way? Belém, Bethlehem. It is the doorway to a whole immense continent that drew the bravest of the great men of the nineteenth century to wander endlessly and for years across that watery, half-drowned world that held the secret, the mystery of man's essential inconsequentiality. It was here and over the mountains to the west in the Encantadas that Darwin and Wallace simultaneously were struck with the idea of evolution that brought God and his divine man-made plans about human perfectibility crashing down forever. Wallace, Bates, Humboldt – rational men, brave and profoundly curious; around the campfires on the Amazon sandbars, suffering that inhuman world, they pondered through the nights and began the construction of the modern godless world. The truth hurts, don't it?

Wallace and Bates, those furious collectors newly arrived from England, have not been ten minutes in the town before they have walked past the couple of muddy streets that form the business section and offered themselves up to the jungle. Less than a mile from the jetty they have come to virgin country rich with plants that they have never seen, that have never been classified. There, having passed boarded-up farms going back to ruin from the encroaching vines, closed-up houses abandoned to the blacks who were making one of their last revolts to eject the Portuguese, out past the bamboo shanties and the swamps and the ditches full of still, black water they found that new world of plants and bugs and animals that would occupy them for the next years. There were 15,000 people in the town that day, and now there are almost a million, a widely spaced out place crowded with newly failed Pará farmers who have been forced to abandon a land suddenly gone sterile. How does one make farms on unproductive earth, on lateritic soil, which, being stirred and worked one time too many, will violently revolt against this rape and set up like cement so that overnight it becomes like rock into which a nail cannot be driven? The ecology of the Amazon jungle, fifty times more subtle and complicated than the intricate balancing of a Calder mobile, operated for centuries when each human who inhabited it had ten square miles to roam in and to harvest from; this was what the jungle could support. The land is poor and leached from the incessant rains, so poor in fact that almost its entire richness has gone into the trees that stand upon it. It was the unproductive nature of the jungle that determined the essential nature of the people who once owned it; they were small tribes not much more than family size, and they were nomads who claimed enormous territories. Are these mobs of men in Belém bankrupted by the land not the vanguard of millions more who, still trying in further places to dominate a jungle, will only turn it into a rain-washed desert of poverty weeds and red, bare gullies? There are terrible hints of the future in this place, this city of poor people who have destroyed the land and been destroyed in a partnership that they had never begun to understand before they were wiped out, owners of farmland upon which suddenly nothing would grow.

Tracing behind Wallace and Bates I leave the wharf and wander under the shade of mangos across the waterfront streets down to the main drag and away from the river. After a mile, having ventured farther than the great botanists, I take an elevator to the top of the city's highest building. From my vantage point Belém has almost disappeared in trees. The avenues are solidly lined, but more impressive are the backyards of almost all the houses – gardens bursting with the great leaves of tropical plants. Looking south away from the river it is impossible to tell where the city ends and where the jungle begins. From up here the island in the river seems much closer and I begin to feel disoriented. Hadn't I read that the river was two hundred miles wide at its mouth? I return to the streets and wander up and down them looking for two stores – one that sells books in English and one that sells maps.

From the building's roof, trying to put myself squarely into this world, I have remembered the last pages of Peter Fleming's very funny and very British book about his Amazon adventure and of how in a race with his guide to reach Belém he had taken a shortcut from the Amazons through a narrow, one-way canal. *From* the river?

I have almost forgotten that all my clothes have been lost until by chance I pass the Cruzeiro office, and having already established an attitude with the airline people that more or less agrees with my own personal feelings – that I will never see my bag again if I care too much about it – I saunter in and ravish with charms and japeries the nice lady in the lost and found department. She makes long-distance calls to all the airports in northern Brazil but comes up with no news. Studying my disgracefully wilted shirt and sniffing daintily she asks if I have money to buy new clothes, and we decide to wait one more day for the offered advance. The Belém manager arrives and is desolated to hear that I have lost my bag. He invites me into his office, makes me coffee, gives me a cigarette, pats my arm, and puts in an enquiring call to São Paulo. While waiting for the call we talk about tourism and how it is destroying the countries it wishes to honor and how all the cities of the world have become homogenized and interchangeable. He agrees that the situation is tragic but manages to keep smiling. He is just one little bolt in the intricate aviation industry determined to put airfields and expensive hotels in every village in the world. It is awful; it is a disaster, but it's not his fault, and he is making good money.

A block from the hotel on a narrow sidestreet I find a map store run by two grizzled old men who look like Turks. When I tell them I am going up the river they laugh and dance and tell me how wonderful it is going to be; one of them makes the same trip every year on his vacation. The river is stupendous, he keeps saying as he unfolds the only map of the river presently in stock and studies it with delight, pointing here and there and clicking off the names of towns and rivers. It is a highway map of the state of Pará – roads built and roads to be constructed, a map of good intentions. It is a beautiful map of green emptiness filled with a million miles of winding rivers and a few brave strokes slashed across the interminable spaces. The rivers are the highways, and they go everyplace. It is the cement roads that will destroy the country.

But I am looking over his shoulder to confirm that other thing that I had been afraid of. Belém is not on the river Amazon. From the map it is not easy to say exactly what river it is on – the Pará, the Guama, or the Tocantins – but it is not the Amazon. The Amazon is another hundred miles to the north. After my exultation I feel a little foolish about this. Still, like the innocent rube who worships an outside urinal mistaking it for a shrine, I have had the emotion. And remember my sweet old grandmother at the symphony concert one night; she was quite deaf and when the orchestra had finished tuning up, she began to clap.

I go back to the hotel and wash my shirt and under the blast of a large fan that swings back and forth like the searching beam of a spot-light take a long nap while the shirt dries.

I read from *Death in Venice:*

Desire projected itself visually. . . . He beheld a landscape, a tropical marshland, beneath a reeking sky, steaming, monstrous, rank – a kind of primeval wilderness-world of islands, morasses, and alluvial channels. Hairy palmtrunks rose near and far out of lush brakes of fern, out of bottoms of crass vegetation, fat, swollen, thick with incredible bloom. There were trees, misshapen as a dream, that dropped their naked roots straight through the air into the ground or into water that was stagnant and shadowy and glassygreen, where mammoth milk-white blossoms floated, and strange highshouldered birds with curious bills stood gazing sidewise without sound or stir. Among the knotted joints of a bamboo thicket the eyes of a crouching tiger gleamed – and he felt his heart throb with terror, yet with a longing inexplicable.

This first clear announcement in the first pages that Mann is going to write about corruption, the unconscious, and the destruction of a man through his passions and his vices. Funny the jungle is for so many a symbol of man's animal nature, that unspeakable hidden suppressed part that is supposed to be straining to get out – a Mr. Hyde with his pointy head and big, yellow gnashing teeth. Even Rousseau, who painted jungles out of a naive heart, put that naked woman on the couch into the middle of his jungle dream.

Mann, who never saw a jungle and, Wallace, who lived in it, how differently they saw it. Mann, the bourgeois exquisite, would immediately see the vulva in an orchid's spread; Wallace, only a fantastically beautiful bloom constructed to attract a wandering bee. Living in it do we remove as much of the sexuality as we may be unable to handle? Or is the scientist a healthier man and less a victim of his imagination?

What a pleasure it is to think of Wallace and Bates and the rumors about them. They came to Brazil together with the intention of traveling on the river; within four months they had split up, each going his own way. A friendly decision though I think that neither of them mentions it. The rumors about Wallace? Well, that he really wasn't a gentleman; he had little sense of his own dignity, of his God-given white English superiority. He would walk through the streets of Belém, deeply abstracted, in the most eccentric dress. Without a coat and with his boots unshined. He made friends with disgraceful people – slaves and savage Indians – treating them as though they were fully human.

Years later out of the Far East, out of Malaysia, Wallace shocked the scientific community (and the theologians) by getting in the last licks that would bring the old "scale of being" concept finally to tottering. We were not, all life, strung along an ascending ladder becoming more and more godlike, with the white European (leaving out the Latins, of course, who were scarcely European and certainly scarcely white) on the top rung and stretched below him between the apes and the Englishmen, the lascivious blacks and the jibbering Chinese. In 1855, scandalizing the scientists, he wrote, "The more I see of uncivilized people, the better I think of human nature, and the essential differences between civilized and savage men seem to disappear." Another time he wrote that except for the places in which man found himself, a savage seemed to him quite as intelligent as a Cambridge don.

Loren Eiseley says of him that he had gone into the jungles in search of birds of paradise and butterflies. "He loved beauty, and among the many rarities he came to cherish was the potential moral beauty of man. He found it among simple people and it never passed away from his heart."

The potential moral beauty of man. This is one of the things that Wallace found in the Amazon, and it made a mystic of him. Only God could have put such potential in the human race, only God could have evolved a creature with so many unused divine qualities so long before he might be called upon to need them. Darwin parted from him sadly. "As you expected, I differ grievously from you, and am very sorry for it," he wrote. "I can see no necessity for calling in an additional and proximate cause in regard to man. I hope you have not murdered too completely your own and my child."

Wallace died in 1913 as a European war decimated a continent and made the contemplation of man's moral qualities an academic exercise. Mann, who saw a darker, more horrifying aspect of man's potential in the black waters of the jungle, turned out to be the prophet of our disaster. Wallace, the giant, is half-forgotten. Traveling on the river Amazon he was entranced with the beauty and the potentiality he saw; what he didn't see, what Mann saw through mists, what we are beginning to see quite clearly is the awful ease with which man can be corrupted.

Two pages later, speaking of Aschenbach. "Good, then, he would go on a journey. Not far—not all the way to the tigers."

Early the next morning through almost-deserted streets I follow a thin but growing straggle of women with baskets. We walk along the malecon, the river half-hidden by wharves, headed for market. The fishermen's harbor in Belém is square-sided and tiny with one of its sides open to the river. It is about the size of a small city block, and when I arrive at five a.m. there is not a drop of water in it. An expanse of mud and upon it some thirty fishing boats lying tilted at awful angles or sunk straight and deep into the muck. A few sea birds, a few vultures perch on something out there, but, like Ecuador, most of the vultures, as though yearning for a truer, more evil smelling corruption, are perched on the roofs of the public buildings. Along two sides of the quay several thousand people wander between the open pathways where the richness of the river lies displayed. Piles of fish, tons of fish shining like silver in the first light of the sun, some small as smelt, some as big as sharks. (Some *are* sharks). Sailors, policemen, beggars, priests, cripples, children of all ages bent under baskets, housewives formidable as battleships parting the crowd, their faces cold and vacant among so many men; old men dressed like judges in formal black suits sometimes for the sake of dignity accompanied by a small black child with a loaded basket. Grinning dogs skinny as death, gathered from miles around go skulking, and in a long row of semipermanent kiosks separating the quay from the street wonderful things from up river are displayed—woven baskets, woven boxes, some of them enormous, some as tiny as a fist; carved wooden saddles, tables loaded with dried herbs and incense, medicines against curses. The whole scene is vibrant and wonderful and throbs with terrible stinks—a typical tourist spectacle. The sun has come up out of the river; the light is soft and golden. Marajó, the great island, where the tourists go to shoot the last of the wild buffalo, sleeps on the horizon. And the market for all its vibrance is strangely quiet as though the river were absorbing all normal sounds or as though beside this river everything must shrink away into an insect buzzing.

As strange as this strange muffled silence is the size of everything. The bay is so tiny; the boats are small with flimsily built cabins, vulnerable looking and painted in bright, childish colors. Everything—the harbor, the boats, the government buildings, the park beyond it, even the people—is in

perfect scale, like a very expensive stage set in exquisite detail for a children's opera about the past. And gazing at this miniaturized world one suddenly realizes something breathtaking about the conquest of the Western
Hemisphere: the actual size of the boats that first crossed the Atlantic. They
could not have been much bigger than these Portuguese-designed craft
with their crudely carved prows and their square, bulky afterdecks, frail-
looking even on the inland waters of the great river. And the men who
came sailing in against this coast to conquer the land and subdue it, those
men of four hundred years ago: they were the size of our present-day
twelve-year-olds. Here in Belém they hadn't changed much. Thinking of
their size, their childish bodies, one wants to magnify the greatness of their
achievement and minimize the sadism with which they carried it out. Once
you stop snickering about it, isn't a five-foot-two Columbus a braver man
than a six-foot-three one? Gregory Peck plays the mythical Columbus,
Woody Allen, the real one. How great man is in his littleness.

The only people in this crowd who seem to be uninvolved are the fishermen; they squat on the decks of their boats strangely apart from all the activity. In their eyes there is a faint alienation as though they can't quite connect the fishing, being out there at night in that great stillness under the
enormous sky, with this confused and rather ordinary bickering over
prices.

One of the fishing boats tied up to the quay has, lying across its deck, two
enormous fish with enormous gaping mouths, their lips touching one side
of the boat, their tail fins, the other. Three fishermen, disgracefully dressed
in torn clothes, sit on the roof of the cabin dangling their legs. All three of
them, it seems to me, are looking rather disconsolate, as though they had
got hold of something almost too immense to have value. I catch the eyes of
the fishermen, smile, and hold up my camera, and they smile back and nod
sadly. After I have snapped my picture – two black mouths, four staring,
outraged eyes, two eight-foot rows of coarse blue scales – I climb down into
the boat and crouch at the fishermen's feet.

"Do these fish eat people?"

"But, of course. These little three-meter ones are just babies."

"Yes. We have them in the river on the farm in Ecuador. We call them
meras there. In Ecuador they say that the *mera* likes gringos best of all, especially German gringos."

•   •   •

Across a street and just behind the harbor is a little block-square park with a dry fountain and a dry pool in its center and straight paths lined with mangos cutting the park into eight pieces like a pie. The benches are all occupied by either old men or shoe-shine boys, and I sit on the edge of the pool to change a roll of film. All the trees are heavily loaded with green fruit, tons of pale green pear-shaped mangos still a month from harvest. As I gaze up at the fruit, from all those millions, a yellow mango, probably the only yellow mango in the city, probably diseased at the stem, suddenly comes sailing out of the sky and plops down in the middle of a path. Across from me an old man comes to attention at the sound. I watch him as he sits there studying it, looking at it steadily for a full two minutes, staggered, as though he can't believe in a May mango. He gets up finally and goes to it and stares at it with his hands clasped behind his back. He puts on a pair of glasses and looks at it some more and after an interminable time bends, picks it up, and studies it intently, rolling it in his hand, peering into its stem, holding it to his nose. It is obviously rotten, but it is obvious too that the old man is consumed with the passion to eat a mango. I sit there imagining that the whole city, living under the promise of this enormous harvest that will soon engulf it, when all the streets and parks and sidewalks will be knee deep in golden fruit, is also waiting in a kind of tension, a citywide lust of anticipation. The old man throws down the mango and wanders away. Two minutes later a shoe-shine boy has found it, circled it unbelieving, picked it up, sniffed it with passion, and flung it away.

Of all the odd things that happened in Brazil one of the oddest now takes place.

Across the street on the far side of the park there is a military barracks of policemen or soldiers. I don't notice it until there is a sudden gaggle of whistles from that direction. Through the shrubbery I can see a flagpole with the first sun shining on it. It is six a.m., and we are going to raise the flag. A hundred uniformed men march out of a low stone building with a wide double door and line up in double ranks. A squad of men approaches the flagpole, there is a flourish of horns, and the Brazilian flag rises limply into the still morning air. Everyone in the park but me either rises from the bench or stops walking. No one comes to attention, but they acknowledge the solemnity of the moment by facing toward the flag. I observe all this with interest; in a strange country (and after the chaos of the fish market) it is comforting to watch a ritual that is completely understandable.

The ceremony has been over for a couple of minutes, the soldiers or policemen safely marched back into their quarters, when two young women come across the park and stand very close to me, shattering that inviolate space that one stranger gives to another and which, by being broken, implies a relationship, quite possibly hostile. They are black but not very and they have the pleasant but brainwashed faces of Brazilian housewives. They are each carrying a basket, and they are talking to themselves nervously and in voices that I am expected to overhear. I overhear their country Portuguese but without understanding a word, though, of course, I know exactly what they are talking about. They are talking about me and what I have just done. I don't understand if they wish to condemn or warn me.

Suddenly I want very much to talk to them and to explain; I can feel an emotion building in me to explain it all to them. In order to slightly change the situation and give them the courage to assault me, I look into their eyes and give them that Mr. Neuman smile right off the cover of *Mad* magazine. Feeling safe now they put down their baskets and take turns with me. What I think I understand is this: what I have done is very dangerous and, if the police had seen me, I would probably have been mistreated and thrown into jail. And really, it is a very small thing to do and a great foolishness not to do. One may be bored with the military, one may hate the oppression and the fear, but still, isn't it true? The flag is a sacred thing. One loves one's country in spite of everything. One has a great emotion for Brazil and shows it by standing quietly while the flag is being raised. Really, it is a small thing to do and will prevent all kinds of trouble.

"Oh, my God, my dear ladies," I finally get to say (and how I love those ladies in this moment and how sad and apologetic that I must speak in a Spanish that they will only partially understand), "I am very sorry that I don't speak Portuguese, and you must forgive me. I have no more than two months in your country. I am trying very hard to learn it, but am finding it almost impossible. Thank you very much for your interest in my bad manners. It was a very personal thing and was not against you or Brazil. I love Brazil, I love the people; they are the loveliest in the world. But I am not a citizen of this great country; I owe no allegiance to it, and I cannot honor your flag as long as it is in the hands of a military junta."

Saying this I discover how I feel and discover with emotion that I actually have strong feelings and that they are foolish and dangerous enough so that even under pressure, and perhaps, if I had the courage, not even under a few carefully placed police blows, would I ever stand at attention while the Brazilian flag was being raised under a Fascist regime.

There is a compassion between us that I'm sure I'm not imagining and that replaces the words being spoken and perhaps makes them unnecessary. However, we go through the whole routine again. The ladies, miming men with clubs and men with their hands chained behind them, explain that I am in danger if I don't shape up. And I tell them that in my country, while I would stand at attention and that under the emotional enslavement of martial music or crisp bugle blasts, even weep and shudder with pride and love, that I hated that emotion, that I was ashamed of myself for feeling it, and that I hated the idea of flags and national pride and boundaries and the ease with which people can be manipulated to kill one another. Jesus, it is amazing to discover that I am a fanatic and to feel my eyes filling with tears and to feel, as an American, a profound yearning for these Brazilian ladies to whom I cannot speak clearly. Embarrassed, I decide to shut up, but we continue to smile and nod for a time.

We shake hands and part. No, we hold hands and part. How I wish that my camera had been loaded and that I had asked to take their picture; I feel deprived now not remembering the faces of two of my best Brazilian friends.

They wander down one of the paths toward the market with their empty baskets and come to the mango, the yellow mango, the first one. They stop and study it in amazement and suspicion as though it is attached to a hidden string and will be whisked away if they bend to pick it up. They turn, raise their hands to me solemnly, and pass on to become part of the crowd.

Trying to keep the river in sight I go back to the hotel for the free breakfast—the wonderful jolting Brazilian coffee that stirs you up like a slug of gin and the silly little paper thin, skinned bananas. At nine o'clock I find on the wall-to-wall carpeting of the airline office, cowering and wetting itself with emotion, the long lost bag looking just as I had claimed—blue and unzipped. The manager of the office and his lost-and-found lady, almost dancing, shower me with joy, handshakes, and squeezes; they press Marlboros upon me and lay one behind my ear. Watching their delight I begin to wonder if this is the first bag lost in Belém—or just the first one ever found. "Nasty, nasty bag," I say sternly. I kick it a couple of times for its naughtiness (it had gone back to Rio) and it licks my hand and whimpers. Everyone laughs at my clever bag. Together we return to the hotel and I gut the poor creature, hanging shirts and pants to air in the blast of the fan. There is nothing missing but three one-dollar bills that I had stuck in an outside pocket for some reason. My jacket moves slowly in the air, limp but still brave. It is only nine thirty but I have already had a full day.

On the River

The slow, lazy, negligent beat of the diesel is like the opening bars of some tremendously long Mahler symphony; it hints that we will be taken to far and awful places but at another's pace. We must now submit to the river's rhythm. All night in the cabin sleeping off and on, very warm in a curtained-off bunk, one of four, I listen to the piston beat of the engine — slow, slow — waiting for it to confront the push of currents, waiting for the boat to get under way. It never changes, and five days later (or was it six or seven?) at the end of the trip, I will still be waiting, needing to have the memory of having struggled, at least for a time, against that unimaginable flood.

At four thirty in the morning I am out pacing around and around the first-class deck rattling the locked doors of the men's toilets. The captain walking among us shortly after departure has seen three classy passengers and has ordered all the toilets to be locked. He is afraid that some of that third-class scum, that rabble from the steerage, will sneak up in the night and piss in the toilets of the gentry. It will take us almost two days of mutinous behavior before the first-class passengers are dealt out great three-pound keys chained to heavy brass plates. They are like recognitions from the bridge of our superior blood and we hang them from our pockets like watch fobs or twirl them negligently in our hands while talking to one another. How proud we are to have official permission to wade through that first-class stink of plugged-up toilets, dripping showers, and urine-soaked floors. But why be a captain of a ship if you can't make everyone feel the lash of your power?

Out of absolute need, alone on deck pooching out my tummy between the railing pipes, I piss into the Amazon. It is a nice moment, this exquisite moment of relief that defines happiness, this meeting of my waters. During that whole year in Quito the flushing toilets in my apartment had been delivering modest but daily contributions to the great father of them all, and figuring quickly it seems not at all unlikely that at this very instant last year's juices have traveled three thousand miles and finally reached the mouth of the river and the sea. What a trip we have had, together again, my juices and I. Filled with nostalgia I peer down into the darkness searching for my past, searching for last year's turd, which I know will be immediately recognizable since it is only our own turds that we can bear to look at with admiration and a sense of accomplishment. But it is dark; the thought is sad. For that whole year everything that was cast into our river on the farm had flowed into the Pacific while I had been dedicated only a couple of hundred miles away in Quito trying to leave my mark upon the Atlantic. We were more separate than I had ever realized until now. (Here in Quito, now, today, I resist the temptation to do variations on this theme, get up, and reverently flush my toilet – and send the best part of me on its way, following down behind brave Orellana, the discoverer of the Amazon, the conquistador – another turd, though it would perhaps be impolitic to say it aloud in this city that glorifies his name. Greetings to *Belém y saludos a la familia.*

There is a fish in the Amazon, they say, microscopic and evil, who will swiftly climb through the curving stream of urinating man, enter and work her way up through that interminable length, and what she does up there I don't remember, except that it is extremely unpleasant. I think of this fish in my first hand-to-hand encounter with the river but don't honestly feel much threatened. At my age that quavering and intermittent stream of mine is more like a hesitant Morse Code sending out an angry message about death than a fish ladder.

Standing on the deck I wait in the darkness for the first light. It comes slowly, leaking weakly out of the east as though there were not enough light pouring in from below the horizon to fill the immense sky and the dimly felt, flat land below it, half under water and flowing away on every side in a staggering monotony. Then it all begins to happen quickly, the stars dim, a band of lemon-yellow light glows on the horizon, above it the sky catches fire, and the few trees along the one visible bank of the river take on color. It is more awesome than any symphony, the lights coming up to reveal endlessness upon endlessness, another kind of hell that Dante, living too soon, simply did not imagine – a world drowning. We are moving against the northern bank and behind the trees that edge it, beaches of grass, floating clumps, ponds floating in grass, lakes, grass-bordered. And past all that, more lakes, winding bands of low-lying grass-covered islands, and behind the islands stretches of water to the farthest distance. On the port side there is no shore at all, the southern bank is miles away; just water, yellow, sluggish, scarcely moving. A long row of pure white egrets, their feet tucked under them and looking as though they were packing sticks of firewood, pass by heading the other way and barely skimming the water.

There is no sun yet; the whole world is still in shadow under a sky that blazes with hot light, yet the birds in their whiteness moving past us seem to be illuminated, lit by some mysterious grace. It is the unearthly egrets, the only living things in all that vastness that make the vastness so overwhelming and that shatter my conception of place and time. A line of pterodactyls with rigid leather wings and the rowed teeth of alligators moving past us in an empty crimson sky could not have been more disorienting. I have arrived at an emptiness that seems to match and make apparent the emptiness and the inconsequentiality of my own life. It is a crushing and cleansing moment of illumination; only an over-proud egotism could have allowed me to take on the Amazonian wasteland and mingle it with my own desolation. But I do, and there is a great trading back and forth of emptiness. What a sense of separateness, what an overwhelming sense of loss those aloof egrets have given me.

At last and for the first time on the trip I feel as though I stand diagnosed. I know what my disease is, and, knowing that, may now begin to cure myself. I hear a voice saying, "You must make a moral stand." While I'm not sure what it means I find great truth in it. I must try to figure it out and obey it.

My mind is split into many pieces. With one part I am wondering about this word "little," which, when applied to man, and especially to man confronting tremendous natural forces, defines him somehow within a context of great courage and nobility. But it is the part of my mind that watches the egrets disappear that I decide to honor with my attention. I recall a memory as automatic as the tears that follow a blow, for I am programed to go weak at the sight of egrets.

Thirteen years before on another river I had gone one morning to a poor man's jungle farm, paddled there from the village on the ocean by his young son—past the old balsa mill and around the bend that hid the sea and abruptly cut off the sound of the breakers, and past the mangroves and, still in the tide waters, had come to the farm. We probably arrived on the tide or how could that child who was not much more than nine years have paddled me so far? It was over a mile. The whole lower half of the farm by the river was a field of muck, scuttling crabs, and half-drowned salt grass. The house sat in the middle of this on stilts.

I had made a contract with the town's children that I would give them gringo chickens to raise if they would first build little bamboo chicken houses for them. It turned out that the kids and their fathers were too poor to buy nails or bamboo, too poor to own hammers and saws. Still, the little boys were crazy to own chickens. How they pestered and begged. It ended up that I had to build the chicken houses first myself, and then raise the chickens up to a pound or so in my bedroom, and then give them away. So this morning I had come out to build the little bamboo cage that would hold the two chickens that he thought he could afford to feed – a mother chicken and a daddy chicken. The boy and I were working out behind his house, and his mother and father, who were very keyed up because I had been invited for lunch, were doing something nervous in the kitchen.

These are details that I have almost forgotten. I truly remember only the crack of the rifle and the egret, and just that one moment is imprinted on my memory like a photograph in tones of gray and the brilliant white of the egret about fifty feet away, its wings stretching out in a convulsive spasm and its legs collapsing under it and its curving neck stretching out straight and outraged as its head first reached for the sky and then fell slowly into the mud. It had happened in that same moment as I had stopped my hammering to watch in joyous amazement as the bird, quite close, came in to land, my look and the gun's explosion so simultaneous that I had felt an awful evil in the power of my eyes (still vividly remembering that a year before I had killed a cow the same way, by laying one hand upon her flank, that dead animal the final unarguable symbol of my final days as a California farmer).

It is impossible to think at times like this, for the stunned body rushes into shock. I just stood there with a blank mind, trembling, and aware of a real horror in the world. While I stood there looking at the dead bird, the little boy clapped his hands and went running across the muddy field to retrieve it; the boy's father came to the window, the gun still in his hand and a wide, relieved grin on his face. We were going to have egret for lunch.

Later that day, at night perhaps, lying in bed and listening to the ocean breaking on the beach, I realized that what I had seen in that self-satisfied smile was the potential moral awfulness of man and his capacity to destroy the world. I had seen the destruction of the river, of all the rivers on the continent. I had seen the destruction of the Amazon. If a man could sight down the barrel of a gun at that pure white bird with its delicately and intricately feathered wings and its sweetly curving neck, and those frail vulnerable legs, a wild bird who had come in innocence to that man's farm and in the alighting, in the subtle coordination of its marvelous parts could not help but have moved that man to wonder—if a man could sight down the barrel of a gun and pull the trigger, there was no hope for the world. (A couple of months later on the beach I watched a *Policia Rural* beating a man with the flat of his machete as he drove him along the sand where the sea had wet it; the man while drunk had raped a nine-month-old baby and was being taken in to die. Somehow I felt less horror watching this terrible tableau than I had felt for the dead bird. There are things that can be atoned for, and as the machete came down again and again upon that man's body there was a look on his face that I can only say was joyful. How he longed, how he yearned to die. All of us who saw him that day in Rioverde knew that he would be dead within the hour, that the policeman under orders would never deliver him up to the law. "I had jumped . . . , it seems." Isn't that sentence in Conrad's *Lord Jim* one of the most terrifying and heart-breaking sentences in literature? Jim atones, but how do you atone when you have destroyed the world?

That year high-school kids all over America were memorizing Faulkner's Nobel speech, those brave macho lines to the effect that man would not only endure, he would prevail—or some such bullshit. I knew that night as I thought about the meaning of the dead bird that it was all bullshit, that a good man with a few belts of whiskey and the Nobel prize under his belt might be expected to and forgiven coming up with some euphoric hogwash for the great emotion of the moment.

        •   •   •

And on another tropical river where the jungle came down to the water's edge, a few years later Ramón and I had bought a farm and four years after that had bought a second one, one for each of us, and I had gone across the river to do my macho act—to live alone on the new jungle farm and see what I could do by myself.

From my shack until the maracuyá vines covered one end of it I could look downstream and across the river to the farm buildings on Ramón's side—and every morning at dawn and every evening just before dark the same line of about fifty egrets would pass by both the farms flying very low over the water, an incredibly beautiful line of birds as white, pure, and glowing as that soul of nature that we have invented for it, a line of birds more intense and poetic than lines of Debussy. Later, because I was the only human on the farm and they had begun to feel safe, they would veer in from the river, fly through the shade of the rubber trees below the house, and circle the pasture. If the cows were out away from the trees and grazing in the sunshine, the egrets would alight, one to a cow, and riding on the backs of the animals peck at their backs and necks for the ticks, blood-engorged and as fat as pennies. That was another fine thing to watch: the egrets riding on the backs of the white Brahmas, the green grass up to the cows' knees and the green, jungled hillside exploding behind them in the sunshine.

From the first day and for the two years that I lived there I dreamed of being able to tame those cows so that I could walk among them as they grazed, and I even dreamed finally that one day I would walk among them with the egrets on their backs. During the first months those crazy cows would go berserk each time they saw me; they would rush away into the brush, go leaping over or through fences to hide out in the middle of the abandoned banana planting. Later they grew calm and would almost ignore me, and later still in the last six months when Ramón was putting the pressure on me to leave, the cows, when they saw me coming down the lane, would gallop up to me, flinging their hind ends in the air and fighting among themselves to be the first to have their necks or their heads rubbed. And the egrets? They loved to ride the backs of the galloping cows, but they would desert the cows and sail away when they saw me. The nearest I ever got to an egret is that one who died as I looked at it.

There was the most marvelous and lively stream of crystal water that ran through the farm. From the mouth of the river the stream formed a part of the northern property line but, after a thousand feet or so, it cut, winding, through the middle of the farm and divided that small part that years before had been planted to bananas from the larger part, a steep hillside cut down its whole length with many deep gullies of smaller streamlets that tumbled and rushed full for a day or two after each winter rain. Behind the bananas were hundreds of acres of flat land, heavily wooded and badly drained, so dark, oppressive, and unfriendly that I avoided this part of the farm for months until I realized that my neighbors were trying to steal it and that I would have to move in and fight for it. The hillside was the wildest kind of tropical forest and in much of the deepest shade it broke the textbook rules; the ground was covered with heavy brush – willowlike bushes but with immensely long branches like whips, elephant ears, and ten-foot-high *jualanga*, a spikey and stinging plant worse than any nettle, the plant most preferred by the most ignorant and brutish of the Negroes for beating their nasty children. For the first three or four months, close to the river, half-afraid to go out further, I burned old pasture, cut down *caña brava* and second-growth brush that was coming back, and built fences for new pastures for the cows. Then, very tentatively, I began walking out along the hillside trying to establish the lines of the farm; it was immediately apparent that we were being invaded on all sides by our neighbors. The boundary line ascended across the face of the hill so that two miles out, quite high now, where there were gaps in the trees (wonderful holes in the jungle like windows in some gloomy building) you could look out for miles across the flatter jungle below and look back at the river winding between the hills with the little Negro huts built on the bluffs above the river beaches, a dozen or so to every mile. What frightened me out there was not only the tremendous silence that was almost loud enough to deafen you and the strong feeling of being absolutely alone in the kind of country made mysterious and dangerous because I didn't know it, but also because there was a family of mentally retarded Negroes who had taken possession of land along our south property line and who deeply resented the fact that we had bought that jungle that they had been invading for years.

The farm was shaped like a funnel, quite narrow along the river (less than a thousand feet) but becoming wider and wider as you moved out into it. At the back it was so far and so hard to get to that I managed to get out there no more than a dozen times; one had to be in just the right mood to go out alone into the darkness. It was miles between the northern and southern lines, and looking out over it from the hillside, and thinking of the magnitude of the job in cutting down that forest and planting all that space to grass, made you sick to the stomach, not only because it was going to be so difficult and expensive but also because there was a deep immorality in the idea of destroying so much jungle and opening up so much land to the sun. The time had come to tame that side of the river, and if we didn't do it someone else would, but this reasoning reminded us a little of the madame who says, "Well *someone* has to operate the whorehouses." Some rich *hacendados* to the south had just bought a tremendous piece of jungle, *Oro Verde*, and planned on putting in pasture and African palm. The two of us would turn that whole area into an agricultural land and destroy the hunting grounds of more than a hundred people. When we cut down the trees would that lovely stream dry up? When we had cut down the trees where would the birds and animals go? Would grass alone with its shallow roots hold that hillside together, or would it melt away in bare and sterile gullies? And out there at the back in the land so flat that all year round it was a cup of coffee in one hand. The cows always tried to sleep in the lane by the house, where they would listen to the Voice of America and where I, lying in bed, could listen to them making grassy flops and belching, both of us equally stimulated, I suppose, by one another's profoundest observations about life.

For two years then I had over seven hundred acres of jungle to play in, to do again finally at sixty all the things that I had done at six in my grandmother's California garden. And more, much more. All the things that I had been forbidden to do. The lost garden of childhood is only Paradise because we have been kicked out of it, of course, and by being forbidden to return will forget that the golden bees would sting, that the sun, burn, and that our hands had come away bloody from those first ecstatic grabbings at crimson roses. I would learn it all again and something else – that the innocence and intensity of childhood comes back only in little unexpected and ephemeral moments, and that, being a man, I was much too corrupt and superficial, much too enslaved by the safety of stale emotions to be able to remake myself, to submit myself to life. If life has any meaning at all toward the end, it is certainly only in one's ability to draw from the well of memory a satisfying amount of intense experience to contemplate, for the things that are forgotten are only symbols for the parts of us that have already died. Part of the middle-class tragedy lies in the facility with which intense experience can be synthesized and bought.

I would go over and play with the jungle and look for little intensities that I could handle; I would order the businessman's blue-plate special. Just as I had no intention of taking on the sensibilities of my jungle-bred black neighbors, whose feelings about the jungle were way too subtle and profound to be casually absorbed, neither would I, sublimating my sexual frustrations, try to expand my feelings into the areas of wild poetic ecstasy. I was a farmer, perhaps a rather highbrow one for the books I read, but a farmer all the same. The beauty I found in any new landscape was firmly based on its agricultural potential, and the most beautiful land to me was land being properly used. There is something sad about pasture growing where tomatoes should be planted; one thinks of Albert Einstein pumping gas for a living.

Still . . . Still . . . There is nothing more serious than play, and those two years were awful and marvelous and ultimately serious as hell, the best and worst days of my life, and when I dream now very often I am once more walking up that stream wet to the waist or standing alone on the hillside. I write about this time with reticence and embarrassment, feeling that in the simplicity of my pleasures there was an element of childishness in-appropriate to my years. What business does an old man have sitting for an hour in a patch of sunlight on that deserted and silent hillside watching a great wasp, insanely active, hunt for, find, fight, and paralyze an enormous spider? If someone had walked up on me suddenly and found me there I think I would have blushed with guilt as though I had been discovered too deeply engrossed in another childish vice. But it was an important and ex-citing encounter, perhaps one of the most profoundly terrible things I saw on the farm, and I felt that I was being plunged deep into awful secrets. But at the same time I was ashamed to have been so wholly caught up and ab-sorbed in a drama so innocent, so divorced from the realities of my real job, of subduing new land and getting new pastures ready for the calves we hoped to have. Sunlight, soft and green, filtered through the high canopy of ceiba or *matapalo*. At times walking in that light I felt a queer delight that made me want to wave my arms about and sing. And maybe I did, though I hope I didn't, for who wants to present oneself as dotty. It is amazing that so many of the things we don't do in public we don't do in private either.

The muse behind my chair is urging me on to further lyric flights. Let me in an instant note down the first things that I remember vividly; if I were writing this at age six I doubt that the list would be much different.

A *juaco*, an enormous black-and-white bird, a kind of slovenly version of an eagle who came one morning and sat for an hour like an omen in the branches of a dead snag thirty feet from the house; the hummingbirds by the dozens darting and hovering in the upstairs space when the maracuyá began to bloom; yes, even the blooms of the maracuyá, languid and intri-cate as orchids but more innocent; a couple of rains in that two years that empties so much water in an hour over the country that, watching and listening to it under the tin roof of my house, soaked to the skin, I felt brought to the edge of insanity, stupefied and humbled under a constant bombardment of thunder and lightning; it was surely meant for me. An-other ten minutes of *that* shit and I would have run outside, knelt in the rising waters, and confessed to *anything*.

And little things: certain great pale golden mushrooms that swelled and exploded overnight into beautifully complicated structures, like the little paper pellets that Proust in his childhood would drop into a bowl of water and watch as they swelled into flowers; they were not designed to last and would collapse under the first breath of air; certain shaded light on certain pools of water where schools of tiny psychedelic fish flashed red and blue and silver as they rose to the water's surface; certain trees that would burst into crimson or yellow bloom, the trees, solid burning color; certain clear nights when the southern sky blazed with equatorial stars, colder, purer, more purely furious in this more newly created hemisphere just beginning to become polluted. On those clear nights if I hadn't seen a human being all day – or for two days, or as happened a couple of times, for *six* days, I was subjected under that cold vast night to emotions so complicated, so mixed between desolation and mystic wonder, all my confusions taking on cosmic dimensions, that after studying the sky for what may have been minutes or hours, I would stagger off to bed and fall, in a kind of shock, into the deep sleep of a dead man. Even the cats were stunned on those rare clear nights when the constellations swung so crazily above us; they would stare at the sky with unbelieving eyes, eyes golden and as cold as ice, and walk along the edge of the balcony on stiff, careful feet, and then, shocked like me into an awareness of their true stature before the immensity of the universe and wanting to hide themselves, would climb, desperate that I not boot them out into the night, underneath the mosquito netting and, burrowing, sleep between my legs.

Joyce's hundred-lettered thunder now booms and echoes out across the Amazon wastes, and I am returned to my body. Let me present it in an abridged form: *Gerumbaflatarooga boom boom boom.* Presto. We are back on the Amazon, and the red disk of the sun is coming up above the water. I have been brought back to today by a gargantuan fart, the kind that if I had made it in high school would have got me immediately elected as class president. But it is not mine; I don't have the constitution to manufacture such monumentalities. It is the work of a newly arrived passenger to the deck who now stands at the railing of the ship peering furiously across the empty grassy spaces of the Amazon – Hedrik, a six-foot, six-inch Dutchman who because of his great size, his shambling walk, and the fierce face beneath his tousled and uncombed hair had become for me one of Belém's principal tourist attractions for I had seen him every day lumbering up the streets beneath the mangos like a trained and perhaps half-friendly bear. Kind of a shock to recognize him now and to realize that Belém's principal tourist attraction is a tourist.

Another blast, a fart to match the greatness of the river, echoes and rolls out over the water, and though the Dutchman is fifty feet away I can only regard it as some kind of a European communication. A morning salutation?

"And a good morning to you," I call. "Was that *beso*, that kiss, for me?" Embarrassed and grinning, barefoot, he comes shambling down the deck hoisting his pajama pants and wiping the hair out of his face with his paws. "A thousand pardons," he says in very good English. "Excuse me, I didn't think you would hear me."

"Hear you? My God, if there were people on shore they would be putting out in canoes right now to save us; that sounded like nothing so much as the boiler going."

"I'm sorry," he says. "I am not well. The awful food of Brazil is stirring everything up; I think I have eaten six hundredweight of beans in the last two weeks. I think very soon I may jet back to Amsterdam on my own, without a plane, you understand? How in God's name do you get into the goddam toilets on this craft? All my cabinmates are making pee-pee in the wash basin."

"Apparently the Atlantic Charter says nothing about man's right to take a shit," I tell him. "But ask them," I say, pointing. "*They* have a set of keys." The three classy passengers have come out into the early morning in smart Parisian bathrobes and with their tremendously long telescopic lenses are snapping picture after picture of a solitary half-drowned tree.

The scowling Dutchman studies the three classy passengers and then studies the tree. "Imagine coming from Holland to look at *this,*" he says, encompassing the whole tremendous waste with one sweep of his arm. Scowling and clenching his fists he wanders away toward the photographers.

Alone again I try to stay on the boat, but it will take more than a fart to separate me for more than a minute from the recent past into which I have gone plunging, that past where something went wrong that I must now try to understand and onto which I must attach the rest of my life. I am held for just a moment under the delight of speaking English again; it has been almost two months since I have communicated anything with ease with anyone, and saying something that is decorative, that is not involved with food, a bed, or other equally boring banalities is as stimulating as a lover's smile.

·   ·   ·

I had not gone over to that other side of the river, to that other, wilder, purer side, believing that I would find only innocence, plainness, the deep emotions in the brighter, simpler colors of childhood. Not that those things weren't there, of course. They were, but mixed as everywhere when the human element is interjected, with the vices, passions, and brutalities of the people who had chosen to live or had been driven to that empty jungle side. They were the people who would be endangered and whose lives would be tumbled about and changed by my arrival. That jungle wasn't just leaves and silent paths and moving sunlight on still pools of water; it was people, too. A year before we bought that second farm I had got a hint of what it might be like on that other side.

There was a family of very poor, desperate, and disreputable hunters who lived about a mile to the south of the farm that we would buy. I don't remember their names or if I ever knew their names. We didn't even know they existed until a murder made stars of that family for a few days – a middle-aged father with his second woman; four or five of his sons, a lighter dusting of daughters. All of the children were incorrigible thieves. In all probability so was the father, but for the sake of the story let us make him innocent for once. All of the children had been denounced and jailed by their neighbors on innumerable occasions, but they continued to ravage the countryside, stealing chickens, pigs, canoes, the battered pots out of momentarily unguarded kitchens, and the tattered clothing that the women hung on the bushes at the edge of the river to dry. They were a scourge and a curse to all their neighbors, who were just as poor, just as desperate – and perhaps only slightly less inclined to steal themselves.

And so one day a couple of their neighbors decided that they had had enough; they took a gun out into the jungle and lay in wait. Whispering together they fueled their rage. As luck would have it, it was the father who walked the trail that day; his youngest son, a child of seven or eight, walked behind him. They shot the old man in the chest, and as he was dying they dragged him off the trail and laid him sitting up against the trunk of a tree. After three days in the jungle no one would know how he had died. While the terrified men were arranging the body, the child ran away, climbed into the convoluted and buttressed trunks of a large *matapalo* and hid himself in one of the caves formed by the sinuous nature of the separate limbs before they grew together. The murderers, when they came to their senses, realized that the child, too, would have to be killed since he could immediately identify them. The child stayed hidden in the tree all day as the two men cruised back and forth in a growing state of panic, beating the bushes and crawling into the hearts of the *jualanga* thickets.

Can you believe that as they searched they called him by name, called him sweetheart and promised him candy mints? Can you believe that the child, out of hunger, was tempted from time to time to show himself and test their intentions?

At nightfall, almost weeping with fear and frustration, they gave up and, squatting down together beneath the very tree where the boy hid, made their plans. They had fucked everything up; they would have to run for it; they would separate and head up along the coastal beaches for Colombia. They did, and as far as I know they are still there.

It was Ramón who told me the story, but it was Arcario who had trailed behind the police and seen the body. He told me the little detail that I can't forget and that makes all the rest all real. When the child led his brothers back the next morning to the tree where the dead man lay, they found that his face was no longer black but absolutely white. The flies had laid eggs in the sockets of his already decaying eyes and filled his mouth with eggs and then covered the whole surface of his face with a million fly eggs like a finely woven, a faintly glowing but grainy shroud. When I imagine this story of thievery and murder I always linger over this moment when the sons early in the morning and in the deepest shade stood before the body of their father and gazing into that white, subtly distorted face confronted a crime for which in large degree they were responsible. What had they thought as they stood there? What might one have seen on their faces? Could I even have looked into their faces in that moment? There is something terrifying about seeing complicated, conflicting, and unacceptable emotions moving over the faces of very simple people; it is like watching the mixing of volatile and dangerous chemicals into unstable and explosive combinations.

A month or two later coming in from work one afternoon I was directed up the hill by Ester, Ramón's wife, who called down to me distractedly from the kitchen and begged me to hurry, to hurry, that there was a badly macheted fellow from across the river who had staggered by a half hour before held up by a woman and begging for a ride into Viche and the local nurse. I jumped into the pickup and drove up the hill; they had not gone far in that half hour. The man was lying full length in a large mud puddle stained red with blood, and a young woman was sitting in the puddle with his head in her lap trying to keep it up out of the water. A small bundle wrapped in leaves and roughly tied with a length of picquiya vine lay at her side in the gravel. She had no expression on her face and all of her subsequent movements were drugged and graceless as though she were already beyond hope and had already given up this man to death. I realized immediately that she was his woman, the woman who lived with him and cooked for him, but that she had no feeling for him; she had been so battered by life that she could not even go through the rituals of mourning, of fear, or of anguish. As I got out of the car and went running to her she looked at me blankly and said nothing.

It wasn't until evening that Ramón told me that they were from across the river and that the man was the oldest of the sons whose father had been killed for their sins, but at the first glance I knew, even before I could clearly see his face, that he was a dangerous man, one of those invisible, unscrupulous blacks who lived a truly primitive life centered on some hidden jungle shanty. I had pegged him precisely; he was one of those absolutely simple men untouched by civilization who terrorized and menaced the people and by the poorest of the people was referred to as "jungle shit." He was almost the first black I had ever seen in Ecuador whom I recognized immediately as having those qualities that infuriated Ramón and made him predict that when I slept alone in an unlocked house I would end up being murdered in my bed. He was a man *capaz de todo.*

He was about twenty-five years old but as slim and undeveloped as a child, perhaps even a child who has been bedridden for years. He was undersized with the delicate, fragile bones and the slack muscles of a man who has scarcely in his life ever had enough to eat. His wrists, which seemed capable of wielding a knife, seemed to be as brittle as egg shells. I don't believe he had ever cut his hair; it hung in hundreds of long, tightly rolled curls, a real Medusa, almost to his shoulders and made him look like some mad, unearthly fanatic from another century. I had never seen such repellent hair; leaves, sticks, dead grass, bits of mud were entangled in those awful locks. He was wearing nothing but a pair of heavy canvas pants black and shiny with dirt, and between his legs halfway between one knee and his crotch the pants had been torn open and a slow pulsing of arterial blood leaked out and darkened the water. Though it was completely irrelevant, for the police had no interest in a man so poor, the girl would later insist that he had wounded himself while working in a patch of platano. But the wound was a downward slash toward the back of his leg. It was impossible to imagine that he had cut himself; in fact it was almost impossible to imagine that anyone else had slashed him either – except perhaps from the back while the man had been surprised in some unlikely posture: climbing over a log or more likely stretched out in a hammock on his stomach with one leg dangling to the ground.

He had fallen forward into the water, and now as I turned him over I saw him full-face for the first time. I was appalled and shaken – not because he was unconscious with the eyes rolled back in his head so that only the whites showed, not because of his pallor, an awful grayness that was beginning to approach the imagined color of his dead father's face while he sat alone for a day leaning against a tree and the flies buzzed in and out of his mouth, but because of my instant perception of him. What I immediately understood about him was this: he was a man completely out of touch with his senses; he was a man who had never been loved and, never having been loved, had never learned to love or to value himself. He had accepted the world's rejection as the true measure of his qualities. His whole life lay there plainly in his face – an emptiness, an incapacity to feel. What twisted sound would come out of him when he laughed? It was impossible to imagine that he had ever heard a tender word or that his parents, who had brought him up, had ever heard or spoken a tender word themselves. How sad and repellent this man and strange that on some level I had identified with him, for as I first looked at him the totally irrational thought had flashed through my head, "Well, at least *I* have heard music."

I think there is a sort of proof that I have not totally invented the inner deprivation of this man by what happened between us three months later. It was the only time I ever saw him again. We passed each other on a trail, coming upon each other abruptly around a curving path that skirted a clump of bamboo of tremendous dimensions. In a certain sense it is possible that I had saved his life; certainly he knew that in the infirmary I had emptied my pockets and given him all the money that I had. He was not the kind of man who would deny a sense of obligation, who was incapable of saying thank you for a favor done. He was simply a man to whom things were done, who stood passively under life's torrents and could not recognize in another's actions any sense of involvement. Does the leaf thank the wind that shakes him from the tree? Does the ant thank the hand that brushes it from a burning stick? I recognized him and smiled and saw from the depth of his eyes as quick as the flick of an eyelash an instantly repressed recognition that had begun to light up his face; then it went blank and dead, and we passed each other without speaking, my own face now as sullen, as rejected as his. Last time I go around saving *your* life, prick.

．　　　　．　　　　．

I had to kneel down in the water to pick the man up, and though he probably weighed no more than a hundred twenty pounds he was inert and as heavy as death. "Get in the car," I told the woman. "In front. You're going to have to hold him in your arms." Without speaking, her face expressionless, she picked up the bundle at her side and got into the truck. I swung the man up, walked that five steps to the car door, and handed the woman his feet, but in that instant as I still held him and before the woman could slide him over onto her lap, I felt his body turn icy cold, and he broke out into a torrent of sweat. It were as though he had dropped into another, more dangerous kind of shock, as though all his cells had suddenly gone slack and released their juices. In one instant he had dropped through another barrier, perhaps a final one, into a purer state that more truly defined his essence. He was nothing now but a Suffering Man. As the woman took him I noticed that the skin on his chest and belly was discolored, bleached and mottled from the jungle fungus that ate away the outer layer of his skin. I was splotched but more modestly with the same affliction; apparently neither of us bathed quite as often as he should have – or perhaps it was the polluted river in which both of us bathed that carried the infection.

Deeply repelled, deeply involved, I surrendered his body with relief and walked around to the other side of the truck, and as I opened the door I was hit with the most powerful revelation, a confusion of values that stayed with me for years and only finally began to make sense this morning as I stand alone in the early morning on the Amazon steamer. What happened was simply this: that as I opened the door of the car I was confronted with Michelangelo's *Pietà*, the body of a dead Christ held across the lap of his mourning mother. The pose was identical; the emotion of awe and pity, the sense of standing before grandeur was far stronger, like the difference between studying a portrait of God, or, blinded and shattered, standing like Moses before the real McCoy. The similarity alone could not have bludgeoned me so; it was more the sudden realization, and on a level that was purely sensuous and had nothing to do with the intellect, that this fainting man, completely helpless and vulnerable, hung now between life and death, contained within himself outside of any of his personal qualities that absolute and rare uniqueness of being himself and that in miming the body of God he had made his own sacredness manifest by being in this moment so purely, so nakedly human.

His trembling legs straddled the gearshift, the nerves rippling in waves like the skin of a horse trying to scare off flies. His head, the eyes closed now, lay half against the woman's arm, half against the car's window frame. On the woman's face was such a look of dumb acceptance, of such uncomprehending acceptance that I began to tremble with terror and pity. Frozen, unable to move, staring at them, I realized that man had not been created in the image of God, that God had been created in the image of man, and that man, stripped of everything, reduced to his essence could be defined simply as that animal who suffers.

I got into the car and started up the road, and when my hand came away from the gearshift, it was covered with blood.

The man was conscious when we got him up and stretched out on a bench in a big empty room in Viche next to the police headquarters where miraculously a government nurse was on duty. She took a pair of scissors and ripped his pants leg to the ankle, gave him salt tablets, and set up an iron stand upon which hung a bottle of plasma; she was as cool and efficient as though she treated machete wounds every day. (She probably did.) When everything was ready she told the man to take his pants off, and he did a noble thing, this man so weak from loss of blood that he could hardly stand; he made a tremendous effort that I think could be defined within the limits of moral beauty. There were several of us in the room now; even a sobbing sister had appeared who apparently lived in the town. There were police in the room and several curious women and children in the doorway. The man whispered something to his companion and struggled to stand, and the woman held him up, shielded him from the people, and opened the package she had been carrying. She took out some bright red underwear like swimming shorts and a pair of clean pants. Groaning and staggering he changed into the underwear, and exhausted lay down on the bench again and suffered without moving the needle of the plasma into his arm, and the needle of the anti-tetanus shot, and the brisk washing of his wound with soap and then with stinging disinfectant. Three hours before he had had the decency to foresee this moment; he had brought clean clothes with him; he would rather have died than to have lain down on that bench and publicly displayed his nakedness.

Driving back to the farm alone I was convulsed with an anger that surprised me and that I didn't try to analyze. It was an anger so strong, strange, and irrational, in a sense so insane, that I didn't dare think about it deeply. This rage, until out of shame I directed it to another target, had been aimed at my father who had been dead for years. I saw immediately as I cursed and railed against him that more basically I was cursing myself. Out of a lifelong disrespect for his philosophy and his ideals, I had been driven into extreme and eccentric positions that increasingly isolated me from my class. It was that first morning on the river that I first remembered that anger and tried to understand it and began to realize that, certainly not wanting to, I had become my own father in my relationship with Ramón and that compelled for some reason, some imperative perhaps as petty and obscene as a few strings of DNA molecules, to repeat an awful cycle, I had become that figure finally that Ramón, like me, had been forced for his survival to repudiate. (It was more complicated than that, of course, for Ramón had also repudiated his own father and by doing so was now fated when I became his father's surrogate to repeat this neurotic drama with me.)

The anger driving back to the farm had lain in the sudden realization that I had never really been free to make my own life and that out of revenge I had dishonored my own potential to become a puppet in a ridiculous puppet show, screaming "yes" to my father's "no," a "no" to his "yes." If I now found myself living in a malarial jungle with black people under the most primitive conditions, it had never been because of any great passion for jungle or ethnic investigations or black people. I had simply reacted against my father, one of whose favorite jokes when he wished to anger me had been, "If that son of a bitch Lincoln hadn't messed everything up and freed the slaves, I'd be worth ten million dollars today." And who had boasted that while he had done some pretty bad things in his life, he at least had never sat at the same table with a nigger. Out of the deepest need to repudiate and disassociate myself from this evil, out of a strange repugnance to have sprung from his loins, out of a necessity to publicly treat his values contemptuously, I had constructed a life whose authenticity I was being forced to question, a more liberal and moral life than my father's (and one that he detested and that made him scream that I was as bad as that other traitor to his class, that son of a bitch, that Jew, Franklin D. Rosenfeld). It was amazing to find myself years after my father's death living a life that ten years before I simply could not have imagined, and which, if it wasn't always pleasant, was at least seldom boring. More amazing, I now discovered, was this need of mine to justify my choice with questionable intellectual intricacies – this wildly muddled attempt to equate art with morality and find in the face of the most deprived, most dangerous, and desperate man on the river, the very face of God.

Strangest of all, it was the emotional power of this experience and all the confusions that grew out of it that made me suspect that there was something great and mysterious across the river. A year later when the chance came to buy that other farm, and in the face of Ramón's occasional reluctance, I could hardly wait to move across and challenge that menacing purity where everything would finally be made clear. Like Wallace, I would go farther off into the jungle looking for the potential moral beauty of man.

The sun is up now, there are people moving on the deck or staring with stunned eyes out over the tops of the trees, the ship has entered a channel and is curving between the forested banks of islands. The first houses have appeared (we will seldom be out of sight of houses from now on) – small and square, two-roomed, tin-roofed, brightly painted in violent reds, blues, yellows, greens, all of them at the edge of the river on high stilts and surrounded by water, many of them locked up and deserted. We are going up the Amazon in the month of its highest flood, and the people have retreated to higher ground.

What troubles one about these shacks is their isolation from one another; there are seldom more than two or three to a mile, and they are like a child's penciled scrawls marring the sweep of the landscape – cramped, graceless, almost identical, looking with their small, tightly closed windows as hot as ovens under the Amazon sun. In their separation which speaks plainly of an unnatural way of living, they are as depressing as the crowded slums of Rio or of Guayaquil. One is reminded of the early settlers in the Dakotas who lived in their sod huts separated from one another by miles of prairie. How many of our grandmothers went mad from loneliness? How many of these poor women on the river are giving in to the despair of living alone year after year? A day or two later hundreds of miles upstream but looking at the same houses the word "incest" suddenly comes into my head from nowhere, and like a miracle, no more than two minutes later a middle-aged Brazilian who earlier had been identified as being from Manaus and a poet of the city will stand at the railing beside me for a moment and pointing out at the flooded pastures and the black buffalo up to their knees in the water and the scattered huts along the river, will say the same word, confirming my intuition. "This is incest country," he will say. "Fathers with daughters, mothers with sons, brothers with sisters; this is a most abandoned and desperate land." Part of the fantasy of travel is in putting yourself into a new situation, and for two months I have been looking at landscapes and asking myself, "How would you like to live *here*?" But asking it now I shudder. It never occurs to me to compare the reality of the river with my teen-aged perception of it.

It is the houses as much as the slow realization that for mile after mile all the forests have been cut down that makes one know that one is moving through a land that lies under an eternal curse and that the awful history of this place is a continuing story of murder, enslavement, and exploitation. John Hemming in his history of the Brazilian Indians estimates that in 1500 when the first Europeans arrived there were almost two and a half million natives in possession of the land; today there are less than a hundred thousand, most of whom live in the farthest reaches of the Amazon tributaries. Their turn is coming. A good part of the slaughter and enslavement of the Brazilian Indians took place on the narrow flood plains of this now comparatively almost-deserted river whose population was murdered and its forests cut down. One moves through this land under the constant awareness of a curse, and it is as crushing as the sun. In all that history of white men confronting Indians there are scarcely a dozen Europeans, aside from the Jesuits, who came out of it with even the shreds of honor, and even the Jesuits, if that hellfire that they preached to dominate their flocks actually exists, are for the most part probably roasting in the infernal flames. Reading the early Jesuit chronicles and knowing that they took themselves seriously one at times feels that one is losing one's mind. "From the Toncantins we gathered 1,200 Indians who came with us gladly for we promised them the security of our missions in Pará where they would learn of God's love. But the trip was hard and the smallpox struck. Out of God's mercy we baptised them on the trip, and 600 of them went to heaven."

But let us leave the contemplation of the river for a while, stream into the first-class dining saloon, drink coffee with bread and marmalade, and then go back on deck to meet our traveling companions. If we don't find them quite as interesting as we had hoped, at least we will have the delight of speaking to them in a common tongue. Except for the three classy passengers, of course, who have found their own language quite good enough since they will be interested only in speaking to themselves.

What we will all soon know is that they are French and that coming from a superior culture, no, coming from the *only* cultured country in the world, there is no reason to accept anything that does not meet their discriminating standards. Three middle-aged French tourists, all of them rather grossly overweight: a chunky man with thinning hair and wearing long khaki shorts that come almost to his knees and hung with three beautiful cameras (wide angle with color film; a telescopic lens with color film; a telescopic lens with black and white). He is not half as impressive as the machinery in which he has draped himself and which, until later he will appear draped in tape recorders, almost totally defines him. Two golden blonde statuesque ladies, look-alikes, like cruel parodies of Barbie dolls whose skins have been fatally aged by constant sunbathing and whose faces are turning tragic, leathery, and discontented. They will have little to do with this trip or at least this trip as I conceive it; in fact they have already made their most dramatic move and have gotten the toilets locked against us. By noon of that first day, appalled by the food, the lack of a decent table wine at meals, and the crudities of river travel, they have offered to pay double passage and have been moved to VIP quarters on the top deck. They will continue to eat the same unfortunate food but alone with the captain after the rest of us, growling about this insult to our sensibilities, have picked at our beef chunks and our beans and gone back to the bar. Everything will be the same for them except that by paying double they have made a social statement and have been isolated above us with the master of the ship in a cabin, which, under the full blast of the sun, by three o'clock will begin to glow incandescently. They also get to eat dinner at eight, a much classier hour than that six thirty bell that sends us all streaming into the dining saloon like cattle through a hole in the fence.

They will be an unseen presence on the ship, though we will be constantly aware of their aura. Their cultured vibrations clash discordantly in that emptiness of river and sky through which we are drifting and we feel that they have not earned the right to so easily penetrate this carboniferous world of three hundred million years ago. They are like drunks in church; they are having an experience that will mean little to them and that they will remember only as that week of the barbarous cooking and the badly ventilated stateroom. But maybe none of us in first class has earned the right to invade this land and to travel on these waterways on a boat that is only incidentally touristic; it is a land too sad, too secret, too complex to be comprehended. We are though, thank God, in a much lesser degree, like curious people who have steeled themselves to spend an hour touring the paraplegic wards of a veteran's hospital.

Is it only the people jammed into the third-class holds below us who have earned the right? Except for a couple of bearded American travelers who have chosen to travel in decent poverty they are all Brazilian colonists with their families. Pretending to be looking for someone, I have delicately peered into their quarters – a chaos of humanity and hammocks crowded together in an impressive dark squalor, everything touching everything else and so intertwined and connected that it is almost impossible to go from here to there for the stretched ropes and the piles of boxes and the squatting bemused children, the wooden suitcases tied with string, the sacks of rice or salt, the sad and modest purchases that they are taking back: bolts of cotton material, plastic tubs, plastic dishes, plastic G.I. cans full of kerosene.

These people are not playing with the river and using its vastness to titillate their emotions. They have chosen to live along its banks and live the narrow, deprived lives of provincials whose egos have been blasted and reduced by the vast distances of an inhuman landscape.

The Baptist missionary, an Englishman, appears on deck. By afternoon he too will have become an almost unseen presence – more truly, a silent presence. Between two and four sitting at a table on the shaded deck where some of us have gathered to drink canned beer, he will be furiously attacked by the wild Dutchman. For all his look of rural informality that makes him seem as though he had just come from milking cows, he is a subtle student of theology, and the missionary, whose only strength is a fanatic faith, is overpowered by the Dutchman's eloquence. Had he read Freyre? Did he realize that the Church's insane obsession with clothing the Indian's nakedness was considered one reason why they succumbed so quickly to the European diseases? Naked, they had bathed in the river four or five times a day; clothed, they stopped bathing and wandered around in their infected rags. Oh God, this Christian arrogance, which made virtue out of murder. And your gifts, what are you bringing them? – guilt, shame, this bullshit that it is noble and necessary to suffer, jockstraps and brassieres, a helpless God nailed to a cross. And all of it dimly lit and contaminated with the illuminations of the capitalist work ethic. Sitting at another table on the far side of the ship and watching the river's bank I will hear only scattered words – "the phallic rock that was Jahweh," "the Mithraic mysteries and the blood from the slaughtered bull," "eating, for Christ's sake, *eating* the body of Christ." The Baptist minister tries to make a dialogue, but he has finally met a fanaticism to match his own; abruptly he gives up and sits with a cross, frowning face staring at the deck. He is like a veteran from the Vietnam War who has come back to his people feeling like a hero to discover that he is regarded as a fool.

Finally, the missionary, driven into hiding, will retire to his cabin and stand for hours in the doorway. When someone approaches along the deck he steps back into the shadows. Late in the afternoon of the following day I sit with Hedrik drinking beer at one of the iron tables by the bar. The table is set far over on the starboard side toward the railing and a lifeboat, and from our chairs we can look down the whole length of the deck past the rows of cabins. From time to time the Baptist missionary pops his head out of his cabin, notes our presence, and immediately disappears again. "The poor man," I say. "I think he wants to pee and is afraid to; he must feel threatened seeing you sitting here so close."

"Being oversize I tend to intimidate people," the enormous Dutchman says sadly. "Should we move to another table? I don't want to threaten him, not at all. As a matter of fact I half-admire anyone whose mad convictions have driven him into such an extreme situation. Teaching Indians in the Amazon jungle about the Garden of Eden is pretty wild, is, what do you call it? Pretty redundance?"

"You sounded a little bit anti-clerical yesterday when you were talking about God."

"Yes, I'm impatient with the conventional wisdom," Hedrik says. "Theology is such a trap of lies and confusions. Our relationship with God is so obvious, our role as men, so tragic and magnificent; I get nervous in the face of that nineteenth-century romanticism."

"Then you believe in God?"

"But of course, of course. I'm much involved with God, and in fact, for some years, deeply confused, I even studied for the ministry."

"So what do you mean, our relationship with God is obvious? Seems to me it's just the opposite. Do we have a relationship? Isn't it, if we have one, absolutely inscrutable?"

"No, to anyone incapable of thinking that white is black, God's intentions are perfectly clear. First, you postulate a Creator; then you observe the world as it is. You do believe in a Supreme Power, I presume."

"I've been trying hard for years," I say. "But observing the world, if there is a God, I don't find Him very loving or very lovable."

"Yes," Hedrik says, suddenly coming to life with excitement, "God is terrible, terrible." He leans forward toward me, grasping his can of beer in a gigantic paw. "That's where everyone goes wrong. Carl Jung saw God once. Bloodcurdling. Pure horror. God isn't your dad; why must we feel that God wants us sitting on his lap?" For the first time Hedrik is smiling. "Does God need tennis partners, people with mops and brushes to shine his golden floors?"

"So if there is a God, no matter how terrible He may be, our job is to figure out His will and then obey it."

"God is God, and He is all powerful, and how can any of us ever do anything that is against God's wishes? Cut through all the theological cant and crap, and that's what you're left with."

The Baptist missionary's head peeps out at us for a second and abruptly disappears.

"Is he really frightened of me, do you suppose?" Hedrik asks. "This makes me very sad. Why don't I learn to talk more softly?" He pulls himself up from the table, excuses himself, and shambles down the deck tucking in

his shirt tails and tugging at his pants. I watch him as he stands in the doorway talking into the cabin, talking less and less as the minutes pass.

When he comes back to the table he seems depressed, and the wrinkles
across his forehead, half-hidden beneath his tousled hair, are deeper. He
takes an empty beer can, crushes it into a nothingness, and tosses it into the
river. "Ach, no," he says, "there is no way to communicate with that man;
he is a brainwashed lump of stone."

"What did he say?"

"That he forgives me," Hedrik says incredulously. "He invited me into
his cabin; he suggested that we kneel and pray together."

"And what had *you* said? Why did he feel the need to forgive you?"

"I told him what I just told you—that God is God and that all of us are
subject to His will, that in fact, being manifestation of His will, we were unable to do anything else. He said that this denied man the power to choose
and that I was in the grip of Satan." Hedrik, his face glum, turns away from
his view of the ship's deck and gazes out over the flooded pastures to the
long straight line of the horizon where three distant forest fires send up slow
straight columns of blue smoke.

"But he's right, isn't he? Aren't you denying that man has free will?"

"Yes, the denial of free will is the foundation upon which one pierces to
the heart of God's intentions. We have as much free will as those Siberian
lemmings who swim out into the ocean to die in their millions. As much as
a pack of dogs following behind a bitch in heat. Look at what we're doing to
the planet? Look, look out there. Isn't it against all common sense? A million dollars a minute is what the world now spends on armaments, those
things that man makes best. If there is free will then we are all insane. I
mean it, if we have freely chosen what we've got, if we have allowed others
to choose what we've got, then we are stark raving mad."

"And so God wants . . . ?"

"Exactly what we're giving him: the elimination of this planet from His
universe. If I were a physicist I could write you the formula for this, an expanding universe with everything moving away from everything else,
faster and faster and approaching the speed of light."

"Oh shit," I say. "Then why did God make us?"

"Why not just say that God has a passion to create?"

"Then why does He want to destroy us?"

"Why do children spend hours constructing something out of blocks
just to knock it down? Why do they always build their sand castles within
the sweep of a rising tide? Perhaps destruction and creation are the same

words. If not, why not just say that God has a passion to destroy?" We sit for a long time without speaking, and then Hedrik asks, "Could I be right? Doesn't it make sense?"

"It makes sense, but I don't believe it," I tell him. And a minute or two later I get up and move away. Hedrik is a man to be avoided.

An American girl and an English-speaking French girl are traveling together; they have met casually in Bahia and joined forces for a time – as far as Lima, where one will go back to Bahia and the other to Paris: Beverly and Fleurette. They are good-looking girls in their middle twenties who were brave enough to have thought they might travel alone, have been hassled on the streets of the Brazilian cities by a thousand machos, and who now, in a constant disgust, will no longer go out into a city, one without the other.

"It took me all the way to Natal to learn how to handle these fucking men," Fleurette says. Apparently she had learned her English on a Texas ranch. "You have to give in to your rage. When I couldn't take anymore I'd just stop dead on the sidewalk and start screaming, 'Merde, merde, merde,' as loud as I could. All the men following me, bumping against me, tweeking my ass, fondling their crotches, whispering dirty words in my ears, pretending to make wee-wee against the walls so they could show off those pathetic enflamed little animals, would scatter like chickens, really terrified of my screaming. It was the only way to convince them that walking up a street by yourself didn't mean you were absolutely a whore. You'd have to yell 'shit' at them as loud as you could before they'd believe you weren't dying to be laid down on some dirty bed in a fifty-cruzeiro pension that you rent by the hour and given one of their twenty-second screws. Believe me, mon ami, these deluded incompetents are the original wham, bam, thank you ma'mmers; these little fuckers are worse than rabbits and there isn't a good lay in a trainload of them." I have seldom talked to a liberated woman from whom I learned so much so fast.

In that same park in Belém where I had been warned about the dangers of not honoring the flag, Fleurette a few hours earlier had had a more ominous adventure. On Marajó, that island as big as Switzerland in the mouth of the Amazon, she had met a young touring Frenchman that she liked. At midnight back in town they found themselves in the middle of the park by the empty fountain doing with their mouths what the French are famous for doing – kissing in that particularly lascivious and unsanitary way that the Jesuits refer to as "trading spit." Unfortunately they were doing it lying down on the grass, and a passing gentleman found this particularly offensive. He made a citizen's arrest, called a squad of police out of the barracks with his yells, and Fleurette and her friend spent the rest of the night in jail. Only the Frenchman was beat up. And not really beat up, Fleurette said, just slapped around and knocked down a few times. "How lucky for you," the police kept telling her, "that you're not a whore – if you're not. In Belém we kill whores for doing what you were doing where you were doing it." Perhaps the police, since apparently they are so proud of it, have killed a few, but these murders were not apparent to me. I have never walked down the streets of any city in the world except Shanghai or wartime London where I saw so many women trying to stay alive in that sad profession.

Fleurette had the idea of bringing the primitive art of South America to Paris to sell. Primitive art in Paris was "hot" right now she said. There were two flaws in her plan: she had no money to buy art, and she had, as far as I could tell, no taste. Her only purchase so far, which she absolutely adored, she said, had been a very small painting that she had stuck away in her backpack. It had been done on canvas board, had cost her eight dollars, and was a very bad copy of something that looked like a United Nations Christmas card – a Bahian woman dressed in hoop skirts of blue and all hung with Christmas tree balls. I like Fleurette and her enthusiasm very much; she is a tough traveler, as tough as a *poilu*, very frank and open. Perhaps she has kissed a few too many casual friends in a few too many strange Brazilian parks, but in Belém she has learned better, and talking to her I get the idea that she has made her point and may now relax a little. She is a liberated woman who has proved that she, like any man, can screw on a one-night basis from here to there without losing her dignity or her self-respect. She has done it, savored its delights, appraised its disappointments, and is now slightly bored with the whole scenario.

At the end of the trip as we are docking in Manaus I will invite Fleurette to visit me in Quito where I think I may be able to put her in touch with some interesting painters. There are a few primitive artists in Quito, engineers and lawyers, who have been working very hard for years and are getting quite good at being primitive. I think they would love to be exhibited in Paris where some of them spend their vacations. And there are even a few Indians out in the *pueblitos*, shoemakers, carpenters, *curanderos* who paint from time to time, though their purer vision is not so quite in demand and like sign painters they sign their names very large and with many distracting flourishes. I give my address to Fleurette and she promises to come and stay with me, and I feel vaguely like a pimp for in the back of my mind I am thinking of another friend of mine who likes to couple casually with any good-looking girl who wanders into his store. It occurs to me that they are going to like each other very much, that they deserve each other, and that together they might be able to see themselves in each other's eyes and make a single problem of their identical situation – one blind alley for the two of them.

But at the last minute trying to match her frankness I will shatter the friendship in a thoughtless moment by breaking the rules of shipboard etiquette. I have given her my address; now she tries to give me hers. And like an oaf I refuse it. "I want to see you in Quito, not in Paris."

"You don't *want* my address?" she asks, amazed, for in her travels she has probably offered this dozens of times without being repulsed.

"Fleurette, I am not going to Paris; I will never go to Paris; I want to see you in Quito."

She looks at me for a long time, completely frustrated, and says again, still unbelieving, "You don't *want* my address." She frowns, shrugs, and turns away.

"Fleurette baby, come to Quito, no? I'll see you in Quito." But she doesn't answer; she moves away. Twenty minutes later we have disembarked and separated forever.

But that was the last day. Let me go back to the first day again and take Beverly on this same journey. I am not the only one about to be changed by the river.

Along with the destruction of my Amazonian preconceptions, Beverly will now arrive to shatter my ideas about cocktail waitresses. Saving her tips from a San Francisco bar she has made enough in less than two years to finance a year's touring in Brazil. The cocktail waitresses I knew in 1965 before I left my country were from Chico, a California town that caught some of the overflow from thousands of Reno bars. They were a sad, neurotic bunch, pretty young women running from outrageous and improbable marriages, trying to bring up their neurotic children, and living in second-rate motels or boarding houses. Their lives were made complicated by the only people they ever got to know and when appraising their situations they tended to become hysterical. One I knew slightly tried on almost every other full moon to kill herself; she finally succeeded. Except for the most aristocratic and wealthy ladies, the cocktail waitresses were the only girls I knew who loaded their conversations with obscene words; since I associated this freedom with the smartest people, I tended to find the waitresses a little more chic than they usually turned out to be. I would usually realize this at three a.m. speeding through the walnut groves and trying to get to Crystal's house before she jumped out the window.

The dirty words are all that Beverly has in common with those pretty girls out of the sixties – her dirty word and her prettiness. But in 1978 even a missionary's teen-age daughters talk like mule skinners. Beverly is the most unneurotic girl I ever met, and she has a radiant corn-fed beauty with her fuzzy blonde hair and her pink cheeks and her very enormous blue eyes that exactly mirror an inner health; she is made more radiant yet by that awful disease she has just caught on the beaches north of Salvador. She is in love.

"A friend of mine does catering in San Francisco for fancy parties; he's probably the best-known caterer now because he has the only really well-trained people. They're Chinese. You know making those fancy little bite-size sandwiches, the little melted cheese things stuck with olive slices and bits of crabmeat – all that decadent shit, there's hardly anyone who can do it anymore on a large-scale basis. Just think about it, think about waking up in the morning with someone on the phone ordering seven hundred pounds of assorted canapés. He calls me when he has a job, and I can pick up an extra hundred at least in three hours. He's a wonderful man, gay, and in that business having a gay boss solves a lot of problems. Well, so he was going to Rio and didn't want to go alone. He offered to pay my way, and I couldn't turn that down. After a couple weeks in the most fantastic hotels, when he was ready to go back, I just decided to stay it was so wonderful down here and the people are so super.

"And I ended up in Bahia and met a man, a lawyer from a good São Paulo family, who said 'Screw it' and came to live in a little house on the beach and make ceramics. We live in a small village right on the ocean, and he's a most simple and loving man, a real vegetarian. So that's what I'm going to do. From Lima I'll fly back to Bahia. I love that life on the beach, all that fresh fruit, the sun, that little village that is full of gay artists. And Jose is going to teach me ceramics, we'll work together, it's time I got into something creative and important."

"That's wonderful," I said. "I love Bahia, but I never could find that simple little village just outside it where I could live for five dollars a day."

"No, the only five-dollar villages left are inland in the *sertão* and anyone who would go out into that waste of heat and dust would have to be a very dedicated anthropologist. On the coast there aren't even any thirty-dollar villages anymore, and look what they're doing to Bahia, the way those big cement hotels have come marching south across the town."

"Yeah, between the hotels and the churches there's enough weight to sink that town into the ocean. But turismo can't wreck the people, and the people is what makes Bahia special."

"There are even rumblings in Bahia," Beverly said. "For the first time black maids are sassing their white employers; there's something interesting brewing in Bahia, in the whole country for that matter."

"Isn't it funny to talk to whites in Bahia; they can't go five minutes without saying how much they love the blacks. They're obsessed just like the taxi drivers in Washington, D.C., where you can't ride five blocks until they're screaming about the blacks. Or like the middle-class people in Quito who just love their little *Indiecitos* – and treat them like dogs. We have three thousand Indians in Quito who live off the garbage dump; that's one per cent of the population."

"Yuck," Beverly said.

"In Bahia I was invited to see the first two hours of *Roots* in the USIS theatre," I said. "The American cultural attaché was scared to show something so brutal to a black audience. He made a long speech beforehand: that it was just ancient history, that everything was different now, and that now with integration everybody loved everybody else. Almost made me want to go back."

"And *did* they take it?" Beverly asked.

"The blacks took it very well, but there was considerable sobbing from the white contingent."

"I served cocktails at a party in San Francisco for Alex Haley," Beverly said. "We were serving scotch and something else with rum, and different people would come up to me and say that Mr. Haley would like nothing but a glass of white wine. I'd never heard of Alex Haley, I was very busy, and anyway, there wasn't any white wine. Then Mr. Haley came over and asked me very nicely if I couldn't please bring him a glass of wine. I promised I would, but I never did."

"The guest of honor," I said.

"Yes. I haven't forgotten what I did. You know, if it had been Saul Bellow or Marlon Brando, I sure as shit would have seen that he got what he asked for – if I had to go out and buy a bottle myself. Until then I'd always thought of myself as a great little waitress."

"I hope you don't think it's going to be easy to be a successful ceramist," I said. "That is a tough racket."

"Jose is very well established, and I'll be helping him; he sells everything he makes; it all goes to that tourist place, the *mercado modelo* in Bahia – ashtrays."

"Oh Christ," I said. "*Ashtrays?*"

"O.K., so what's wrong with ashtrays," Beverly asked, bristling, as though she already knew.

"Nothing, I guess. It just makes me sort of sad all of a sudden, and I wish you hadn't told me." I did feel sad all of a sudden, but angry, too, and the anger was what interested me since it seemed that lately my life was turning into anger and that more and more I was making uncharitable judgments. We didn't talk for a time. We were coming upon and passing a small town with a sawmill at one end of it; the ground for acres around was pink and red with sawdust. Hundreds of logs floated in the river tied up in rafts along the bank, the great, squat hardwood logs of the Amazon so heavy that they barely floated. The town was a single row of houses built along the bank with a church in the middle of its row. It was bright blue; all the houses were painted the same color, and the whole scene vibrated, the pinks, reds, and blue, making the eyes spin with pleasure. The scale of the buildings, the way they fitted against the trees, the subtle complementary colors all hinted at a planning intelligence, and because there were no people anywhere in sight there was a grandeur in the simplicity of the scene. (Nothing wrecks an architectural scene quicker than to put a human being into the center of it.)

I am still finding the Brazilian country towns strange and unreal for their silent quality of being empty. I have passed through hundreds of them between Rio and Belém, little rural centers that, through the daylight hours, seem to be deserted or populated only by women; the men will begin to be noticed only at nightfall when they will appear at the edges of the roads walking slowly into town with hoes or shovels or machetes laid across their shoulders like incredibly heavy weights. This river town is more deserted than most for all the women have left it and come out toward our ship in canoes. (Will we be suddenly pinned to the decks with the spears and arrows of these Amazons?)

There are about thirty canoes roughly made of milled planks, flat bottomed and awkward-looking compared with the gracefully carved *Cayapa* canoes that the people use to float upon the river on my farm. In each canoe there is a single woman with the youngest of her children, and all of them are paddling furiously to come as close to us as they can. The faces of the women are sullen, the faces of their children are blank.

As we sweep past them we see that they are not truly Amazons; they have not cut off their right breasts, better to aim their arrows. They are just women in their twenties with the faces of forty-year-olds, dressed in cheap cotton, their hair straight, long, very black, very badly cut. In the wake of the ship they will stop paddling for a moment, and as the swells lift and toss them three times, they will raise their faces to ours, stare blankly as though they were blind, and then, awkwardly manipulating their canoes, head back for town stolidly paddling. It is sad even the first time to see so much energy expended for so little pleasure, but as the days pass and as hundreds of identical women repeat this thing over and over, it takes on elements of horror and becomes almost a symbol that almost totally illuminates their deprived and brutish lives. It is like a cry of desperation enacted in sexual terms in the rising and falling of the waves of the ship's wake that lifts the women, an instant of emotion as brief as the flaring of a match. They will go back to their houses and wait; in another week the ship will be returning to toss them on a river momentarily come to life, to movement and glitter.

(On the fourth day, six hundred miles up the river, one girl will wave to us as we pass. Not having lost hope yet she is sending us a more intense and piercing message. A young girl, quite pretty, she is in a freshly ironed dress, her cheeks are painted, her lips, scarlet. As the waves lift her she searches the faces along the railing, her own face radiant with fantasy. Thirty seconds later she is far behind us standing upright in the canoe in the boiling wake of the ship that catches the sunlight and turns the river to bronze. She has raised both hands above her head, and the fists are clenched tight – pure Munch. Seeing this, hardly able to believe it, one's first impulse is to rush to the captain and scream, "Stop, for Christ's sake, turn back. There is an abandoned castaway out there." It would be the simple truth.)

We were past the town now and Beverly was still not talking. "O.K.," I said finally, "Maybe this is why what you said made me sad . . . what I began to see in Rio, that tremendous city of what? Eight million? Ten million? . . . that the cities don't work anymore. It's almost as though they had been designed to reduce people to objects, to bugs. Bahia doesn't really work; Natal, Recife . . . they don't work. They are crammed full of people who look just like those desperate women we just passed. They have awful jobs that they hate – if they're lucky enough to have jobs. Didn't you see those zombie faces rushing through the streets of Rio?"

"I didn't see that at all," Beverly said crossly. "In fact, quite the contrary. But go on. What's that got to do with ashtrays?"

"Just this: that the world has turned into a place where you can no longer find work to do that doesn't make you ashamed. The jobs that men must do are insults to their potential, and it's not just in Brazil. People filling out forms. My God, they're cutting down all the trees in the world to make paper, to make forms to fill out – to throw away. People standing at windows in offices just to tell you that you've come to the wrong place . . . or screwing bolts on the top left side of unidentified flying objects . . . kids on motorcycles taking piles of papers from this street to that street. Look at the buildings; they're all new and they're beginning to crack wide open. The faucets leak but don't look for a plumber because nobody knows how to plumb anymore; the lights go off for three hours at a time; try to call someone on the telephone. Nobody does anything real anymore, nobody likes their work, it is all plastic shit work. So, just looking at you and hardly knowing you, I'd guess that making ashtrays won't give you much more than a month's satisfaction."

Beverly, staring very hard down into the water, said, "We should all be raising bananas like you, so little snot-noses in Boise will have something to slice over their cornflakes."

"Exactly," I said. "I was a farmer, and that was pure luck. I've always had noble and important work to do."

"And there were no ashtrays in your house, of course; you just used old banana skins."

"Oh Christ," I said, "the world needs ashtrays, and I think the world is full of people who would love to make them. Now, if making ashtrays gives you joy and fulfillment ... "

"I'm in love," Beverly said. "I'm in love with a sweet man who makes ashtrays, goddamit."

"I've known of girls who whored because they fell in love with pimps," I said, smiling. Beverly looked at me for a long time and finally began to laugh. "Are they pretty ashtrays?" I asked.

"Yuck," Beverly said.

We had some nice talks in the next few days – about books, movies, and Brazilian machismo. Beverly had a tendency to sit in one place without moving, and I would have to tell her from time to time that the ship had now crossed to the other side of the river and that she was missing something spectacular. I don't think she liked the river or the effect that it had on us. It was strange that traveling through that enormous land we were not compelled out of a sense of our smallness to huddle together. On the contrary, all of us were dispersed as though each of us had been shot out into deep space, and we stood for hours staring out over the incredibly flat land as it moved past us, monumentally immense and monotonous. It was like a kind of therapy, or if you did not want therapy, it drove you to the bar and the cans of cold beer.

Being twenty feet above the river on the first-class deck it was impossible to guess to what extent the country had changed since the first Europeans paddling in canoes had observed and described this land from the level of the water. For them the banks of the river had been a solid wall of trees; for us, higher up, we could often see over the trees and into the grassy lands that sometimes, almost treeless, faded away to the horizon. For miles, for whole half-days, almost the only trees were those that grew in a narrow line along the banks of the river on a strip of slightly higher ground, like a dyke formed by the river throwing out its solids to make a deeper channel for its flow. The bottom of the river for a thousand miles, from Belém to Manaus, was below sea level, an amazing fact that confused us. In some sense that we couldn't understand, we were traveling into the center of South America on a river that flowed uphill.

But let us dock at Manaus one more time and say goodbye to Beverly. And then go back again to square one and meet a few more passengers. I hope you didn't think this was going to be an easy trip.

.　　　　.　　　　.

We are docking in Manaus. I have either just insulted Fleurette or will in the next five minutes for we are all lined up at the railing, all of us I imagine feeling the usual sadness of the traveler, that feeling of having been cheated by seeing an exotic city like the legendary Manaus finally revealed in all its banality.

"Bev, what's the name of that little village north of Bahia, you know, the ashtray center of the world? If I ever come back to Brazil I'd like to see it."

She told me and I wrote it down on a piece of paper (now lost) and then she said, "Shit, I had to strain to remember the name; this trip has put it a million miles away back there; it even seems like years ago."

"In another ten days this river won't be real either," I said

"In another ten days I'll be back in San Francisco," Beverly said. "You know, you suddenly wake up and find you've been acting in a fairy tale."

"The Manaus poet was telling me an Amazon fairy tale," I said, "about the white river porpoises who turn into irresistibly beautiful men and in the moonlight call to the girls. You can know they are enchanted porpoises and not men only by feeling their heads; they all have a big hole in the back of their heads. When the river girls get pregnant and their fathers ask who did it, the girls say it was the *fodo*, the magic man that no girl can say no to, and the fathers accept this."

"Well, in my case," Beverly said, "it looks like I'm the one with the hole in my head."

"You're not going back to Bahia, back to the ashtray king?"

Smiling in a funny was as though she were still living through a kind of dream, staring down into the water of the Amazon now black as Coca-Cola from the Rio Negro, Beverly slowly shook her head.

There is another American on this trip, a guy in his middle thirties always dressed in crisply ironed khakis and a severe short-sleeved Brazilian shirt. Studying this guy some of my rage against bourgeois standards will be dissipated for he will turn middle-class vulgarities into a kind of nostalgic slapstick. He has been traveling around South America in a pickup truck and with a very constipated dog. The truck is lashed to the top deck and the constipated dog lies on its front seat day after day in desperate canine catatonia. He is a very sensitive dog who would not dream of fouling the ship's decks, and he lies there contemplating his lower intestinal convulsions and wanting to die out of shame and boredom. He is a large, fuzzy, faithful, intelligent type from Alaska, a memory out of my childhood disguised as a dog. But now in Brazil he is patched and plagued with skin diseases and heat rash, and he has lost his identity, his dignity, his virility, his dogginess. He has been hauled around through too many tropical countries and has spent too many hours locked up in the furnace of the front cab. Being a dog he cannot know how lucky he is to have traveled so extensively, so expensively, and he acts as though he now accepts this trip with a kind of dull despair knowing that it is a punishment for something awful that he did as a teen-ager. The man's name is Don; the dog's, Harry—or is it the other way around? Each time we dock at a town Don will pack his Harry, or Harry will pack his Don, out over the lower railing and they will scurry off behind the steamship buildings looking for a patch of grass or a little plaza already christened and made appropriate with local dog turds. Harry, his coils all turned to stone, will hunch up, groaning and heaving, straining until his popping eyes water. Watching him, sharing his suffering, though our own bowels are in quite a different condition, our eyes mist.

But the dog, much pleasanter to write about than his master, is only a digression. We must stick to our pure and rigid story line and discuss the man who owns him. Studying him I realize, as I had realized in the Bogotá airport building, just how fast the world had changed while I had been down in the jungle confronting another, a more illusory reality. First, to eliminate confusion let us decide that his name is Don. Second, a short anecdote to explain why it may seem that I wish to treat him cruelly.

On the farm almost a year before Ramón told me that I had to leave, I had been visited by my old wartime pilot, Jack. He was a retired colonel now with an outrageous pension, PX privileges, and several thousand Air Force planes at his disposal. He flew to Ecuador, spent about ten days on the farm, and in horror at the ascetic lifestyle I had finally achieved, began giving me, among other things, all of the clothes he had brought with him. Being practically naked at the time, not because I couldn't have bought pants and shirts, but because I hated the idea of wasting a day of my life in their purchase, I gratefully accepted these gifts.

In 1943 Jack had been an ideal Texan—slight and lanky, so slim that it must have been sheer nerve and patriotic fervor that made it possible for him to drive and tame his B-17 for ten and twelve hours at a time. But almost thirty-five years later he had become as portly as a—well, as a retired colonel. He had taken on the forty pounds that life in Ecuador had burned off me. One of his gifts had been a pair of G.I. fatigue pants that even on Jack hung loose. I had packed them when I left for Brazil, hauled them around for two months, and now steaming up the Amazon decided that the time had come to flaunt them. They were way too big for me, I admit that, but they had a certain *Je ne sais quoi* in this river *ambiente*. The pockets alone were so big that one of them, had it had two holes in its depths (depths that I could hardly reach without squatting) would have served to decently clothe me.

So here I come strolling down the deck in my marine greens, twenty extra yards of critical war material billowing about me like the Star Spangled Banner, and here comes this asshole, Don, in his Gucci loafers and his tight, pressed pants. We have spoken before but just barely, and now, his eyes opening in surprise and beginning to grin so widely that I would not have been surprised to see his false teeth pop out and clatter to the deck, he calls, "Hey, old man, the war's over; you planning some kind of guerrilla attack?"

Which, having given me the idea, I immediately begin to plan. It is the morning of the first day, still quite early, and I have not yet had those first few cups of coffee that make me charming. Matching his grin, for we are now in mortal combat, my mind blank but whirring like a computer, I stare at him for about ten seconds, and then without having any idea what I am going to say, say, "Oh, don't talk like an asshole; at least my balls aren't pooching out."

Don flushes, glances down quickly at his front, and says in a hurt voice, "Why, heck, my balls aren't pooching out."

Still mocking his smile, blessed by the divine muse for the first time in my life with the nimble gift of repartee, I answer, "With pants like that I bet they would if you had any," and serenely, like some old queen from a low bar I pass him by and sail down the deck more or less sure that he will not strike an old man.

Do you remember back almost to the beginning of the world an old man with a stubbled beard and no teeth who used to sit at the camp fire next to Roy Rogers when Roy was plunking his guitar and singing cowboy songs under a Hollywood moon? And those Hollywood stars wired to the arms of cactus, stars as big as popcorn that winked and dazzled as insistently as police headlights, five seconds on, five seconds off? This old geezer used to spew out great splats of chewing tobacco when the script called for authentic Western color, and when it called for Western humor he would squint up his eyes, go "hee hee hee," and touch the tip of his chin to the tip of his nose in a repulsive display of toothless versatility. This was his only talent. Waves of high-pitched, pre-teen-age glee would ripple through the audience where I sat through the Friday afternoon triple feature. I must have been the only one who didn't laugh; I found the old fart absolutely disgusting. (I have been researching this guy all day since my description of him makes him seem invented, and may now declare that his name was Gabby Hayes and that he was Roy's sidekick in at least six hundred cowboy epics. Does the name ring a bell, give you the shudders, make you give thanks that we must only endure childhood once?)

Funny that Don makes me think of this superfluous old man who rode through the hills of childhood spitting and cackling. They have little in common except – what? – that gaping mouth? . . . no, hardly that even. Don's teeth may be worn down to the gums, but I would swear they are his own. They share more than that sly, faintly lascivious working man's grin. And yes, suddenly I connect those two. Don is also a man without star qualities, the Gabby Hayes, the Ronald Reagan out of the high-school years.

Don is that superfluous figure that we must put into the memory of mob scenes to remind us that we live in a world populated by other human beings. He is life size, cleverly colored, made of heavy pasteboard and may be set here and there as circumstances require. Oh, that ordinary smiling face that reminds us that ninety-nine percent of what we have gone through is all forgotten and that in fact it was so dull that there is no other way to handle the past. In how many memories of others, I wonder, does my own face fulfill this same function?

But, of course, it is a lie to say that he has no qualities; a moment's examination will give him plenty, and I cannot so gleefully denigrate this harmless man simply because he found my pants too large and flapping. He has spent years in the Yukon and Alaska working on the highway or the pipeline. If he was able to squirrel away thousands of dollars a month that doesn't mean that he didn't have character to endure those winters of sub-zero winds sweeping down from the north pole or the mosquitoes of August. And he had the character to save his money and invest it in this trip, and there is character too in the very fact that he is making it, and (minus Harry) making it alone. It is his other qualities that interest me – or rather the quality of his other qualities. In the most comical and shattering way he will answer that old ad in the magazine, a question that down on the farm in Esmeraldas I had pondered for years – "What kind of a man reads *Playboy?"*

Don tells us immediately and proudly that Rio was the high point of his trip; there he had traveled in the smartest international jet circles, had gone everywhere, had met everyone. We who have traveled in Rio and gone no place except to the public museums, the public beaches, and the public gardens and have met no one who is now not already forgotten are anxious and filled with envy. Had I not dreamed of meeting Maria Bethania, humming along with Milton Nascimento, bowing down before some grandchild of Machado de Assis, or shaking the hand of Amado? How had he done it? Had he moved into the penthouses of the very rich and seduced the elite by flashing that shameless smile, a smile that, though very different, reveals him as being as tremblingly vulnerable as Chaplin? Did he use his charming dog as bait? Impossible.

No, it was pure luck, He had met Anita Americo, the famous gossip columnist, had in fact shacked-up with her for a time after having picked her up one night, dead drunk in a disco lounge. She had introduced him to a hundred of the glittering stars of stage and screen. They needed Anita A. They need to find their names in her column. Carmen de Costa, remember her? that gorgeous doll with the immense knockers. She played the part of one of the prostitutes in that so far rather unrecognized epic about the death squad. What a little piece of acting. Born to the part. Remember the blood when they killed her off in an early part of the first reel? Gallons. . . . Santos Dumont Rodrigo Páez, the young lyricist of "Riki Riki Ti Ti Ti Bananas," a sort of rock samba that with luck would soon catch on and sweep the provinces. . . . Simon Groeschman, that talented kid from Recife who had that neat act at the club Tyrol. Remember? The solo tap dancer who yodeled? . . . And many, many more. Don had met them all. He was *in*.

How could dirty-talking Fleurette, that corn-fed Beverly who gazed into the river hour after hour without speaking and the ridiculous white-haired gentleman in the flappy pants compete with Don's memories of the Rio *haute monde*? We couldn't of course, but we assumed that he was part of our little group and that we were stuck with one another for his inability to speak with anyone else. For two days we ate together, listened to his *Playboy* jokes out of the pre-pubic-hair issues, and guarded him against abandonment when the ship would dock at some little town for thirty minutes and he would pack Harry in his arms over the side to prowl some back alley looking for a doggy piece of turf. "Don, Don," we would yell into the night, "Come back. Can't you hear the captain calling?"

On the third day by way of the ship's ladder he ascended into heaven and transcending his linguistic limitations joined his peers, the three classy passengers. We were proud and amazed that he had so quickly found his own kind and that they had so enthusiastically embraced him in their exclusive group, for his only French, I'm sure, consisted of not much more than *"Voulez-vous zig-zig?"* – and how many times can you say that expecting yucks?

For the rest of the trip we hardly see Don. He winks at me when I pass him on the top deck where he sits next to one of the French blondes rubbing suntan lotion over her leathery back, but he does not say much aside from an occasional, "Well, hi there; how the heck are you?" He now eats with the captain at exclusive hours, and at night drinks beer in some special little place that the rest of us never discover. In a sense it is as though he had gotten off the boat at the end of the second day.

On one of those first mornings on the river, very early, we begin to pass the Daniel Ludwig pastures on the north side of the river. It is without doubt the greatest of the man-made spectacles, far more impressive than the Great Pyramid of Cheops, an incredibly immense pasture that stretches along the river for a hundred miles to a distant row of mountains at the horizon. Nobody but an American could have conceived of something so big, so simple and flawless, and in fact it could probably not have been conceived with the conscious part of the mind; it is something right out of the subconscious. We pass it hour after hour, and the imagination, delighted and stunned with this grossness, begins playing with figures. My God, how big can it be? It is surely twice as big as any other pasture in the world. Fifty thousand? A hundred and fifty thousand? Two hundred and fifty thousand acres? Holy shit, a cow pasture as big as Norway. The ship is hugging the bank, we are very close, but it is impossible to identify the kind of grass it is. From its color, from the way it has taken over the land it might be *elefante* or *saboya*, those tropical grasses that explode with sunshine and rain. This carpet grows so thick and pure and has made of the earth something so feminine and yielding that it seems as though one might fall from five thousand feet into it from an airplane and, unhurt, gaily bounce on this green trampoline. From five o'clock until almost noon I stand on the deck mentally at full attention and saluting, and that pasture slowly builds in intensity into an incredibly moving statement about man, as romantic, as thunderously seductive as some late nineteenth-century symphony (Schönberg's *Gurrelieder,* Strauss's *Zarathustra,* Saint-Säens's Organ Symphony). Ignoring the vulgarity, one stands before this monument to an idea brought to a perfect and terrifying perfection and fights (and loses) an impulse to break into tears. In that whole trip of a thousand miles from Belém to Manaus that pasture of Ludwig's is the only thing I see that speaks hopefully of the Amazon's future, that hints in the purity of its workmanship, in its imaginative grandeur, that men will learn to use this country without irrevocably destroying it, an intuition that is absolutely false.

Hidden behind the distant mountains is the rest of the Ludwig homestead. Among other things: a twelve-thousand-five-hundred-acre rice patch, a million acres of jungle cut down and planted to fast-growing pine, whole mountain ranges of bauxite and a great river about to be dammed for power. There is a two-hundred-eighty-five-million-dollar paper factory amusingly built in the form of a great barge being towed up the river behind us, the poet from Manaus will tell me. Ludwig, an almost extinct species, an alive-and-kicking billionaire, is having at eighty-one a fine last celebration, a billion-dollar party. Until today I haven't seriously thought about such things, but now wanting to understand I write down the zeros thus: 100,000,000 and study it for half a minute before realizing that this is only a lousy hundred million and that it takes ten of them added together to make a billion. Old malarial fevers suddenly flare along my legs from the crotch to the knees; it is like a sexual arousement.

He is so rich and the things he is doing are so momentous, that he stands outside our everyday morality. By experimenting with a continent, by setting natural ecological forces into disarray that may make deserts out of savanna or destroy the world's delicate oxygen-producing factory, he is fooling with the lives of hundreds of millions of people, but like a Nixon or a Napoleon or an Alexander his crime may be so tremendous that it will never be regarded as criminal but only as an historical event.

As we travel along the outer edges of his kingdom I search the bank for a sight of this mythical old man. It seems to me that on a day like this he ought to be out there counting his cattle, but I see neither man nor beast, just this sea of grass laid over the landscape. Drawing a line along the equator (a line that is not as long as some) from this farm on the Amazon to my farm on the Esmeraldas, I join us together in the brotherhood of shared ambitions. Taking a chance, in brotherhood, I mingle his pastures and his cattle with mine. I am just playing with the idea and think he wouldn't mind that for five minutes I have given him another fifty acres, another forty cows. *My* cows have white egrets riding on their backs, and a lot of that fifty acres I have planted myself. Each of us in his own way has been drawn to the tropics, and moved perhaps by identical emotions in the face of the jungle's inhuman arrogance, charged with the impulse to confront it, to cut it down and plant grass among the rotting trunks of the fallen giants. In our insensitivity we are brothers, Ludwig and I, and if he has made more of a splash in Brazil than I have ever made in Ecuador, it is only because he has a little more money. Hell, I don't even have *half* of what he's got.

But Mr. Ludwig and his billion dollars and this cow pasture before which I can only bow my head and shudder with admiration, are things so unreal, so shamelessly romantic that they can hardly be contemplated under the hard light of the sun. There it is, that monstrous pasture, rolled out before me and made real.*

.   .   .

My pasture was only a dream, Ludwig's is just as dreamlike but absolutely real. Still joined in a brotherhood with which I am not entirely comfortable, I wonder if we had suffered identical sexual fantasies in our early teens and if, trying to exorcise those jungle monsters who tempted us to wallow in unspeakable practices, we had both to the limits of our abilities committed much greater sins. We had cut down the jungle and tried to eliminate the menace — our true natures — that lay hidden or threatening in the awful shadows of the black trees.

At the far western end of Ludwig's pasture just outside the boundary of his property the boat docks for a few minutes at a town called Almerim. In trying to remember it now nothing much comes to mind: a water tower back toward the scrubby jungle behind the low wooden houses; a main road that cuts through a bluff and joins the two parts of the town; three pickup trucks that move through the one or two streets as aimlessly as

*AUTHOR'S NOTE. Long after this trip was over I discovered that Ludwig's pasture was not a pasture at all but the world's largest rice paddy. Does this explain why I saw no grazing cattle?

though they were being blown by the wind. It reminds me of Los Angeles in the twenties, a place of vacant lots, impermanent houses set at great distance from one another. As usual like a little blood clot called déjà vu the town's population has gathered on the dock and blankly stares at us as though we had just floated in from Venus; as usual fifty women in fifty canoes drift around the ship, their empty faces menacing with despair; as usual Don and Harry have gone trotting off looking for grass; and as usual just as we leave and as part of a ritual that is repeated in every town on the river, a small boy throws a bag of something that looks like shit high up near the bridge where the captain stands thoughtfully sucking at his shiny mustachio.

Wanting to think about Dan and his pastures, I am, under the irrational tyranny of a mind that skitters here and there like a fart in a skillet, against my will standing on the shaded deck and thinking about Don.

•   •   •

O.K. I will think about Don and save Dan for that lovely time just before sleep more sweetly takes over our fantasies. The last trumpet blasts of Ludwig's symphony hang shimmering in the sunshine behind us at the edge of town. And I am thinking about Don and music and that dying black man and that rage against my father that the black man had precipitated. That day by a conscious effort of will and out of shame I had cut off my anger against my father and directed it to another larger target – the whole bourgeois *ambiente* that my father symbolized.

Repudiating my father's values, which were solidly bourgeois to the point of farce, I had repudiated the whole middle class and had wasted a lifetime's energies in sneers and jeers. In time I had developed an almost foolproof theory about a world-wide conspiracy directed by the bourgeois against the people of the world. It was a conspiracy that aimed at the enslavement of the world's masses through economic domination, and its objective was the absolute ownership of the world's goods and the construction of a system that would convert everything into the shoddy crap that only the bourgeois could afford to buy. A man would be judged as either a success or a failure, as either good or evil, as either respectable or beneath contempt by the number of gadgets that he could fit into his house. The rulers of the world have become, in enslaving the masses of the poor, completely enslaved themselves by their sad possessions. I had been reminded of this in the Bogotá airport and had felt a shattering despair when I thought of Ramón's children no longer the children of a poor man, and of how they would have to be corrupted and mortally wounded as human beings by their upward movement into the middle class and the new false values that would be imposed upon their sensibilities.

There is no way to live with the illusion of being made happy by the things that one owns, especially in a country like Ecuador where a comparative handful of people own everything, without developing an armor of blindness that makes one not only insensitive but contemptuous of the overwhelming poverty through which one moves. Perhaps worse than the contempt is the hypocrisy of pretending to be outraged while living a life devoted solely to the consumption of things that almost the entire population is unable to enjoy. I am thinking of a recent dinner party in one of the more modestly priced French restaurants where each of us ate sixteen dollars' worth of food while talking about the corruptions of the world and the plight of the poor Ecuadorian Indians, most of whom live in the absolute feudal degradation that arrived in the 1540s with the Spanish conquistadores. Talk about engaging in an orgy of unspeakable acts. Our sin was not in enjoying good food but was much more complicated and suggested the whole disintegration of our moral sensitivities. How could we have left that restaurant stuffed like pigs and half-drunk on Chilean wine and French brandy and not vomited the whole thing up in self-loathing when we encountered the barefoot citizens of Quito ransacking the garbage cans in deserted nighttime Avenida Amazonas? How strange and awful; we know that living this way is gross and unnatural but we keep on doing it. How many of us who can't bear to hear the shrieks of animals being slaughtered revel in the delight of licking the grease from our fingers after slicking up a plate of spareribs?

It is not only the destruction of our morality that allows us to isolate ourselves in the separate world of our exquisite bourgeois sensibilities. Even our taste buds have been numbed and perverted by the chic *ambiente* and the outrageous prices, the smart wallpaper that mimics fabric, the handsome French posters, the candles on the tables, the Indian waiters in their ridiculous costumes.

For a time, wanting to dazzle my jungle friends who came to Quito to visit me, I would take them to these fancy restaurants and introduce them to our civilized cuisine. I wanted them to like it, to be seduced by the rich sauces, the extravagances of oil, butter, mayonnaise, the grossnesses of flaming crepes suzette. I wanted to introduce them to these things as a revolutionary act that would help them to see themselves as deprived people. In all their lifetimes they have never imagined this endless changing of plates, the soups, pâtés, salads, fish, and meat. I want them to eat with resentment, with a growing outrage, the first little flame of political consciousness. Maybe feeling cheated they would want to join together and try to change things. But they are not so easily fooled, and their rage when it comes will be built around things more fundamental than a butter sauce. Their mouths are not seduced, their passions are not awakened by candlelight and European *ambiente.*

Pedro, Arcario, Julian, Wilson, Cangrejo: slim young Negroes from the jungle who have come up to visit in the only clothes they own or clothes borrowed from their brothers – bright shirts, flaring pants – and who now sit in a Quito restaurant huddled up in the sweaters or jackets I have had to loan them against the nine-thousand-foot chill of a Sierra night. They look slightly disreputable and menacing in these clothes that don't quite fit, but in their slimness, which hints at want, they are infinitely more beautiful than the guests at the other tables – the middle-class tourists with their thick necks, their tremendous flabby asses, and their flushed red faces that scream of imminent death by cardiac arrest.

Tonight it is Arcario who picks at his food, the entree, an avocado stuffed with shrimp. And tonight it is Arcario who will lean across the table and whisper, "But Martin, this shrimp is rotten, and look at the black strings in this avocado; it's rotten, too." Arcario is the jungle innocent telling us the truth, that the emperor has no clothes on, that this salad we are paying for at two dollars a plate is little better than garbage. On later visits he will beg me in the late afternoons to please not take him to a restaurant. "Can't we just stay here and cook up a nice batch of rice and tuna fish? And a whole bottle of beer for each of us?"

With three children and one in the oven he is very poor. The cheapest brands of tuna fish that he can afford to buy occasionally for forty cents, the black half-rotten meal that is sold as cat food or to the poorest people and that stinks of rot will be replaced tonight, he hopes, with a can that costs a dollar, Van Camp's Chicken of the Sea, oh my God, *que rico.* The purity of this response is overwhelming. And in Julian's case his ability to overcome his dislike of this suspect restaurant food whose inferior quality is disguised beneath rich, highly seasoned sauces, the sharp insistent hunger of a body starved for protein and that drives him to eat and eat and eat, is overwhelming, too. All night I will listen to him groaning and farting, and stepping carefully between the bodies of his sleeping friends, pattering off to the bathroom to be sick. When I refuse to cook for them and drag them off to some restaurant to eat strange food that is past their comprehension, I feel a vague guilt now as though I were taking them to a pornographic movie that would by teaching perverse techniques confuse and complicate the pure, straightforward intensity of their romantic and passionate sensibilities.

.   .   .

Twelve years in the jungle had sharpened my vision and given me my own fanatic interpretation of reality. Deprived of the details that might prove me wrong, namely perhaps, more than anything, just rational or thoughtful men with whom I could speak, I had constructed a disastrous philosophy of nice simplicities in black and white. Like a child who out of a couple of books like *Kak, the Copper Eskimo* and *Wild Animals I have Known* can construct the whole North American continent in all its millions of details, I had out of my own need and my own warped vision built a future world where man, if he still wandered through it, would once more wander naked; he would kill with clubs again. I was convinced that the bourgeois in its angst, the pains of which it could only momentarily assuage by buying something else on credit to display, would end up by destroying the world. Buying a speedboat to prove that you exist and that you are good is like taking an aspirin against cancer. Living what I thought was a real life involved with real things—trees, clouds, running water, the vital and honest responses of poor people—I found the bourgeois incurably ill and knew in my heart that when they came crashing down or when they were brought crashing down by the rage of the world, that they would bring the rest of mankind with them. Wasn't this conviction itself born of Spengler and Kafka and the other desperate prophets blatantly bourgeois and a manifestation of my own bourgeois angst?

I had a three-band radio out there and from time to time I collected old *Time* magazines in Quito. It is easy enough when the atomic bombs are going off in Nevada, Siberia, China, and the South Pacific to predict that all is about to be lost. You can even predict wholesale and crushing disaster from lesser things: in the insane wars that break out with more and more frequency like suppurating infections, in the ever more corrupt and inhuman domination of nations by ever more shamelessly corrupt politicians, in a constant economic crisis that seems to shout that all the systems in the world are beginning to shatter, in a world population that is growing past its capacity to feed itself, in the steadily declining per capita earnings of populations in the poorer countries, in the pollution of air and oceans, in crime statistics, the madness of ridiculous religions, in the madness of racial hatreds, etc., etc., etc.

But the jungle has made me sensitive to even lesser omens, and now like Blake I could see the destruction of the state in the starving dog. These perceptions, which we all have, have made me insufferably conceited and I feel that my little talent may not be in planting bananas but may more truly lie in prophecy. (Maybe everyone's talent now lies in prophecy; maybe the man who merely says, "Bread no longer tastes like bread; tomatoes no longer have flavor" is prophesying terrible things for our plastic future. Jesus, can't you see the end of the world in a slice of Wonder Bread?)

So here I am on a boat idly watching Don and Harry, not even thinking particularly of Don but more perhaps of the music that Ludwig's pasture has brought to mind – the over-rich music of the last Romantics whose lush Ludwiglike cloying orchestrations warn us that our poor emotions are much too easily moved, captive to swelling chords and pounding rhythms, to volume and swollen conceptions.

Just below me on the lower deck Don drops his dog with a little thump and almost simultaneously over on the left that little plastic bag of shit splats against the ship's side. It is like the double Zen blow of a Zen master offering illuminations, and I experience a little double-barreled click of enlightenment, two thirty-watt bulbs that dimly flicker on in my head, one of them casting light on that old fanatic conviction about the bourgeois conspiracy and dissolving it and the other, a musical perception which, when I have time to consider it, may imply that an artist more than anything is only the paid employee of the bourgeois, the bourgeois' paid clown.

Looking into the smiling face of Don as he climbs aboard a ship that has already cast its ropes and is about to continue its slow pulsing over the yellow waters, I realize that this poor man who yearns to have the social graces of a jet-setter, and who is trying so hard to ape the cool and puerile sophistications of the middle class is a part of no conspiracy, that there is in fact no conspiracy at all. He is simply like everyone else, as human as my dying black – foolish, corruptible, and easily seduced by the most easily available of the earth's pleasures. Like everyone else he wants to better himself, to own things, to be happy.

It is not an especially optimistic thought for it implies, well, it implies almost anything that you might want it to. For instance, to be grandiose, it can imply that since man has turned over his destiny to the machines he has lost his capacity to make decent choices, or that in choosing something new, bright and plastic covered, loud, fast, and expensive, he is choosing that thing, since he has lost God, that will take God's place and offer something of meaning in his awful journey.

Well, having lost God myself I am up that same creek when it comes to finding meaning. Still, if I am not an especially happy person, I am no unhappier than most and feel in my depths that what meaning there may be involves the obligation to celebrate life – that the meaning of life is found in being alive enough to live it. My little thought for the day. It is like being given the key to a locked box, something neat and deep, and I walk around the box but it doesn't seem to have any keyhole, any lid, any hinges.

And the potential moral beauty of man? Finding that must have something to do with the riddle and must be tied up with what has been lost since the machines took over. Jesus, into the vacuum of an empty mind made more vacant by the vastness of the river, what pompous and pretentious thoughts have come pouring in. And what a small part of the whole.

I am half-angry, accusing, confused, grabbing at every flickering thought and trying to make it into some kind of an answer. I didn't like being kicked off the farm; it had meant that my work had had no value and that things would go along as well without me; it had meant that I was old and useless, gastado. But now it occurs to me that all that is just part of it and really, fundamentally, all that I am pissed about is this one thing: that after years of effort I had made some kind of truce with the simplest and truest kind of life; I had fled out of the bourgeois in the only way I could, by embracing poverty, and in one moment of desperate screaming rage Ramón had cut me off from that life and had booted me right back again into the middle of the middle class.

Up the river about ten miles from Almerim there is another small town built into the curve of a little bay. Just above the town there is a point of land, a bluff of black rocks topped by a thick growth of trees; around this point comes a flood of swift boiling water. It is almost the only swift water on the whole river that we will see, and it probably means, though the thought occurs to me only now, that some tributary winding to the north and draining some tremendous Amazonian area has received ten days of hard, steady rains that have now gathered into this swift and turbulent flow. The agitated water catches sunlight and blinds the vision, but through the sparkle and blaze of sun and water a canoe expertly paddled by two men emerges and approaches the ship. Before they have come close enough to be clearly seen as individuals they display the marvelous skill of river men in the deft and economical way they manage their craft and in the way, like a duet of ballet dancers, they complement each other. In their ease, in their absolute grace and mastery, they honor the river, they stamp the rushing water and the bright sky with their humanity. A part of me watches this while I am engaged in gloomier thoughts, but like one of those fancy machines that can record a tv golf spectacular while you are watching a tv football spectacular, the material is all collected for a later rerun. I have filed the fishermen away and will recall them later; now I simply watch them as they hail and stop the ship. Their canoe is filled to the gunwales with hundreds of slim silver fish about the shape and size of trout that one would be proud to have caught. We float slowly backwards on the river while the captain and the fisherman dicker for this catch of fish that will feed us all, but after ten minutes the fishermen, who have been patiently waiting for the captain to make an offer that will not be an insult to his high position, speak together briefly and then abruptly push off away from us. The amazed captain yells after them, some final but still ridiculous price. "Eat shit, *mi capitan,*" one of the men yells back but in a tone that is nicely conversational. He scoops a dozen fish into a basket and, smiling, lets them fall back into the river one by one. A soft insolence. Tonight we will eat sun-dried beef speckled with fly larvae again. At least some of us will.

·   ·   ·

Maybe it is two, maybe four a.m. I have gotten up out of need and gone into the first-class toilet. Someone has forgotten to lock the door; it hangs open and slowly swings when the ship changes course; the floor is awash with its own slow tides. I stand at the railing dressed only in pants and shoes and gaze into the night where far across the river a small town made out of eight lights looks enormous as it stretches across a piece of shoreline. How sweet and caressing the air. Moths, drawn from the shore, swoop and stagger in our lights.

Someone is standing at the railing toward the stern by the deserted bar, which is locked up but still brightly lit. He snaps his cigarette in a long curving trajectory into the river and strolls toward me; it is the Manaus poet dressed in pajama bottoms and the white shirt, double-rowed with strips of lace that older upper-middle-class men of the tropics still sometimes wear. The style is Cuban or Panamanian, something left over from another century, something a little vulgar, a little foppish. Ah well, we forgive him; he is a poet, after all – a middle-aged poet with a bourgeois pot – his face tells you that he knows he isn't Dylan Thomas.

"How you Americans stick together," he says in almost-good English. "No one can penetrate into your intimate conversations. That pretty blonde girl, how I would love to engage her attention. But now is my chance; you are alone; God has answered my prayers. May I practice my English with you?"

"But you speak English very well. Not, of course, that I won't be delighted to talk with someone who knows the river. They tell me you're the poet of Manaus."

"*The* poet? Hardly; just one of many – and less and less. With middle age one loses the lyric gift."

"But how can you not be lyrical in Manaus, the very heart of lyricism? Parrots flashing through trees, the great silences, jaguars peering down through greenness at naked Indians, clear curving streams."

"Ah, *you* are the poet of Manaus; I'll give you your certificate in the morning. But you will see soon enough the dead Manaus that was created by the Romantics – and that never existed. As the great man said, 'We are condemned to civilization.' Manaus has embraced Progress. Today we make electronic equipment, motorcycles, plywood sheets, and refrigerators in all the latest decorator colors from teat pink to puke puce – a city of slums and factories owned by foreigners."

"That's a description of almost any Brazilian city, isn't it?"

"Yes, but who could have dreamed that it would happen here, a thousand miles up the river. We have traded, finally, the decent isolation of the last century for the modern kind. The river life was never beautiful, but we had achieved a certain style that integrated man and nature in a profound way. In our dependence the shopkeepers still owned us body and soul, of course, but we had begun to shake off that Portuguese mercantilism and had begun to take possession of the land and the great flowing rivers; we were turning from traders into farmers and men who knew how to move through this inhuman world. There was a certain drama in our isolation, an illusion perhaps, but it gave us dignity."

"Oh wow," I say. "Let me practice my English on *you.*"

"Oh dear," the poet says. "Let me apologize. This is something I feel very deeply about, and I tend to overdramatize my despair. I am quoting from chapter one of a book I hope someday to write."

"Aren't you hard on Manaus? All I know of it is the airport building. I was there a couple months ago. The inside areas are heavy and oppressive, but it's beautiful in a way, a really classy statement."

"And just as honest to the realities of Manaus as those leather phalluses that the actors wear in *Lysistrata.* Everything out here is symbols. Someone sitting behind a desk in Brasilia decided that Manaus would be Polar, a central point around which the Amazon would be developed. And what does an anchorpoint need? Varig's fantastic Hotel Tropical, a new paint job on the opera house, an air-cooled modern airport. Presto, the Amazon is developed. Then the bureaucracy and the factories come in and everything turns into confusion. The farmers have come in off their farms to wait on tables or get a factory job at two dollars a day. Now we have to import most of our food; the small farms are going back to brush or are being bought up by the big cattlemen. We're a duty-free port, you know, a kind of second-class Hong Kong, deeply involved in smuggling contraband. Every cruzeiro that is spent here helps to destroy Brazil's trade balance. No, the only honest symbol of this poor place is the leper colony; you should visit it just after breakfast in the Hotel Tropical. Though I think they no longer run buses out that road, and you'll have to walk."

"Walk?" I say, doubtfully. "Well, maybe. I'm pretty much walked out to tell you the truth. I've walked at least a thousand miles through Brazil."

"And what have you seen?"

"I swear to God, I don't know what I've seen. Nothing I understand. Why do Brazilians think of themselves as owning a rich country? What is this "economic miracle" that Netto pulled off? I seem to see through the smiles and the tinsel the most desperate of countries, the most shamelessly manipulated of countries. You are the best people in the world, but aren't you rushing toward some awful breakdown? How can you fool yourselves? How can you keep going when the richest tenth makes forty-five times more than the poorest tenth? That is the world's worst distribution. No society can endure . . . "

"O.K., O.K., O.K., you have seen more than some," the poet says. He sighs and stares out into the night. "Yes, you are right; we are heading into an awful future. But don't think that the *militares* don't know it. They are in a panic, too. How awful for them, this knowledge that in saving us from Communism they have destroyed us by delivering us into the hands of the West."

"If you are condemned to civilization (who said that, Machado?) wouldn't you rather be screwed by a blue-eyed Nordic type than by one of them godless Mongolian potato-nosed kulaks?"

"Maybe we don't want to be screwed by either one," the poet says, laughing. "Funny you should put in into sexual terms, though; I have been thinking of the Amazon in the same way. Look, are you sleepy? Shall we talk? Let's sit down at one of the tables, and I'll practice on you. This trip up the river always depresses me so; let me talk it out."

I follow the poet back to the bar and we sit down under the bright lights. "I can understand your depression; it is sad to travel through this man-made desolation."

"But this isn't man-made desolation," the poet says. "This is the Amazon floodplain, the Varzea, the richest land in Brazil. Every year like the Nile the land is renewed with millions of tons of silt that washes down from the Andes. This isn't where the desolation is, it is out there." He waves one hand toward the horizon, and as though to confirm his statement, there is a very distant flicker of lightning where his hand is pointing. "About two percent of the Amazon is floodplain. Man can't destroy it; it is land that is self-healing. Another two percent is savanna, open grassland, much of it lying at the edge of the Mato Grosso where the jungle fades away into open country. Flood plain and savanna, that four percent that man might safely exploit."

"Four percent of the Amazon is a tremendous amount of acres."

"Of course. We are talking about 6,000,000 square kilometers. But let's talk about this in sexual terms. I've been thinking of the Amazon in terms of rape — and was reminded of what happened in 1976 when your Skylab satellite just happened to take pictures of a one-million-hectare forest fire in southern Pará. It turned out to be the Volkswagen ranch, and they had been given permission by IBDF to clear no more than 9,000 hectares. A million hectares of jungle burning up and nobody in Brazil even knew it. Volkswagen got their wrists slapped with a six-million-dollar fine, but a smart team of lawyers probably saved them."

"But how did they defend themselves?"

"Who knows? They probably said, 'Goodness gracious, somebody must have dropped a cigarette.' But don't think it is only Volkswagen that is controlled by monetary considerations. At this very instant there are hundreds of fires raging out of control on a hundred different properties. This is the cheapest way to prepare land for pasture."

"There's some nice new ecological backlash developing. If you're against a million-hectare forest fire, you're against free enterprise; you're a Commie in disguise. Or if you're not a Commie but on the other side, you're a bourgeois who wants to preserve the status quo and the romantic, untouched places you can fly to for a month's vacation."

"Brazilians are a little sensitive about the world telling us what to do with our own land; the Amazon has been everybody's business; you Americans have always been intensely interested in our raw materials and have moved your gunboats over the river as though it were your private reserve.

Only fanatics want to preserve the status quo. Those few of us who worry about such things simply want the Amazon to be exploited in a rational way and for the national good. Surely this area is worth more than just supplying menial jobs to Brazilian peons in the forest camps. One of my best friends in Manaus works for INPA – a tremendous organization carrying on Amazonian investigations. Their job, don't laugh, is to try and save Amazonia. My friend is one of the top foresters; *his* job is reforestation. Ten percent of the forest is already cut down, and it's got to be replanted. But so far, he says, nobody knows anything about tropical reforestation. This is an empty book. Still we keep right on going; in 1976 we were destroying 100,000 hectares a year; God knows what it is now.

"Well, this is a mean, insensitive world and we can't live completely outside its madness. We are condemned to civilization, yes, and you know, many of us wouldn't even mind if they cut down every tree in the jungle if it would solve the country's problems. If killing off the rest of the Indians is a vital part of a plan to save Brazil, then I'd say to the Indians – Integrate or die. The same with the crocodiles, the manatee, the turtles, the jaguars. But if they must all die, if this is the price of civilization, for the love of Christ, let it be for a noble purpose. To die for nothing, to die as part of a rapacious insanity; that the Amazon, *my* Amazon, end up as a desert represented a few years from now as a couple of hundred moth-eaten tiger skins nailed to the walls of sportsmen's dens – my God.

"Ah, poor Brazil. We scatter ourselves across the continent like leaves in a whirlwind, driven by hunger and desperation, moving from one disaster to another. We move in, create a desert and move on. And now we have come to the end, to the last great challenge, this great empty space that up to now has withstood every assault. You know, in the long run, nobody has ever made a happy dollar off the Amazon. Ah, that virgin whore; what a rage we've built up against her, what resentments.

"For four hundred years we've been trying to fuck this place, and now with your Western tools, your bulldozers, chain saws, napalm, and your war surplus defoliants, we can finally do it."

"But surely it won't happen," I say. "Nobody will let it happen."

"We are talking about rape, my friend, and who in the passion of rape and fully engaged in his lust, will listen to reason. And we are talking about the people who think they will make money committing rape. Rape and money, what an overwhelming combination. We are already almost to the end of the Amazon story; there are terrible powers dedicated to its destruction. Even you, who are no longer exactly a young man, perhaps will live to see the final act. The girl has been gagged and tied; she has been carried to the cliff's edge and flung over; she is plunging down to that final smash."

"Ah, poet, poet," I say, "for Christ's sake, let's not talk about rape anymore."

"Just one more thing," the poet says, "and then I'll leave you. Talking hasn't helped much, I'm afraid. Rape is a kind of murder. This Amazon business—what we're really trying to do is rape God. We've got to destroy the last of his immense creations. It is our revenge on God for condemning all of us to death. Man's last great cosmic fuck is an insolence in the face of the creator. We have to say, 'If You have given us all this only to let us die, then You have given us nothing.'"

The Joining of the Rivers

By the night of the third day all of us
have had nine meals together; we have set up patterns, established family
groups, staked out territory at the tables in the dining salon. The middle-
aged Brazilian poets eat with middle-aged Brazilian poets – or men who,
under the blows of this river landscape, wish they were. The young jetters
fly wild patterns at a corner table. The three classy French passengers have
disappeared tonight. Having paid the double fare, they are hiding in their
cabin waiting to eat at a classier hour at the captain's table. I eat at the
gringo table where English is spoken, but there are not many of us, and
there is room for more. Tonight a new couple join us, two handsome young
Brazilians who have bought one of the few smaller double cabins. All day
walking the deck I have seen them through their open doorway sitting and
gazing at each other or moving their hands across the other's face. They are
dazed with that love that excludes the world, and I am puzzled about why
they would travel through the great spaces of this river when they will see
only themselves. Their faces are transfigured with love. They are in their
middle twenties, the girl, beautiful with a calm grave face, enormous black
eyes, and long straight hair; the man, quiet and inward looking with his intelligence focused in thoughtful eyes. They sit directly across from me, and
we smile from time to time but without speaking.

Don tells *Playboy* jokes and nervously searches at the other tables for the
French tourists. Expecting to eat with them he is afraid that they have found
another more interesting table. Fleurette and Beverly poke at the food and
say funny things about it. Let us face it; it is food that deserves to be made
fun of, and mocking it will be the only pleasure it will give us. I have the
only map of the river on the boat and everyone borrows it trying to figure
out where we are on this long yellow intricately looping flow of curving
channels, bays, and island beaches overhung with trees. We all study the

map but reach no agreement. This river at its flood has no connection with the map. *No importa;* the captain probably knows where we are. He has begun to spend less time locking up the toilets and more time on the bridge staring sternly and sucking at his mustache. Everyone spreads marmalade on his bread from the big jar that sits before me and which I joyfully offer as a sign of my good feelings for them. Just as the meal is ending the young man across the table speaks to me. "Excuse the question, sir. Marlui wants to know. She says you can be only one thing. Are you a writer?"

The question comes like a blow. It has perhaps arrived at that only moment on the trip when it could pierce and devastate me. I don't know what to say; it seems like the most painfully personal of questions. Smiling foolishly, looking from one to the other, I begin to answer, making stuttering sounds like groans. I can feel my lips begin to tremble. At the same time I feel strangely lifted up and somehow released from a long tension. It is as though some part of me has immediately accepted the special power of an outside intuition to define me in a way that I have never dared define myself. I know immediately that, though it is a natural, perhaps no more than a graceful question, it must be answered honestly – not to these two attractive strangers, but to myself. I have arrived, I hope, at the last crisis of my life.

I feel like someone who has been castrated and with the wounds just barely healed is suddenly asked out of the emptiness of a great confusion about himself, "What are you? Are you a man?" To answer honestly will define the man forever. And this comparison is no poetic conceit; in a sense it quite precisely pinpoints my perception of what has happened to me. Within a year I have been castrated three times, if not in reality, at least in the most disturbing symbolic way: first, by being driven into a premature retirement that has separated me from my life, from work in which I had been totally engaged; second, by having in one terrible three-day period almost all the teeth yanked out of my mouth; and third, by this two-month trip in which I have drifted empty and aimless and half-sick through a world in which I have been completely irrelevant. Old age had arrived in a rush before I was ready to accept it; I had been swept like a little pile of dead leaves to the edge of a grave.

Though I have written a couple of books, I have never thought of myself as a writer. I had written them in those pre-dawn hours when the land still lay in darkness or on days of heavy winter rains when the cattle huddled in the brush dumb with misery. Out of conviction and dedication I had always considered that all my passion was centered on farming. The things I had written in a notebook while I waited for the sun to come up and the day to begin had been done with the same enthusiasm that a corporate lawyer might devote to the learning of card tricks. But how can I be a farmer without a farm? As I stand there staring at my new friends I realize with a rush of regret, with a terrible sense of loss that I will never go back to the farm, never walk sweating up the hillside beneath the big trees, never wade the creek, never stand alone at night on the empty deck of that disgraceful house listening to the cows belch and fart below me in the lane while the stars blaze above us in a southern sky. I have lost my courage for that particular kind of life; it requires a toughness that has leaked out of me.

In my secret heart, feeling insulted and rejected, I had told myself that I would never go back to the farm until Ramón came up to Quito and begged me on his knees. But I realize now as the answer to this question begins to form itself at some level as deep as my bowels, that I had set impossible and ridiculous conditions and that proud, hard-headed Ramón – on his *knees*? – would never beg, would in fact rather lose the farm than admit that he was incapable of managing it alone or that he had been wrong in forcing me to leave.

And so the answer to this question, which makes me gag and stutter, though it takes no more than a few seconds to consider and to answer, is filled with tremendous emotion. In a way it is the final confrontation to a question that I have never wanted to face, and since college and while my father lived, never dared face when the very limited nature of my very modest talent for writing became apparent. Marlui's face lights up as I say, finally, "Yes, I'm a writer." I think it is the first time since I was twenty years old that I have said this.

"I knew it," she says smiling. "Your face. You have something in your face that Marcos has. I knew immediately; Marcos is a writer, too."

"And Marlui sings," Marcos says. "A devastating talent; you will see."

"Will you sing for me?" I ask. I have the strongest urge to take her hand across the table.

"But of course," Marlui says, laughing.

The waiters are trying to drive us from the dining room but the three of us talk for a minute explaining and identifying ourselves, the old dog's nose to dog's tail routine. Marlui's English is very shaky and she is shy about making gross mistakes; Marcos is a little better, a little braver. He is a journalist photographer; later he will show me some of his published articles in *Veja*, a magazine like *Time*. He is the owner of the Land Rover on the top deck and is parked next to the truck with the sad dog locked inside. Marlui and Marcos are about to drive through the Mato Grosso, Manaus to São Paulo, a long and difficult journey. He is doing a series of articles on colonization; Marlui wants to record folk songs and wants to sing to the people; she has given concerts all over Brazil. His English breaks down on this next point, but I think what he is saying is this: they are also going to break the law; they want to do some political campaigning for a senatorial candidate who is opposed to the military, and they want to collect taped interviews with desperate farmers who have been reduced to extreme conditions by the careless planning of a callous agricultural policy. The three waiters have lined up at one end of the saloon and are glaring at us.

"Shall we meet at nine o'clock in the lounge?" Marlui asks. "When things are a little quieter. I'll sing then if you wish."

"Yes; that will be wonderful. Until nine."

Something tremendously interesting and important has happened to me, and I want to be alone for a while, stand alone in a quiet place and try to discover how I have been changed. There is no doubt at all that I have been changed, and in an instant. I feel strangely opened up as though I had been turned around and pointed in a new direction, as though I had been given a job to do, some little something that I could wave in the face of death and say, "Not yet; come back another day; can't you see I'm busy." It is a real "born again" feeling, but I suspect, just as fuzzy and undirected—a surge of energy, a hot glow of joyful emotion in the gut like a slug of whiskey. But I doubt if this feeling would help me get a page written. However, I must now be interested in such things and carry the burden of an unhealthy curiosity, must accept, too, a certain diminishing and coarsening of my perceptions. I will be like a traveler who, toward the end of his journey, begins to carry a camera and finds his vision detoured and distorted, reality now seen as something that can be arranged or lighted for the camera's eye. I will be that man who behind his distress will feel a glow of delight for the great picture he has taken of a starving child.

On the covered deck by the bar the tables are filling with people; disco music blares; the same tape has been playing over and over all day. A couple more renditions of "In a Little Spanish Town t'was on a Night Like This" and I might be capable of some ugly act. Like blowing up the boat? Some of the steerage passengers have infiltrated our exclusive area but, not daring to sit at the tables, are standing at the railing in the shadows and drinking cans of beer. They will soon be called to eat and will line up with their own plates and spoons like G.I.s in an army mess line. Down toward the bow a couple of men are angrily rattling the locked doors of the toilet. Fleurette has been taking a constitutional, like a hunter stalking, round and round the deck; she is walking fast and has a discontented look on her face. I have stopped for just a moment to say something to Beverly when Fleurette comes up to us and says, "I've checked them all, passengers and crew; there's not a decent stud on this boat; a disaster."

"Well, thanks a lot, Fleurette, and screw you, too," I say, but in a way that makes her laugh.

"Baby, I didn't mean *you*. But do you want to dance all night?"

"No," I say. "No dancing, thanks. I'm going up on the top deck."

It is night now. The boat is working itself through a narrow channel and is hugging the southern bank. There are no lights on the top deck. Later couples will come up in the darkness to kiss, but now I am alone. That slow, slow, diesel beat. The river is black and the trees are a darker blackness; we are very close to the trees and floating above them; there is the damp, rotting smell of vegetation and the tidal smell of mangroves and sea animals. The stars are out, and there are millions. I stand at the railing looking down through the tops of trees, thinking that this is how it must look to a night-hunting bird who soars over the land looking for something to kill. After a time we pass a clearing with a small hut on stilts sitting in the middle of a little garden of yucca and bananas. It is lit from within by a single candle. It looks exactly like the little house that Cantante built for Cira when he brought his other woman across the river to live. Behind that soft orange light lies an immensity of night and trees, and the little hut in this desolation is as vulnerable as the candle flame that lights it. I search back in the darkness as we pass by; that little light and the forest behind it has the power of an overwhelming nostalgia as though it contained all of the past. Cira is dead now and who is raising her children? And can it be possible that I will never see the farm again? I can feel myself leaving the boat. Without struggling, as though I have abruptly thrown myself into the flood, I am sucked in and borne away on the river's flow.

·   ·   ·

From the house where I lived alone I could look through the rubber trees and past the big avocado and the guavas down to the river and across it to the southern boundary of Ramón's farm where we had sold building lots to the people of Male for eight dollars apiece and where there was now a small village of perhaps a dozen houses. The priest from Viche had even come in and organized *mingas* with the people and a little half-built chapel made of cement blocks and split bamboo sat on a little bluff in front of the town.

There was a constant moving of canoes up and down the river, and almost every day tremendous rafts made of balsa, laurel, or bamboo would pass by. Some of the rafts were fifty feet long. They were beautiful, and when they appeared around the bend in the river and swept silently past, people would stop talking or working and watch them in awe until they disappeared. They carried whole families heading for Esmeraldas, and as they floated by it was like being allowed to peek in on intimate scenes of rural life. Children sat within the shade of little lean-tos built of *ranconcha*, a broad six-foot-long leaf with undersides of silver that shone at night under lights with a dull sheen like the bellies of fish. Around charcoal fires in sand-filled boxes women cooked platano or fish or rice in blackened and dented pots, and while some of the men swam or fished or slept, others standing in the stern would navigate with fifteen-foot-long sweeps and keep the raft from spinning. The sweeps were bamboo poles with great carved paddles attached to their ends; they were shaped like mandalas.

Some of the rafts were piled with coils of picquiya, bunches of platano or bananas, piles of coconuts or sacks of charcoal, but the main profit would be in the sale of the raft itself. The raftsmen would sell everything but the rudders; I think there must have been status in carrying a rudder, for the laden men walked proudly, and identified to us as river men, felt no need to explain with words just who they were or why they wandered so far through territory where strangers were regarded with suspicion. They tended to be silent and self-sufficient types with powerful arms and chests and heavily muscled necks like columns carved out of stone with rather thin and undeveloped legs. Their bodies identified them as much as the rudders they carried.

In the stillness at night the passing of the rafts was mysterious and unreal. Some were dark and silent, a blackness like the shadow of a cloud drifting over the face of the water; some were alive with radio music, candles, camp fires, and the voices of singing people. Lying in bed at night I could hear families quarreling or drunken friends finally facing something that had lain between them, or sometimes angry men passed down the river yelling obscenities into the darkness, cursing life or their poverty or the corruptions of the police. If I were half-asleep and in one of those periods when my own life was unreal and dreamlike, I would listen to these very real and beautiful things and sleep the rest of the night in a kind of delirium, caught in the idea that I was the one who was afloat and moving, that I was adrift and moving past the singing women and the dancing men. In the summer when the water was low and the current sluggish, the sounds from the rafts as they slowly moved past the farm lingered in the air forever. But after February when the rains came and the river filled with dead trees and animals and tore at the banks there was less music from the rafts: there were less rafts. And when they came, they came swiftly and swiftly disappeared.

For about four months until July the river was often at flood level. Sometimes for three or four days when it rained steadily and the whole country was flushing itself out and the great trees came rushing past at fifteen or twenty miles an hour it was impossible to move back and forth over the water except at the greatest hazard. A drunken farmer sent his seven-year-old daughter across the river one day in a small canoe to buy him another bottle of *aguardiente*; she was tipped into the current and drowned in the first minute. A couple of the big rafts, we heard, had arrived in Esmeraldas and been driven by the force of the flood into and under a great wall of trees that blocked the river at the ocean sandbars; everyone had died. Ramón, who had grown up on the ocean beach at Rioverde and had spent his first twenty years as a fisherman netting shrimp or fishing for *pargo* out past the offshore breakers, would never admit that there was any water in the world over which he could not move freely and without fear. When, as it sometimes happened, I had to sit on my side of the river and listen to it all night grinding its teeth above the battering of the rain on the roof – having eaten nothing all day but a couple of eggs at breakfast and at night two big warm beers and a pile of fried rice, the reason was never the danger of coming across to me with a basket of food that left me hungry and angry. The outboard motor simply could not make headway against the force of the river.

At five o'clock in the morning drinking coffee I would hear Ramón trying to start the outboard motor and through the maracuyá vines on the top deck would look downstream and see a cloud of gas fumes floating above the water where the canoe was tied up. It was less than half a mile away.

It made me nervous to listen to the pop and dying sputter of the motor for I knew that twenty minutes of pulling and jerking on the starter rope would put Ramón in a foul mood. I was more than ever aware then of the resentments that both of us were developing over this oppressive dependence. I had gone across the river to free us both of the complications that had grown out of the closeness of our relationship; they were conflicts that were natural; both of us now insisted on making ultimate decisions about the management of the farm; we both wanted to be boss. To cut through this knot, to radically simplify our positions and clarify a situation that wasn't giving either of us much pleasure, it had seemed smart to buy another farm. Each of us would have his little kingdom, each of us the freedom to make his own ridiculous decisions. What a shock to realize after a few months of freedom from each other that we were still so intimately connected by this insane problem centered on food and that now instead of achieving some degree of independence I had put myself into a frustrating dependence on Ramón for the bread I ate. A few months before, Ramón had accused me resentfully of turning into his father; now by some weird switch that neither of us had anticipated I had become like a yowling babe demanding sustenance.

For an hour the canoe would creep up the river hugging the shore, pass the farm on the far side, and then three hundred yards above the beach below my house, swing out into the current and arrive in half a minute, swept down and across on the boiling water. All that work to bring me a case of beer, a couple loaves of bread, a carton of cigarettes, or whatever vegetables happened to be for sale in the Esmeraldas market. When Ramón was a day or two late I greeted him with sulky or piteous looks.

Ramón as a great landowner with tremendous responsibilities felt a certain lack of dignity in having to bring me food. He always arrived with one of the *macheteros* who had the job of hauling the crates and baskets up the little hill to my house. Ramón didn't want me carrying cargo up from the river either; I was a landowner, too, and in a place where the rules were precise and inflexible. *Hacendados* did not pack things, blacks did. Ramón had brought the canoe across the river with the greatest skill and courage, but he had not carried the motor down the steep bank to the canoe – nor would he carry it back. He was a river pilot, not a peon.

"Well, here I am; the morning lost. There's a truck coming in at ten for a load of bananas, and here I am. Over here."

"Yeah, well, I was waiting for you yesterday. Didn't anyone see me yesterday? I was down on the gravel bar for four hours. Waving and yelling like a fool. Four hours sitting there waiting for a canoe to come along. Nobody. Nothing. I haven't eaten today."

"I haven't either," Ramón said.

"And I didn't eat much last night."

"I didn't either," Ramón said, his face tight and desperate."

"Ramón, we've got to change this system. If I don't eat something a couple times a day I tend to become ugly."

"Yes," Ramón said, "indeed you do."

"If you want to see a performance of monumental ugliness just leave me over here a day without cigarettes."

"Oh Jesus, that something so tragical never happens. You know, *hermano*, for years you have been talking this bullshit about the nobility of poverty, and now for the first time you've got a chance to get a little taste of what it's like. But no, a day without eggs and you begin to panic; a day without bread and you collapse. Bread and eggs, food for the *ricos*, food poor people don't even eat. Why don't you think about sharing the experience of the poor man who is under the tension of wanting to smoke a cigarette without the two cents to buy one?"

"Goddamit, I'll go without when it's necessary, but not when I'm just sitting over here forgotten. And I hope you haven't decided to teach me how to be *pobre* and *humilde*. That's not your work, thank you."

"I'm not trying to teach you anything; I'm doing the best I can; I want to bring you everything you need. Sometimes I have other things to do, like selling a load of bananas."

"Let's change this system then; I'm not a big enough man to sit over here depending on you. I need my own canoe. I'll cross over and take the pickup and drive around all day looking for food."

"Sorry," Ramón said. "No canoe. That is something I will not allow. You are no river man and you wouldn't last five minutes out there. Even if you could get down and across, how would you get back?"

"I'd just as soon drown as starve to death."

"Sorry, no canoe. You must now cultivate the manly qualities of patience. Coming over here was your idea, not mine. I was never in favor of this madness as you well know."

Ramón's wife and children now lived in Esmeraldas, and the children were going to private schools. Ramón's situation was almost as complicated as mine, perhaps more so since he was a typical Ecuadorian macho who felt degraded by having to do woman's work: cook his own meals. At those infrequent times when I went across the river I was always appalled walking through Ramón's upstairs kitchen—unwashed pots caked with burned rice; ominous, slimy chunks of platano soaking in the muddy water in which they had been cooked; slices of stinking, salted fish; piles of weird fruit: *zapote*, guavas, *mamé, abas, chontaduras*; things I scarcely ever ate except in some final desperation. Without Ester to cook for him he was regressing to that simple poverty-stricken time of his youth. I was less flexible and insisted on maintaining my delicate and impossibly high standards —bread, eggs, tuna fish, vegetables. I went through a can of curry powder every ten days trying to obliterate the blandness of the food that in its unvarying sameness had begun to gag me.

At the beginning of the dry season I planted tomatoes, Swiss chard, and green peppers around the house, and between July and November harvested the fallen avocados from the big tree at the foot of the hill below the pastures. With these things and with beer, rice, cooking oil, and cigarettes I got along except for the intense competition that began to develop. In the mornings I would take the machete and walk out along the property lines trying to establish the boundaries and frustrate the dreams of my neighbors who had invaded the land. Walking into the shade of the big trees, climbing up through the darkness of the northern hillside miles out away from the river where the sounds of the outboard motors were little more than an insect humming I felt as though I were escaping from the world and that no one could possibly know where I was. Everyone up and down the river, of course, knew exactly where I was, and I would come back late in the afternoon to find that the three tomatoes and the two green peppers that were now ready to harvest and that I had planned on having for dinner had disappeared. Or Amado would drop by on his way home two miles up the river from some farm where he had taken a contract to clean pastures or cut down trees. He was the most shamelessly innocent of my friends though perhaps one of the very few who didn't rob me. He would come into the house for a cup of coffee and with the trained eyes of a poor man instantly appraise every article in the house. I swear he could see through the walls and count the money in my pocket. "Give me those empty bottles; give me those old magazines; give me a can of tuna fish; give me a beer; come on, be a pal, give me a pack of cigarettes; give me that old shirt." And then, standing in the door and getting ready to leave, his eyes would pierce the leaves and count the outside harvest. "Give me three tomatoes and two green peppers. Don't be miserable with me, you hear."

At night, caught up in the heaviest kind of sleep, I would be brought fully awake to the heavy thump of an avocado hitting the ground a couple hundred feed away. One ... two, three ... four; all night long. At dawn, knowing exactly how many I would find, drinking a cup of coffee I would walk round and round the tree collecting dinner. Except that many times the fruit was already gone. Pigs, ants, rats, old ladies, children would have beat me to it. We were all of us over there in the same boat, perpetually hungry in the jungle that for only a few months out of the year offered much in the way of nourishment.

I was competing with the local people for all the decent fruits on my own land, or what, being a gringo, I regarded as my own land with the rights to harvest the things that grew on it. Corrupted by a title of ownership, many times hungry, how I resented the starving old women who looked upon the jungle as the only thing that God had given them and which they might glean. The women picked the fruits, the men hunted the animals. They killed everything that moved, every little sloth, possum, *cuizumbí*, every little *juanta* or *juatín*, those nocturnal slow-moving creatures with enormous eyes that thought they were hiding under the big leaves or that they couldn't be smoked out of their burrows and torn to pieces by the dogs. I mourned the deaths of the animals and alone in my richness ate tinned beef or Danish pâté or canned tuna fish. One morning sitting on a log in the forest and smoking I listened to Chango's dogs down in the stream's canyon hysterically yelping up a storm as they chased something. Suddenly, twenty feet away a small deer, trembling and panting with exhaustion, its tongue hanging out, its eyes wild. We stared at each other for a full minute in a kind of mutual horror, contemplating its death, and then it staggered off and disappeared. When Chango and his dogs came up ten minutes later I sent them off in the wrong direction, but I was sad all day. It was almost the only deer I had ever seen in Ecuador, and it seemed that I was watching almost the last one on the coast. A five-mile strip of jungle along the river could no longer supply the hunters with the meat they needed; the country was being stripped clean; even the little bobcats, the jaguars, were being killed off for their golden spotted skins. (When it is time to club to death the sloth for cooking, he covers his face with his paws and great tears stream out of his eyes. His cries as he waits for death, they say, sound like the heartbroken sobs of a girl.)

·   ·   ·

About a hundred yards upstream from my house and at the very edge of the property line, Socrates and his relatives had built a half-dozen huts of split bamboo and thatch. The house of his son-in-law, Marcelo, was so close to our fence that all the garbage from his kitchen ended up in our pasture. They were the most disreputable people on the river and were hated and feared by almost everyone. They owned the land along our southern boundary or claimed it at any rate. And they also claimed to be owners of several hundred acres in the very heart of our farm. Socrates was a leftover from the Stone Age with the brutal punched in face of an Australian bushman. He was illiterate, stubborn, stupid, his brains half-destroyed, probably by childhood malnutrition. He talked at you without being able to hear your replies. He could not accept the fact that the jungle, except his piece, of course, could be privately owned – and especially by a foreigner. He had, during those years when our abandoned farm had been taken over by the bank, planted about an acre of platano within our borders, and far out in the middle of that back piece, which was flat, poorly drained, and consisted of a cold, dark soil that was completely strange and whose qualities I couldn't begin to appraise, cut down the trees, an acre here, an acre there, and planted pasture grasses, a half-dozen coconuts, a half-dozen whiplike and anemic coffee trees. Now most of our farm was his, he said.

His own farm was planted to almost nothing except for a few bananas that through the years had spread across our property line. When there was a market he harvested our bananas and was outraged when we accused him of stealing. How could something that he and his neighbors had been doing for thirty years be stealing? His horses and his pigs had lived on our farm for years, the pigs rooting up the abandoned front pastures or spreading Panama disease through the old overgrown bananas. We stretched a fence along the boundary and asked him to control his animals. How could he? He had no fenced-off pasture of his own. He tore down our gates and threw the lengths of bamboo into the brush. Fences and gates outraged him, they were foreign and confining things outside his culture, symbols of Yankee arrogance. Still, while he insisted on his right to pasture his animals on the Tierra Nueva property, he lost control when our cows would wander through the open gates and ramble through his brush-choked acres. Pigs and horses did no damage, he claimed. It was our cows that were a menace, the cows of a rich man screwing up the property of poor and humble black folk.

During the two years that I lived over there Socrates or his drunken relatives slashed at least six cows. I would find them from time to time hidden out in the brush standing in shock with their tails cut off or their heads slashed open, or deep cuts full of blood on their hips and flanks. This kind of brutality drove me half-insane with rage especially since there was nothing I could do about it except stand alone in the forest – trembling, weeping, screaming. I had no proof. When I accused Socrates or his *pistoleros* of cutting the animals they would simply look dumb or angry and deny everything. I could have paid them back only by slashing the horses and the pigs, and in the depths of my fury I would consider and reject this possibility with horror, appalled at the irrationality to which I was being driven.

Socrates and his whole drunken gang were mortally threatened by our arrival and by the new order that we proposed to lay over that seven hundred acres that we had bought. Like most of the people on that side of the river they had only in the past few years been forced by the killing off of all the game to become something more than jungle hunters. They straddled their new life, neither hunters, farmers, nor day laborers, with indecisions, with deep confusions. The destruction of the only life they had known, that of hunters who lived outside the economy, had left great rents in the fabric of their lives they could patch up only with *aguardiente* and petty thievery. What a gang of drunks they were. Some of the younger sons or nephews, one of Socrates' brothers, lived in a perpetual alcoholic daze, and they spent weeks at a time lying in hammocks at the river's edge and, until the batteries ran down, playing their four or five records of Cumbias and empty whorehouse music, over and over. All day long. All night long. When there was no music to engage them, they would bicker – or perhaps it was the music that drowned out that petty bickering that at times flared into anger and screams and that I could hear from my house through the long nights. I think they hated each other as much as we hated them. What had prevented them from becoming farmers when all the jungle animals had been killed off was the simple coincidence in time of the bank's taking over our farm at the end of the banana boom in the late 1940s. The first owner had committed suicide, the land lay empty and deserted, Socrates and his relations moved in, harvested the fruit, cut down the trees that they could sell for lumber, and put their animals to pasture. When we bought the farm and began to fence them out they knew the true panic that comes with a change that they knew they were going to be unable to handle. I hated Socrates but didn't fear him. It was his drunken son-in-law, Marcelo, whom I feared. He was a brutish thirty-year-old with what I would guess was an IQ of about 45, so sullen that even his family avoided him, so secretive, brooding, isolated, and resentful that he had scarcely learned how to talk. It was Marcelo who had planted the platano on our land; it was Marcelo, though I could never prove it, who had wounded our animals. He was a notorious thief and had been caught several times with slaughtered pigs that belonged to Cantante, one of my neighbors to the north. The police, who earned about a hundred dollars a month plus what they could shake out of the people, knew about him but avoided a confrontation. Underneath the different clothes they were brothers. Our cattle-owning friends who were also being invaded told us that Marcelo represented a menace that would only disappear after we had hired gunmen to shoot him down. This seemed, at least at first, like a slightly extreme solution. He was an ugly presence on that side of the river, hostile and threatening, and because of his mental retardation, capable of any irrational violence.

I would meet him on the river trail a couple of times a month, and we would pass each other without speaking—Marcelo squat and hulking, grossly muscled, spit drying in the corners of his mouth, his eyes half gummed shut with matter, and his enormous sex, bulging and semi-erect trying to burst out of the cut-off pants he lived in. His feet were monstrous spreading triangles, scarcely human, and I learned to recognize his tracks returning home on the muddy trails far out in the jungle where he used to walk behind me, hidden in the trees and checking me out—his motives a mixture of simple brute curiosity plus a wish to terrorize me. He was the head *pistolero* of Socrates' little mafia, and because he was a perpetual but invisible presence he took on some of the qualities of the *cuco*, the *tunda*, that black jungle spirit who lures men to their deaths with his sweet songs on the far out forest trails.

I don't believe I ever went to sleep on that farm without considering the very real possibility that Marcelo, a hundred yards away and perhaps tonight just a little bit goofier than usual, might, directed by his demon, creep up to the house and shoot me in the back as I ate supper or at midnight crawl up the outside of the house and decapitate me as I slept. I kept a club and a machete under my bed and used to put myself to sleep by imagining his death. It was a fantasy that gave me a good deal of pleasure, and I lingered over the details: how his skull would disintegrate like a pumpkin as I smashed it; how he would tumble off the house as I sliced at his arms. He was the only man I had ever known in my life whom I would have murdered, with delight, and with the conviction that I was performing a noble act.

The farm lay between two opposing groups of families; to the south Socrates dominated a half-dozen small farmers and had enlisted them in a crusade to drive us from the land. He promised that when we had retired he would divide up certain areas at the back of the farm and give them away as rewards for their support. To the north a dozen families lived in the hillier, almost worthless land, some of whom years before had been frightened away from the river bottom by Socrates and his brother. Old Felipe, for instance, had once owned Socrates' farm; how he lost it I never found out for the story was very complicated, involving forged maps and a verbal will croaked out to somebody by a dying illiterate old man.

Felipe and one of his sons, Cantante, were also invading our land along the northern boundary, but they were not fanatic about it. We bent our line to give them half of what they had stolen and paid them for the remaining pasture they had planted and that we claimed. They didn't especially like our arrival but accepted it as part of the inevitable change that was transforming the river as the land at an accelerating tempo passed from abandoned jungle into the hands of the big *hacendados.* Cantante even asked Ramón to be his youngest baby's godfather.

Cantante, like many of the younger men on the river, had two women; untypically, the women hated each other, and for a time Cira, the older of the two, had left Cantante and gone across the river to cook for Ramón and me just after Ester had gone to live in Esmeraldas and we were left alone. But shortly after I came across the river to live, she went back to Cantante unable to face the gossip of the women who hinted that Cira was probably doing more than just cooking for Ramón. Cira got in the habit of walking up the river trail to my house about once a week to sweep the floors, pick up my dirty clothes for washing, and give me the latest sad news about her disintegrating relationship with Cantante. A couple times I had brought her bright-colored pieces of dress material from Quito, and she recognized this as an indication of my special feelings for her. She was indeed a very special kind of woman, illiterate and absolutely simple but rigid in her honesty, her loyalty, her unforgiving refusal to accept Cantante's concubine. She raised three children with love and sternness, beating them cruelly when they stole but working ceaselessly to feed and clothe them. For a year I watched her face turn hard and bitter and the big bright smile full of delight and teeth fade from her face. Consumed by a steady rage she grew old before my eyes. I said nothing, trying only to soften her pain by talking in generalities about the fickle and childish nature of Ecuadorian machos and the ease with which their lives could come unhinged at the wiggle of a pretty ass. Cira, on the other hand, was more open, more concerned with my own disintegration. She saw before anyone else that I was not handling this new life with much grace and that old age was suddenly crashing down upon me. "I don't want to say that don Ramón is always right, but this time shouldn't you listen to him? You don't look well, and he is very worried about you, you know; he hates the idea that you are over here alone with no one to take care of you."

"If he is so worried let him bring me a little more food; food is my only problem."

Cira under terrible economic pressures was a woman who possessed almost nothing but responsibilities. I was shaken when she began to bring me pots of chicken soup. She was in no position to share her meager rations and was depriving herself of food that she needed much more than I did. I begged her not to. She brought me a young pullet, the finest of a new hatch, and told me to guard it well and that one day it would lay eggs for me. In time it did. Ramón brought me a rooster loud and vulgar with red and golden tail feathers, and a few months later I had a flock of chickens scratching in the yard or wandering through the kitchen.

Sometimes for days the chickens were my only company – until Ramón brought me a gravid cat, and after that my house filled up with chicks and kittens, too. In a sense those animals were the only company I needed.

I had spent ten years with poor people, full of illusions about them and out of pity and rage ready to forgive them almost everything. Their sense of involvement with life, their capacity to endure through endless periods of deprivation and catastrophe were qualities I found heroic. But now for the first time I was plunged into the reality of a poverty that couldn't be disguised by Ramón's presence to intervene for my protection or to explain in a softer way certain irrationalities and brutalities. I had come over to this far side wondering if I could handle the jungle, never suspecting that it was the people, not the forest, that would fill me with despair. On one side of me lived a group of drunken louts who, if they had had the courage, would have killed me; on the other side, my friends, the ones who came to my house in the late afternoons – to visit me when I was there or to rob me when I was gone.

One of my friends had been Jorge. He murdered his wife with a machete and instead of running for it turned himself over to the police. Another friend was Jorge's brother, Arcario. He came to me after Jorge had been in jail for two years (still unjudged) with the story that for ten thousand *sucres,* about four hundred dollars, Jorge could be freed. So much for the lawyer, so much under the table here, so much there. "You are his only friend," Arcario said. "He begs you for the love of God to give him the money. He'll pay you back in work." I was suspicious; I had visited Jorge in jail a few months before. He had never looked so well or smiled so openly. "Living in the jungle is pure shit compared with this," he said. He had gained twenty pounds, was a soccer star on the prison team, watched television, and lolled around. On Sundays in the late afternoons the whores came in; they brought guitars and their dancing shoes and danced for the prisoners on a little outside bandstand behind the television set. After working as a day laborer for twenty years cleaning pastures for *bananals* with a machete, being in jail was like being a guest at a perpetual fiesta. All except for having a woman only once a week; that part was a drag. I was suspicious – and resented my suspicions, which seemed unworthy of me; I gave Arcario the money for his brother.

Three days later Ramón stormed across the river. "You'll never learn, will you? I've warned you a hundred times. Why in God's name do you keep on listening to Arcario? Why didn't you talk to me first?"

"O.K., O.K., what's wrong?"

"Just this," Ramón said, looking at me in a pitying way and shaking his head. "Here comes Arcario at six o'clock this morning down the road with a brand new chain saw over his shoulder. Well, the only good thing about it is, he'll leave you alone now for six months. He won't have the guts to show his face."

But Ramón was wrong. Arcario came to the house bringing me gifts of grapefruit and *chontaduras.* "Don't be mad, don't be mad, Adu. It's going to take longer than we thought to get Jorge out. It was his idea that I borrow the money, buy the saw, and sell logs. I swear when the time comes I'll pay it back. With the saw I can make plenty, believe me."

"Arcario, you pile of shit, you disgraceful liar. What kind of a man are you to cheat your own brother? And what goddam trees are you going to sell? You don't own any goddam trees. Now you're going to steal trees, too, eh?"

"Adu, Adu, don't talk like that; you'll make me mad, I swear."

He had stopped by on his way up the river, and he invited me to go with him. A jealous husband had cut off the head of a worker as he slept in his hammock and Arcario wanted to join the little crowd of curious people to see what a headless corpse looked like. He came back a couple of hours later shuddering and saying he wished he hadn't gone. He might have waited ten days more and seen the same thing repeated – and on the same farm. It was the big Oro Verde hacienda now being rejuvenated by a group of rich cattlemen who were contracting gangs of migrant labor. They were cutting down the trees, fencing off the land, and planting the old hunting grounds to pasture and African palm.

·　　　　·　　　　·

For over a month Cira did not come to the house. She and Cantante had gotten in a fight and he had slashed her legs with a machete. Unable to walk, she sent one of her children up the trail to pick up my dirty clothes and sweep the floors.

•   •   •

Jorge's six-year-old son came by the house three or four times a month. His mother had been murdered, his father was in jail. He was living with his grandmother; his uncles, Amado and Arcario, were helping out with money or food from time to time. He would knock on my door and when I opened it would immediately and invariably say, "Give me twenty *sucres.*" Just like that, but without a bit of hope in his face. Sometimes I gave him bread spread with jam, but I never gave him money. How could I? The next morning when the news got around there would be a dozen little kids at the door—and they would be there every morning. They would be like the hungry dogs that came each day on an incessant and hopeless search and were never fed, starving and desperate and without a purpose, dogs without a master. Perhaps as much as for the food they were searching for someone who wanted to own them. One crust of bread and you would own a dog forever; he would never leave your doorstep. Jorge's son was beautiful, but his life was as lost and hopeless as a dog's. How awful to know at six that you are part of the world's garbage and living on borrowed time.

•   •   •

Jorge's son stopped coming to the house. He had stepped on a thorn or scratched his hand with a splinter of wood and died the excruciatingly painful death that comes with tetanus.

•   •   •

I was in bed one afternoon when Ramón and Adolfo came across the river with a basket of food. Shivering and wrapped in a sheet I went downstairs and let them in and then went back to bed. "It's lucky you came, Ramón; I've got malaria again."

"O.K., let's lock up the house, you've got to see a doctor. Come on, let's go."

"I don't need a doctor to tell me I've got malaria. Just bring me that stuff to cure it."

"For Christ's sake, you won't go to the *doctor*? You just want to stay here and *die*?"

"I won't die if you bring me the cure. Look, what doctor can I go to? Some quack in Esmeraldas who'll give me aspirin and some worm medicine? No thanks. I'd have to go to Quito, and I'm not up to that. Ramón, I'm sick; I don't even have the strength to cross the river."

"We'll carry you then; I'll take you to Quito. But let's go." He began snapping his fingers in irritation and saying with each snap, *"Vamos, vamos, vamos."*

I could feel the not entirely unpleasant delirium coming back and wanted only to be alone, to sink into that weird and multicolored world of fantasy where the most irrational thoughts turned into forms and for the time that I dreamed them held me with their profound and lying insights. "Ramón, I'm not going to argue with you, and I'm not going anyplace. I know what I'm doing. All I need is that stuff, what do you call it?, that three-day cure."

I disappeared under the mosquito netting and prepared to set off on my journey, but I could see Ramón standing at the top of the stairs, not looking at me now but staring out over the pastures where the cows browsed and past the grass and the bananas to the hills. *"Usted no es capaz,"* he said finally. "God, how I hate this farm. That you insisted on buying."

"O.K., so I'm stupid, but let's talk about that later, shall we?"

"That won't be easy," Ramón said. "I'm not coming over here anymore. You make out your lists, and I'll send someone across with the things you need. But I? No. I look at this farm and it makes me want to vomit. This farm that is going to kill you."

I drifted away for a time and when I came back Ramón and Adolfo had gone. That afternoon Adolfo came back with the medicine; it was not what I needed, not the cure but the suppressant, but I took it and got better. I didn't see Ramón for four months.

I had been over there for little more than a year and now found myself almost completely alone. But in the sweetly sad and softly corroding anguish of loneliness I was less unhappy than before when I had been involved with people. Almost with relief I drifted into a simplicity that I felt I could handle, the bare-boned purity of a life stripped of confusions, of people whose motivations I no longer understood nor trusted. It was almost like starting again and laying down foundations that would be more solid and upon which I might build something, something. I had had disastrous relations with almost everyone, responding to anger with anger, suspicious and slightly contemptuous of the ones who smiled. I was glad not to have to face Ramón for a time but outraged at his rudeness in abandoning me. He was one foundation that I couldn't repudiate; he was the only witness to ten years of my life, the only one who shared a common memory that would simply dissolve into smoke without his presence. In a way, for good or bad, he was someone I had made. And now he was like a kind of disagreeable younger brother whom I found ornery and boring but who, being a member of my family, I was stuck with. Things would straighten themselves out. With time we would begin to communicate again. I was so sure of his underlying feelings for me that I didn't even miss him. He was like a frozen asset, a wealth that was temporarily tied up and unavailable.

It was the others in whom I had lost faith. What does Julian want when he brings me a basket of avocados from the first tree to bear in the creek bottom? A loan of money that he has no intention of repaying? And what is so great about bringing me avocados that he has harvested from my own trees? Steals a thousand and brings me a dozen with a joyous face that reflects his feelings of generosity. And Antonio from down the river, a hardworking farmer with a hut full of kids, but a guy I hardly know coming one evening to visit for the first time. And saying, "I want a chain saw too. I'm just as good a friend of yours as Arcario."

Arcario comes by and asks me to be godfather to his youngest son; this will make us *compadres* and involve us in a profound and formal relationship so delicate and complex that not even Ramón has ever contemplated such a move. ("No," Ramón said. "We must never be *compadres*. This would mean that we could never fight.") Reluctantly, and though I am not a Catholic and though I hold out for months, I finally submit. Without a priest, alone with the baby and Angelica, the *comadre*, we repeat the Apostles' Creed three times, and dipping water from a coffee cup make the sign of the cross on the sleeping baby's forehead. A week later someone, and I would swear it is Arcario, comes by the house while I am gone, rips the rotting boards off the kitchen wall, and steals a crate of empty beer bottles.

I am as ready as anyone to be true to my real feelings and to hate what I find hateful, but now I have lost my capacity to judge, to define morality. I was like the naturalist who admires the tigerishness of the tiger who will rend him when he turns his back, like the parent who cannot hate the child who steals nickels from his pocket. But of course they weren't tigers and they weren't babies; I could no longer imagine what they were.

It had taken me sixty years to learn one of my last hard lessons: the world is lovely but not to be trusted; the tropical rain forest with its earthquakes, floods, and torrential rains is less menacing, is easier to deal with, and is more satisfying than enduring the confusions of those human relationships that, corrupted by class differences and economic disparities, were polluted with mutual deceptions and incomprehensions. Still, I knew too much about my own class to wish to become involved with it once more. I couldn't go back to that. The smugness, the insensitivity, the self-absorption of the middle class, their obsessional hunger to fill their lives with property, their desperate fear that economic and social convulsions were going to impoverish them, no. I judged them, perhaps unfairly, and saw them with my father's vices superimposed over their faces. Living so long with poor people I saw a world that was absolutely unacceptable and a tremendous and defrauded population just beginning to fill with a final rage that couldn't much longer be contained. The people in the basement were setting fire to the building; how stupid of the people in the upstairs suites that the smell of the smoke seemed only to paralyze them. There were two realities that people in America could scarcely begin to imagine, two intimately connected worlds. There was no communication between them, no awareness of the linkage or the delicately constructed dependence that each had for the other. The rich and the poor, the robbers and the robbed, the masters and the slaves—neither world realizing that it had created the other, that it would not exist without the other.

With timidity, ignorance, and what now, standing in the darkness on an Amazon steamer I begin to feel, with arrogance, I had tried to move a few steps out of my world into one that I thought would prove to be more authentic. It hadn't worked. To defend that little bit of turf that I claimed as my own, that stage upon which I could act out the illusion of having purpose in my life, I was now inclined to eliminate much of the human element.

Are we not all born with a certain bias, an innate proclivity for feeling either that man is more good than bad or that he is more bad than good? This basic way of looking at mankind probably even determines the way we vote. Do we join a political party that demands more freedom to more nearly achieve our potential, or a party that wants more restrictive laws to curtail our evil instincts? Did I, who had always believed in more freedom, still believe in the face of the abuses that had been committed in its name? And how relevant was freedom in a world whose population was now doubling toward eight billion, most of whom would live in constant hunger? Wanting desperately to feel, as I had been born to feel, that man was innately noble was perhaps one reason I had been forced to move away and mock the kind of society where the illusion of man's essential goodness became farcical. Now I was being forced to move away from the poor, too, because they only confirmed an increasingly bleak vision: man could not be defined in moral terms. He was, for all his human attributes, constantly vulnerable to the violence of his passions. He seemed to have been programmed to self-destruct and to find true and profound satisfactions only in those fruits that hung over the abyss and that he could only harvest at the greatest peril. I remembered that awful sentence of Swift's, "How I detest that animal called man," and repeated it with satisfaction though I knew it wasn't true and in fact found man most endearing when, true to his impulses, he sacrificed himself to his flawed humanity.

Our lives are controlled by the fantasies we create to explain and justify our inclinations. And so, since we move within the grip of our illusions, each illumination that frees us from an illusion carries along with it a sense of failure. Life is a series of failures, of realizations, awakenings – and of new paths in new directions taken through the tangle of new illusions. There is no way to pin down life and justify it except by translating it into your own particular and private language. Living in a senseless world we need to have the impression of moving through a world that isn't completely senseless, and so now without even thinking such thoughts but driven into an extreme situation, I began more seriously to look for satisfactions in the natural world, the world of trees, rivers, clouds, and sunsets and living that sensual and unexamined life that is falsely claimed to be not worth living – a statement that is like saying that listening to music without words or precise intent is not worth listening to. If it was a crippled life it was also a painless one, and really, was I less alone than millions of old codgers sitting on benches in the big cities or lying on cots in cheap hotels and staring at the ceiling? I was still faced with enormous challenges, could still function as a farmer. Time turned from a flowing river into a lake upon which I floated outside of an awareness of time's passing. Time stopped and the unchanging days took on aspects of cosmic meaning. Now I could stand for an hour under the power of the egrets as they rode on the backs of cows or move with the cows as they grazed slowly through the grass or, filled with a sense of standing close to some ultimate mystery, watch a wasp paralyze a spider with its sting.

Now I moved further out toward the far boundaries where hardly anyone ever walked, contemptuous of Marcelo, and where if I did run into someone – a bunch of women fishing for crawfish with baskets in the creek, Cantante hunting with a dog, a scowling Socrates half-hidden in shadows, some nameless black chopping down a tree for the sloth that was clinging in the upper branches – these things came as no shock. It was like watching something that belonged in the landscape. It was like wandering through the pages of a child's brightly colored book. How simple life had been until Crusoe, thunderstruck, gazed down upon that single footprint in the sand. I wanted to go back to that time before the footprints, the cannibals, the feasts of human flesh. And I was luckier than Robinson, who had only the Bible for a companion. I had Tolstoy, Proust, and Conrad.

When time stopped it was easy to become complacent about one's death. A death that might come sooner than later was the price one paid for living a free life at the edge of danger. Like a race-car driver I accepted the risks; the excitements far outweighed the risks. Now that I was getting old I had a horror of becoming superfluous. Sometimes hacking weeds out in the sun I would feel vague constrictions around the heart. (A diet heavy on beans, rice, and bananas tends to make one gassy.) But as I stood there diagnosing myself, breathing carefully, it seemed that being struck down with a machete in my hand was a dignified, stylish way to go. I shuddered thinking of my father in a rest home at seventy-nine, senile, incontinent, and desperate, and hanging on, hanging on. I wanted to die on the stage, shrieking out my lines and going through my business, not sitting in a wheelchair out in the wings with nothing to do but exhibit myself to the wardrobe mistress. I figured I had put myself into an impregnable position and that no one could threaten to drive me from the life – and the death – that I had chosen. I stood up to the tearful, tragic letters from my mother and the free one-way airplane tickets to Los Angeles or San Francisco sent to me by friends who couldn't believe that I lived as I did because I wanted to.

To make sense of death; to make it a period at the end of a paragraph instead of appearing in the middle of an incompleted phrase; to fall with a sudden, pleasant thump like a ripe avocado instead of hanging up there, rotting but still robbing the tree of its vital juices; to die at a good time, logically, putting finally some sense of order to a life that has been as ridiculous, as chaotically meaningless as anyone else's: these were preoccupations, though they occupied me less than it would appear here in these pages, which I am finding so difficult to write. Death is a great part of the jungle; it hangs over everything where the most exuberant life bursts from organic dissolution; out there (and at sixty) one is nicely programmed to contemplate death's mystery and to see one's death as being hardly more important than the dying tree choked by vines and rotten at its heart but still standing in an anguished dignity. Even the awareness of my own physical disintegration became blurred; my symptoms bored me. It is easy in a climate where one is neither too hot nor too cold to forget one's body; to someone who has slept under blankets and fought to warm up one's feet before falling asleep there is some ultimate luxury in living where one can sleep naked in a bed and without even a sheet. And so if I didn't feel completely well much of the time I explained it by remembering my age. Never having been sixty before, how could I know how it felt to be sixty? Besides, after a dozen years on the coast I had already survived malaria, histoplasmosis, hepatitis, and leishmaniasis; their echoes slowed me down, perhaps. Considering everything, I figured that I was doing rather well, and even when great chunks of teeth began to break away from their foundations I was nudged into a philosophic stance. I piled the awful pieces on a ledge beside the window, and the rooster sneaked in one day to gobble them up. Great. The law of the jungle. My teeth were still useful; it gave me pleasure to own a rooster who chewed his corn with my old discarded grinders.

.   .   .

Well, it took no great perception to see death standing at the side of Jorge's young son. Children on the river were tied to life by the most fragile connections; over half of them died before they were three years old. When Jorge went to jail it became almost inevitable that his son would not survive. Years before his death, out of the deepest despair, I had accepted the obscenity behind these unlived lives and felt with the people that it was a blessing if one were poor to die at birth, spared the humiliations and deprivations of the poor man's destiny.

Cira and Marcelo, the best and the worst; now it was their turn. They died out of an inevitability that became apparent only after they were gone: Cira, paddled across the river by a daughter and coming to Ramón with a crushing pain in her head, a pain she could not bear. Ramón took her to the hospital; she was tranquilized and spent the night in the house of a friend. And early the next morning rising up off her mat she was killed instantly by a massive hemorrhage, a bursting of the blood vessels in her brain. She was under thirty; she died of rage, in revolt against the injustices in her life.

And Marcelo? He disappeared for a few days. He had gone up the river to drink with someone and never came back. Four days after he left his bloated body was found floating entangled in some tree branches that hung over the river. Until the autopsy, when one of our *macheteros*, Quevedo, was taken across the river by the local police and ordered to take his machete and slice off the top of the skull and open up the chest cavity, everyone thought that a drunken Marcelo reeling down the bank had stumbled, struck his head on something, and fallen into the river. The autopsy revealed, however, that he had been shot in the back and his spinal column shattered. Murdering him was something that I had done so often in my imagination that, had I been there at the time, I might have been tempted to go to the police and confess. As it was I simply felt exultantly guilty, as I think many of us did. It was impossible to pin the guilt on anyone; there were hundreds of us capable of having done it; we all shared the glory.*

The week he was murdered I had gone to Quito. People I now met on the farm had begun to talk about my hair. For some time the comb had been coming away from my head with choked tines, and when I felt around up there my fingers slid across a half-dozen spots as smooth as billiard balls. A friend from Quito had come across the river for a weekend; she told me I looked like a moth-eaten rug. I had no mirror and paid little attention, observing only that the spots were moving around, colliding and rebounding at logical angles as though, having been described as billiard balls they were now involved in a game of snooker. As they wandered here and there a thin mosslike furze obliterated their trajectories.

And now after months of sulking, Ramón came across the river. His face as he walked up the hill was smiling and conciliatory; he was ready to forgive me, but when he came close his expression changed to one of disbelief and anger. "Oh Christ," I said, "are we going to start fighting even before you say hello?"

"What's happened to you?" Ramón asked.

"What's *happened*?" I asked sarcastically. "Well, for one thing your goddam rooster ate my teeth."

Ramón had brought Aladino across the river with him to carry the baskets of food up to the house. Aladino was from Rioverde but came to the farm to work a couple of months each year when he needed money. He was an incredibly handsome man, and he knew it. He had made a comb out of nails driven into a piece of hardwood, and he spent a lot of time fluffing out his Afro. He carried a woman's mirror in his back pocket and checked himself out at frequent intervals, smiling into the mirror and dazzling himself with his black skin and his perfect teeth.

"Dino," Ramón said. "Loan me your mirror." He took it and without speaking handed it to me.

O.K., so it was time to go to Quito and see a doctor. Like a good river man, besides having little faith in medicine, I had tried to ignore those invasions that I couldn't see—the fungi, bacteria, and viruses that brought one

---

* AUTHOR'S NOTE. Four years later, while I was traveling in Brazil, Socrates, father-in-law of the half-wit Marcelo, was also murdered in almost the same spot. Climbing down the ladder of his house in the new darkness of another night for his pre-sleep pee he met someone down there who had been waiting for him.

down. It was the body's job to cure itself, what else was it good for? Let my gurgling glands and lights produce the medicinal juices that I needed. But peering into the mirror to encounter this sour-looking white-haired gent, I met something so crude that it struck at my illusions about time's passing and the ability of the body to stick Band-Aids in the right places. In four months my hair had turned white. Studying it in fascination and dismay I felt like the hero of some horror story by Poe who, struggling out of imprisonment in a coffin or a den of gibbering skeletons, gazes into a mirror to the vacant, staring eyes and the long, tangled locks gone white in a single night.

.   .   .

In back of the pastures about a half mile from the house and in a long narrow space between Socrates' line and the edge of an arroyo that plunged down into the creek where the sun seldom shone and a terrible tangle of stinging weeds and bamboo made it almost impossible to walk, there was a four-acre patch of bananas from which we harvested almost nothing. The ground was sandy, the banana plants were diseased and stunted with Panama, the leaves yellow and drooping. I decided to clear this area and replant it to another crop — coconuts or *elefante,* cacao or platano. Scattered among the bananas were fifty trees, some of them enormous; they had grown back up in those thirty years that the farm had been deserted. I had to cut them down, burn them, dig out the stumps, and roll them down the bank; some of the stumps were bigger than Volkswagens.

It took almost nine months of steady work, and it was so hard, so boring, and at times seemed so impossible to do alone that it became obsessional. My whole purpose in living became concentrated in removing from that field every stick, every weed, every root, every trace of anything that could remind you that it had been jungle. At the time, if I thought about it, I was proud of my resolution. Tonight on the river I see it in a different light, feeling that I am now remembering it more truly and that that fanatic effort, which proved to be my last on the farm, was a kind of insanity. Sometimes after I had been hacking away for six months, when I was burning piles of stumps and logs, I would wake up at midnight and feel impelled to walk out through the pasture and the terrible darkness of the *bananal* with a flashlight and push the wood together to keep it blazing. Now I don't remember why it seemed so important, but at the time it engrossed me and let me wander through a profoundly symbolic fantasy as real and as unreal as a dream that had little to do with the modest improvement that I was making in the value of the farm. The fantasy was a charade. Was I, standing at the threshold of old age, trying to prove that I could still do a day's work, was I probing my body's limits, looking for the weak point? More likely, though I no longer took his words seriously, I was responding to Ramón, who, trying to get me off the farm, was denigrating everything I did and trying to convince me that I was no longer of value.

For a couple of days a couple of times a month the clearing project was interrupted. We had a tractor over there now, a muddy two-mile road through the bananas, and we were hauling out twenty or thirty tons of bananas every month. I was the only one who knew how to drive the tractor and was expected to be instantly available when the crews came across the river to cut and carry the fruit to the road where another two-man crew riding in the wagon with me would pick up the piled bunches and then pile them again on the gravel bar at the river's edge. For everyone but me who had only to drive the tractor, it was the most brutal and exhausting kind of work. We were constantly fighting a deadline, rushing to get the fruit to the packing sheds and off to the banana boats that had suddenly and with only a day's notice arrived in Guayaquil. We put in fifteen-hour days, sometimes unloading the last stems at midnight, and in bed, dead-tired but unable to sleep, I would listen to the motor canoes as they crossed and recrossed the river all night long.

There is among poor people on the coast a certain status connected with handling bananas; it is a sense of pathetic involvement with the world's business, a feeling of sharing in something tremendous that is made up of trucks, steamships, and men who cruise through the coastal regions in Land Rovers dressed in white linen and smoking big cigars. Nothing else can explain the ease with which we almost always found people at a moment's notice who were willing to almost kill themselves in this awful work. They had the pride of Western cowboys who see themselves as movie heroes and are happy with that sixty or seventy dollars a month plus board. Another reason, perhaps: the sporadic nature of the labor, which more honestly reflected their natural work rhythms. Twice a month they engaged in this violent and hysterical work that left them exhausted but for which, considering what they would have earned as day laborers, they were well paid. The cutters, for instance, the aristocrats of the business (they came first and left early), who walked with their crews through the *bananal* selecting the bunches ready to harvest could make as much as fifteen dollars a day, a fantastic wage in a Latin American country where the success of any business dominated by American capital is predicted on slave labor.

The lights burned all night in the little packing shed next to Ramón's house where a dozen people worked and where another crew with banana bunches across their shoulders climbed up the steep bank from the river. There were even some eight-year-old kids (how they fought for the honor of this work) who stuck little printed stickers on each bunch of bananas after it had been washed and its butt end sealed with a red paint. The sticker was smart and jazzy, Chiquita bananas it said, and it completely misrepresented the sordid quality of the riverside life and the poverty of the people and the rags they wore and the way they staggered from exhaustion and lack of sleep.

Sailing up the Amazon river I am thinking about the packing shed and realizing that it is an intrusive memory put in the way of the chronology to slow up or block that final thing that happened that I have scarcely ever considered and that I am afraid to think about now. . . .

The packing shed at three a.m.; one of the few times I ever saw it. I remember it as a kind of stupidly imagined hell: the packers slapping the bananas into boxes as though they had been condemned to do it through eternity, a steady drizzle of rain, someone laying sheets of plastic over the piled boxes, the little kids licking and pasting, and outside under a roof of palm leaves Cira at three a.m. cooking up pots of rice and fish over charcoal, making dishes of food that she will sell to the workers who haven't eaten for fifteen hours. Ramón hasn't been to bed for two days and has collapsed; he is sleeping in the cab of the pickup truck; there is one more load of bananas to bring across the river, and I will go back to my farm in the empty canoe. The big truck from Guayaquil arrives, and as I start down the bank, I can hear it backing into the shed and crumpling the sheets of corrugated iron.

·   ·   ·

We hauled out bananas only four or fives days a month; the rest of the time I was alone dragging tree branches to fires or digging out stumps with a shovel, an axe, and a machete. After months the little field opened up to the sun, and from the edge of the bank you could see out for a couple of miles over the tops of the bananas to the stream, the hills along the southern boundary, and the river. It had been a silent place, the heavy foliage had absorbed all sounds, but now opened up and clean, the hillside came closer and the place was full of birdsong, the harsh no-nonsense music of Ecuadorian birds, all clacks, squeaks, snappings, metallic shriekings. Sometimes it sounded like a machine shop. When it was almost ready to plant I felt elated and proud as though I had accomplished something monumental; I don't know of anything I've ever done that gave me such pleasure; I had made something pure and jewel-like in the middle of a writhing, giddily proliferating jungle. Even the cows loved it. When someone forgot to close the gate the whole herd would sneak up to stand in the clean dirt, gaze dramatically over the forest tops to the river, and, taking deep breaths, bellow in satisfaction.

Once in a while Ramón came over to the farm again, but he did not go back through the *bananal* to the field where I was working. He was fully occupied clearing pasture, milking cows, harvesting pineapples, and shipping bananas on the other side. He was reluctant to show any interest in this farm of mine for which he had developed such a blind, irrational loathing. His manner with me now was completely changed, and he criticized everything I did. When I told him that I had hacked out a trail along the property line that now extended three miles back along the hillside, he pointed out that it had taken me months to do something that a two-dollar-a-day *machetero* could have done in a couple of weeks. The road through the bananal was turning into deep ruts; after rains it was almost impassible. Ramón would intimate that I was forgetting how to manage a tractor and that anyone with a little care could be getting out the bananas without turning the loads over, continually having flat tires or broken hitches or driving into swamps where it was necessary to completely unload the wagon and then push the tractor out onto a stretch of firm ground with ten men. "You are sending me fruit so beat up and bruised that we have to throw half of it away," he told me. When the cows broke out and climbed up the hill and trampled Felipe's young cacao trees or when they wandered up the river past the southern farms to take one bite out of each banana stem that was piled on the shore and waiting for canoes, Ramón would shrug impatiently when I gave him some neighbor's bill for the damages and asked him to pay it. It was impossible to control the cows with all those maliciously opened gates, but Ramón talked as though I were completely incompetent and that any half-wit would not allow such things to happen.

What a snot Ramón had become. If I now accepted the relationship that he had imposed on us, that I was the father from whose domination he must now free himself, I had to accept also that I had produced an extremely unpleasant little whelp. We were in a battle that he couldn't possibly win, and like a bad loser he had turned sulky and sarcastic. When he came over to talk and bring me food he was as tiresome as a whining child. He wanted me off that farm; he couldn't hear me when I explained over and over that my determination to stay had nothing to do with him. I would sit at the kitchen table drinking coffee, half-smiling, dreamily half-listening while he cut me down. I hoped he would leave me soon and return to his own side so I could go back to my field and keep the fires burning, pick up the last sticks, fill and level the holes where the stumps had been. Some day soon I would drag him out there and show him that I was still capable of doing magnificent things.

For almost a year I have been able to get this far in remembering those two years that I lived alone. I have come in retrospect to the end of my life there and tonight on the Amazon will face that last month. It is something that until now I have scarcely dared to consider; it is too full of rage and humiliation; I have always thought of it as some ultimate and shameful betrayal. I have been like someone who has been wounded in a crash, lying cut and broken in the wreckage but unwilling to pass my hands over the wounds and appraise the damage. But tonight on the river suddenly without fear my mind is hurrying toward those last two confrontations with Ramón. I have the feeling that not only will I appraise the damage, but that I may even discover that I had caused the wreck. I want to be released from my self-pity; a strange new possibility presents itself—that in getting things straight my problem will no longer center on forgiving Ramón but on asking him to forgive me.

I feel as though I am about to see everything in a different light; it is as though, finally having been defined as a writer and having accepted the definition, I must now see things more clearly, must more honestly pierce through my wounded ego to a new truth. I must take a moral stance.

.   .   .

At two o'clock one afternoon a gringo from the banana company in Guayaquil rushes onto Ramón's farm in a Land Rover and tells him that in twenty-four hours a truck will come by to receive eight hundred boxes of fruit. Ramón on his side doesn't have bananas to fill eight hundred boxes and will have to harvest my side, too. He gathers a crew to cut and haul and then in a panic collects another crew and brings them across the river. I am not at the house and neither is the tractor; half-running, the men go out through the pasture, the bananas, and up the little hill, and for the first time Ramón stands at the edge of the field that I have been clearing for almost a year. The field is completely clean except for one enormous stump that I have saved until the last and which I have been working on for over a month. It is the hardest kind of wood, and I have dug an enormous hole so that I can walk around and under it. It is much too heavy to move with the tractor, and I am trying to burn away some of its bulk. (The day before I had been disking with the tractor, but the three-point hook-up was not working well and I had got the tractor stuck in a ridiculously small hole, no more, really, than a slight indentation.)

When Ramón comes to the top of the hill and looks across that pure, empty space as clean as some of those fields that I had made on the other side, he sees the dead tractor, and he sees me standing in the bottom of a great five-foot-deep excavation, covered with dirt and sweat and hacking feebly at a root with a machete.

What I see when I look up is a madman striding across the field waving his arms and yelling things in a Spanish so rural, so out of the lost jungle villages of Ramón's childhood that it is almost African. I am too absorbed in the work and too tired to immediately make sense of this fierce figure yelling gibberish and coming toward me, but I climb out of the hole and wait. I try to catch his words, but all I can understand is the first couple, *"Que muere,"* that you die. He comes up to me, tears gushing out of his eyes, his face mad, and he clenches his fists and raises his arms above my head. Young Oedipus. From his deranged look I know that what he wants to do more than anything in the world is smash me to the ground, and without trying to defend myself I wait to be struck down. I think that during this ritual tableau, which doesn't last more than a few seconds, a kind of dumb smile never leaves my face. I am too stunned to react; more important, I have begun to play a role. This whole awful moment is an exact rerun of something out of my adolescence when I had stood before my father in his bedroom, trembling with rage, my fists raised above his head, and yelled, "You son of a bitch, I'll kill you." And my father, hands at his sides, half-smiling, but ashen-faced, looking at me with an expression that was almost admiration, saying, "Oh yeah? Oh yeah?"

Now, aping my father, I look at Ramón stupidly and say, *"Ah, si? Ah, si?"* because I don't realize what is happening and have fallen back on someone else's lines. A moment later I feel a slowly growing anger; it has nothing to do with whatever it is he has said or the way he has said it, but because he has done it publicly in front of the workers. It is a humiliation as brutal as a rape before witnesses, but in this moment so intense and personal, a moment more intimate than we have ever had before, what appalls me is not that he has degraded me but that he has degraded himself. The workers stand in the background, embarrassed and horrified, for if it is something that lasts only for a minute, still, it is like a mental breakdown, a secret and forbidden glimpse into Ramón's soul.

He turns away and walks over to the tractor waving the men to come with him. As they rock the machine, disconnect the disk that is riding wedged high against the rear tires, Ramón, still furious, calls over his shoulder, "You're the only fool in Ecuador who can get a tractor stuck on level ground."

I climb back into the hole but, too upset to work, sit on a root and smoke a cigarette. My hands are trembling, my mind is blank. I have already begun to forget the last couple of minutes, feeling only a new vulnerability, feeling only that I have met a passion that I may not be strong enough to stand up against. I sit in the sun, get up and throw a few burning chunks of wood together, and sit down again. Making my mind empty I observe a curious and wonderful thing: a rain of cosmic particles falling out of the sun, a driving rain of energy glittering in the air, falling into the earth, into the trees. I am being offered some kind of a solace that at the moment I can't accept.

Ugly Alfonso, the sweetest of Ramón's men, stands at the edge of the hole smiling down at me in dismay. His look is devastated; he is as shamed as I.

"What was that all about?" I ask. Alfonso, smiling and shaking his head, doesn't answer. "I couldn't understand him; what was he saying?"

"It wasn't pretty what he was saying," Alfonso says.

"No, I don't imagine it was. What did he say?" Alfonso doesn't answer, and I say, "Come on, Alfonso, tell me."

"Well, he said you could die if you wanted to. You could drown yourself, stab yourself, poison yourself, shoot yourself. But you can't do it here on the farm. You have to go to Quito to do it."

"The son of a bitch has always been eloquent," I say. We look at each other, smiling and shaking our heads helplessly.

"Will you help us haul bananas?" Alfonso asks finally. "We have eight hundred boxes to get out by noon tomorrow."

"No," I say. "I will not help. You can give that message to the big cheeseburger. No more, no more."

"I don't understand," Alfonso says. "*La gran queso-hamburgesa?*"

"Your new tractor driver," I say. "Ramón, the mini-whopper."

It is almost a month later when Ramón comes across the river for the last time. It is getting dark and I am cooking something to eat by candlelight when he brings me in a basket of food and leaves it by the door. He greets me but I don't answer him and stand at the stove stirring something in the frying pan. Ramón stands in the doorway neither in nor out of the house; for almost the first time he has come over alone. I have just had a very bad week. The good weeks have been good, but the bad weeks have been awful, awful. Someone (was it Arcario? Julian? Cantante? Jose? Amado? Which one of my good friends?) had stepped into my open house while I had left it for fifteen minutes to open a gate and call the cows to a new pasture, and with the searing perception of a poor man had found a stack of thousand *sucres* bills that I had hidden in a stack of magazines. He had peeled off eleven of them, almost five hundred dollars, and left me half. A couple of nights later a raccoon or a possum had gotten into the downstairs storeroom where the chickens slept on long bamboo strips and before I could get down to use Marcelo's club on him, he had killed half the chickens. The others, some of them slashed open or with broken wings, were hysterical, and the next morning they took to the brush. When the chickens were all killed or had left, something worse than being robbed had happened. I looked toward the hills with cynical eyes. Even that beautiful field I had made (now planted in measured rows to platano) struck me as foolish and inappropriate in this wild place—a pearl in a trough of hog slop.

After a couple of minutes of silence Ramón clears his throat and speaks. "This is the last food that will be coming over to you." His voice is low, very calm, very tight.

I turn and stare at him coldly. "I thought I had been ordered to die in Quito."

"No," Ramón says, half-laughing. "I've decided to cooperate, and incidentally, I'm sorry about that."

"You can't keep me from getting food; I'll find someone to bring it across to me."

"You don't understand," Ramón says. "No one will bring you food; no more food is coming over here."

"I see; you're driving me off."

"Exactly. There's food here for three days."

"What about the cats?"

"Fuck the cats."

"You want it all; you want to be the owner of everything."

"Think whatever you want. But if I wanted it all why wouldn't I leave you over here? You'll be dead within six months."

"Dead, dead, what the hell do you know about dead? . . . What about the cows, the farm?"

"Fuck the farm. I'll put someone over here, and if I can't, if we lose everything, at least you'll be gone. . . . Can you be ready in two days?"

I stare at him for a long time and he stares back without blinking. "Ramón, you'd better get out of here now."

"I'll send some boxes over for you tomorrow."

"Get out, goddam it, get out."

After he has gone I stand by the stove, blind with anger, nauseated, stirring food that I will never eat, cursing under my breath.

It is dark outside now, so dark that I can't see Ramón, who has walked through the garden and now stands just outside the heavy screening about two feet from my head. I hear him clearing his throat and go rigid.

"There's something else you don't understand. You think you just belong to yourself. You don't; you belong to us, too."

"Oh, Ramón, you fancy talking Negro with your golden tongue. I'm so sick of your eloquence. You can always do something rotten and then twist it around with your fancy talk."

"Oh Christ, Martín, can't you see? can't you see? You don't belong here."

"Where don't I belong?" I yell. "Where don't I belong?"

But Ramón doesn't answer; he has gone.

The most important thing in the next three days is to catch the cats and get them back across the river where they will be cared for. Julian makes me a little bamboo cage, and when Alfonso comes over a couple of times a day with empty boxes I fill them with books or clothes or pots and catch the cats one by one and send them away. On the third morning there is almost nothing left in the house but the little gas burner, a coffee pot, and one cat. I carry him down to the canoe, but when he sees the river he panics and, biting and scratching and screaming in fear, makes me fling him away. When I get over to the other side my arms and hands are streaming with blood and my T-shirt is dripping with cat shit. I am not reluctant to so exhibit myself, to make a last dramatic exit, and my condition – blood, shit, and tears of humiliation – seems aesthetically appropriate to what the moment demands. Whimpering, I go out with a bang. That afternoon I am settled in Quito.

A few months later after ten days in a hospital I am cured of things I never knew I had. Why should I have felt, being sixty for the first time, that it was not normal to get up ten times in the night to urinate? Ramón, that bastard, had been right. My liver, kidneys, and bladder had been heavily infected with jungle bacteria. I had been pissing a broth of pure *E. Coli*. (I think that to this day I have never told Ramón that I had been taken to the hospital in a coma and that I had almost died. We have made our peace, but I still can't endure the thought of having to listen to his interminable and self-satisfied I-told-you-sos.)

Five months of Quito and the total absence of purpose in an empty life and it was time to go to Brazil. A week before I left, Arcario came up to visit me. He called me *compadre*; he wanted to know when I was coming back; he missed me, he said. I'll bet he did. I was the only one over there with things worth stealing. We have both come upon hard times. He told me that my golden-tailed rooster still haunted the farm. He had fled down into the creek bottom and lived alone in the stinging weeds; at night he slept forty feet up in the branches of a *matapalo*, and at dawn, answering the arrogant calls of Ramón's roosters on the other side, shrieked out his wild, insane proclamations of domination. Everyone hunted him, he would make a nice stew with rice and green peppers, but he was jungle-wild now, a seldom seen shadow in the brushy bottoms. I felt a terrible nostalgia listening to Arcario's story. That crazy rooster was my surrogate; I felt that he was that small part of me that still remained—to scratch and strut among the leaves, chase falling seedpods, look with unblinking eyes into the sparkle of sunlight at high noon in the creek in the bottom of the canyon. He was that small part of me that had begun to find moments of uncomplicated peace in the uncontemplated presence of natural things and who had even been given as a last gift that mystic revelation of a rain of energy streaming out of the sun.

⋅ ⋅ ⋅

Someone is calling and has been calling for some time. I turn around in confusion and see Beverly standing at the head of the ship's ladder in a shaft of light and peering into the darkness of the top deck. "Hey, Beverly, over here." As she approaches me I come back to Brazil, or part-way at least, or part of me at least. It is a curious moment for I seem to be traveling on two rivers at the same time, and in an especially intense and complicated way as though, while fragmented and spread all over the continent, I have never been more whole. And now suddenly out of nothing, a totally meaningless and unconnected phrase forms in my mind, the words all spelled correctly, the commas all more or less in the right places; it moves across the front of everything like that moving sign in Times Square that wishes you a Happy New Year – "The rivers, like those intricate unfurling sentences of Proust, which, while they continue to reveal and illuminate, also move mysteriously to encompass tremendous ambiguities." It passes across my mind again while I memorize it, a meaningless sentence, a gratuitous flashing like a second of madness, as revealing as a burst of light from a struck match that illuminates nothing but itself. Was it a sentence I had read someplace and was now remembering, or was I inventing? Either way, it was nothing that I owned.

Beverly and I stand together for a minute looking out over the tops of the trees into an immense darkness. On the far horizon long cold streamers of lightning reveal two separate columns of cumulus clouds that rush boiling into the sky. There is no sound of thunder.

"That Brazilian girl is in the lounge; she's waiting for us. Do you think she can sing? She seems small to have much of a voice."

"I would bet that she can sing. Did you look into her eyes?"

"Are you really a writer like she says?"

"Yes, indeed I am. Do I seem small to be a writer?"

We stand watching the lightning and straining to hear the rumble of thunder.

"Oh God," Beverly says. "Three more days. By the time we get to Manaus I'm only going to be two-inches tall."

"I don't think we'll get to Manaus," I say. "I mean, I don't think I will. You know in a movie how in the last three or four minutes you can tell it's coming to the end? Manaus isn't a part of this trip for me; I'm coming to the end."

"Has it been that bad?"

"No, on the contrary. I feel pretty good, sort of connected again."

"Yeah, the river is good for that," Beverly says. For a while, you know, I was sort of pissed about those ashtray cracks. But at least you got me thinking. I was just talking to the poet from Manaus. You know what he told me? That this stupid river used to run the other way."

"Yeah, that's what they're saying now. South America and Africa used to be joined together; the Amazon and the Congo used to be one river that ran due west along the equator. Then South America floated away and that pushed up the Andes, and the river had to reverse its flow. That was a couple of hundred million years ago, slightly before our time."

"What a mess," Beverly says. "All that moving around. All those mountains shooting up, the volcanoes, the earthquakes, tidal waves. Jesus. I wonder where the Congo used to go."

"Oh, my God," I say, suddenly realizing. "It used to run past my farm in Esmeraldas. My God, it's all one river—the Congo, the Amazon, the Esmeraldas."

Apparently this revelation is less important to Beverly than it is to me. "It's a small world," she says mildly. And then a moment later, "But it really isn't, is it?"

"But what a wonderful connection. Really, it just blows my mind."

"I don't know. You can always make connections, but so what? That kind of a connection, does it make life any easier?"

"Sure it does," I say. "Making connections is what it's all about." I grab her arm and, bending into her face, wink lewdly, and we laugh.

Lightning flashes for whole half-minutes at the horizon; miles away, silent, it runs back and forth between the two cloud pillars. "We'd better go," Beverly says, finally. "Oh, hey, look." She rattles something before my face. "If you have to do pee-pee come to me; this key fits the gentleman's too."

"Gee, thanks, I hardly know what to say."

"I treat my friends right," Beverly says. "Never let it be said that friends of Beverly have to do pee-pee on the top deck."

"Loan it to me now then, and I'll see you in the lounge." I leave her and start below, but at the top of the ladder, gazing out for just a second at those fierce illuminations on the horizon that look like nothing so much as atomic war, another sentence, fully constructed and ready to be memorized, moves across my mind. I watch it in amazement wondering how it will end. "At night the street lights shining into the leaves of a mango tree. As intricate in its design of lights and shadows, its gradations from purest black to luminous spring green, as profoundly orchestrated as a musical statement. Like an Afro haircut in the sun, an incredible and mysterious design of light and shadow, sunlight blazing out of blackness." Amazing. I hurry down to the lower deck, rush into my cabin, dig an empty notebook out of the old blue bag, and copy out these weird messages that have begun to arrive. I am either turning into a writer or I am going crazy; one possibility, of course, does not exclude the other. I wade into the gentleman's and make pee-pee.

In the lounge Marlui and Marcos sit on a long leather sofa with Beverly and Fleurette. Facing them in chairs: Don; the Dutchman, Hedrik; and the three French passengers. The poet from Manaus stands in a far doorway, but he is overwhelmed by the foreign presence and, being sensitive, wishes to be invited to join us. I motion to him and he comes in and sits down beside me. Marlui says something to him that I don't understand, and the poet beams with pleasure. In another corner of the lounge three teen-agers are singing to a plunked guitar, but it can scarcely be heard above the taped music that rocks and throbs through every corner of the ship.

"Really, honest to God," I say to the poet, "Ramona? Ramona, I hear those mission bells above? They were playing that when I was eight years old. Ramón Navarro and who was the girl, Dolores Del Rio?"

The poet laughs. "We Brazilians are a very loyal people to the music that we love."

Marlui has thrown off her sandals and sits with her feet crossed under her and hidden beneath her skirt. She smiles at us and strikes vague chords with a guitar that seems too big for her; her face is beginning to grow vague and withdrawn. Marcos comes over where I sit and gives me an open copy of *Veja*. It has a long article in it that he has written about the colonization of Rondônia. I can't make out the words, but the poet is reading over my shoulder and nodding his head. "We've asked one of the officers to turn off the sound system so Marlui can play," Marcos says. "Here are some pictures I took in Rondônia." He hands me some enlargements on glossy paper: a fifty-acre piece of jungle with everything cut down and burned, stumps and ashes, looking like a battlefield; a large truck in a downpour of rain that has just arrived at a forest with the colonists who will take possession of it; an empty, bulldozed landscape from which every sign of life has been removed and in front of which a young Indian girl holds a child with veined and tortured hands; a thirteen-year-old prostitute sitting on a bed with a friend, another whore in her twenties who looks as tough and ravaged as a fifty-year-old man.

"Terrible, terrible," murmurs the poet. And he says something to Marcos in Portuguese.

"Marcos speaks English," I say. "Will you speak English so I can understand?"

"I was saying that these pictures are three years old and that since then devastation is rushing over the land, uncontrolled. Our friend here who is going back won't recognize the place. I've just flown over Rondônia from Pôrto Velho to Cuiabá; I sat at the window of the plane and wept like a baby. The whole thing is under attack—parallel roads every thousand meters that stretch from horizon to horizon and for hundreds of miles, multitudes of farmers trying to raise crops that will never get to market on roads that have already begun to wash away. They say the soil is fairly rich, it lies at the foot of the Andes and its minerals haven't leached away yet. So much the worse if it's good; Indians who are stupid enough to live on rich land must die for their crime. And poor whites will have to die when the São Paulo lawyers decide to move in. Of course, if it turns out to be poor land, as I suspect perhaps it is, it will shortly turn into a desert."

"This is the story of how it goes," Marcos says. The government is crying for colonists, and they move in – poor men from the northeast and landless peasants from the south looking for cheap land. The northeasterners as a general rule find it almost impossible to adjust to this new jungle world; it's like bringing in Arab nomads. So these poor devils squat on empty tracts or buy worthless deeds that have been forged by crooks who will sell the same land over and over. And the colonists move in and start cutting down the trees, the Indians oppose them, a colonist is killed, and posses of men hunt down the Indians. The Indians stand and fight and are killed or they flee to some distant and isolated jungle on another river."

"Or the government flies the Indians off to a reservation where half of them will die of flu or measles," the poet says, interrupting.

"And it's not just your Western bangy-bangy, the cowboys against the Indians," Marcos says. "The whole area is in chaos. It's colonists against colonists, everybody against everybody, but mainly the rich against the poor. The rich have their own police, their own gunmen. You might be interested to know that one gang of *pistoleros* was run by one of your own Peace Corps staff members."

"He must have been a Nixon Republican," I say.

"Actually," the poet says, "he was probably carrying out in a most fearless way the present wishes of the government. The small farmer concept hasn't worked; the government wants the big companies to move in; poor people are simply part of the infrastructure now; the companies will find themselves with great masses of conveniently located cheap labor. If the land in Rondônia is good, and I'm not sure it is, then the whole state will be cut down in the next six to eight years. And ten years after that it will all be owned by a half-hundred millionaire companies."

"But what about this law that says you can only cut down half of your property and that the rest must remain virgin jungle?"

Marcos and the poet look at each other and smile. "If you respect this limitation, and there are many who don't, you simply sell your uncleared half to a new owner. He is allowed to cut down half. No, look, this is the greatest crime against the planet in the history of the world; there are many who think that it will be the greatest disaster."

"And no one is going to gain," Marcos says. "Everything is going: Indians, colonists, animals, trees, thousands of plant species, the climate, the earth itself. Everything is going, everything – and all for nothing."

"Not quite for nothing," the poet says. "The *militares* said they needed the Amazon highways so that they could protect the Brazilian borders. When the Amazon is a desert we won't have to worry about being invaded; that's one problem solved."

"At least, you'll have pasture for a hundred zillion cattle," I say. At least, Brazilians will eat meat."

"That idea is wrong for two reasons," Marcos says. "We already have tremendous herds of cattle here owned by people like Volkswagen. Their plan is not to sell meat to Brazilians who can't afford it anyway but to fly it to Germany, deep freezing it at high altitudes. Now how does Brazil benefit? How many jobs does a cattle ranch offer and at what wages?"

"And the second reason?" I ask.

"At least eighty percent of Amazon soils are classified as poor," the poet says. "The Indians know this, and they know how to manage the jungle. You can take about three crops off a piece of cleared land and then you have to let it rest for fifty years. They understand this other thing that has so confused the scientists – the larger the trees, the more sterile the ground. The Indians – after all this land is theirs – understand the truly subtle and complicated ecosystem much better than the smartest scientists. How typical of us that we're driving off or killing the only people who know how to manage the land."

"Yes," Marcos says," that's the second reason, the fragility of this highly leached soil. The hoofs of cattle, for instance, are absolutely destructive. A little overgrazing and the grass is gone for good."

Marcos and the poet are enflamed by each other and working closely together in close harmony creating a requiem for the river. Their words are chilling. "Did you read about Liquigas in the Mato Grosso?" the poet asks Marcos. "They had to keep about 14,000 cattle on their pastures for a couple of extra months because the roads washed out and the trucks couldn't get in. In sixty days they wrecked their pastures for good."

"What we're learning," Marcos says, "is that everything we're doing is wrong, and the tragedy is we're doing it on a gigantic scale. Now we know, after building thousands of kilometers of roads, that you can't run highways through this country without destroying the Indians, without spreading syphilis, leishmaniasis, alcoholism, without turning the country over to any private madness, any public or private corruption. Now we know that the small farmer can't make it on this lateritic soil, and even the large cattle ranches are running into terrible problems. We are beginning to know that without an infrastructure it is almost not profitable to cut down the trees. What's left then? The minerals in our mountains, the hydroelectric power in the river, and the fish."

"A few years ago out of desperation to come up with something, the agriculturists in INPA suggested the intensive farming of small plots," the poet says. "INPA had been watching the Japanese farmers in Bragantina turning an ecological disaster into a mild success. They were raising chickens and black pepper as a single operation; it was a clever plan. The sale of chickens fed on commercial feeds paid most of the expenses, and the chicken manure fertilized the pepper plants. All the textbooks got excited; they had an answer at last. . . . This year a new jungle fungus moved out of the forest and wiped out the black pepper farmers. One more thing that isn't going to work."

"There is a real future in our minerals," the poet says. "We have tremendous reserves and we've only begun the exploration. Mining, while it would probably be completely destructive, would at least be a localized destruction. But mining takes hundreds of millions in railroad lines, river ports facilities, the building of whole cities. The government would like to get the minerals out by turning over all our bauxite, tin, iron, and magnesium to the American giants. Some solution, eh?"

"By flooding twenty percent of the Amazon with six tremendous lakes we're building hydroelectric stations now," Marcos says. "Nations love big things to symbolize their grandeur, and we would put an atomic facility in the middle of Brazilia if we knew how. The Amazon has completely frustrated us; what is there left to do if you can't make a profit off this land but to put it all under water?"

"Light and power for ghost cities," says the poet. "No, no, we would love to blame everything on the United States, but the reality is very different. You only own about half of us so far, and we could invite you to leave if we wanted to. I think you would go nicely, wouldn't you? Wouldn't you go nicely if you knew what you were doing to us?"

"Oh, we would probably go," I say, "but I don't think we would go nicely. After all you owe us about fifty billion, don't you?"

Suddenly the sound system goes dead; the slow, pounding beat of the diesel motor is now throbbingly clear and immediately we are able to appraise the quality of the suffering we have been enduring. It is like having lived for days with a rotten tooth that abruptly stops aching. Without that Montovani sound the ship seems to float higher and to glide more easily in the water as though released from a sad weight. We all look expectantly toward Marlui, but just across from us the three teen-agers are still singing, and Marlui will not compete; she sits in a kind of isolation, smiling dreamily and playing a few unconnected chords.

"While we're waiting," Marcos says, "Marlui wants you to hear this tape. It is coming out in a few months as a record." Just before I clamp the ear phones to my head the poet leans to me and says. "But about the Amazon. I have good news. I'll tell you about it later if I may." When I turn my head to answer him he is exchanging deep looks and enigmatic smiles with Beverly.

I sit in absolute silence, Marcos clicks on the machine, and with guitars, piano, violins, and percussion, Marlui begins to sing. Her voice is strong and low, intense and pure; it is absolutely her own with the power of emotion truly felt. I am ready to be moved, of course; something tremendous but amorphous has been building for the last hour. Without knowing it but with an odd anticipation I have been moving toward this moment when, faced with another's emotion and sharing it, I might see myself as now living with new and expanding expectations. It is this anticipation that had made me know that I was coming to the end of this journey, that in some odd way great curtains are now slowly closing behind me. They are the curtains that will domesticate and institutionalize the past and by isolating me from it allow me to reject once more the sense of being superfluous and old. And so when the music bursts out I am immediately and without resisting caught up and imprisoned within it. I begin to heave and shudder.

Bad Brazilian music is very bad indeed, but Brazilian music at its best is the most ingratiating in the world – the subtlest black rhythm, the most sophisticated European orchestration, and rent through like the sudden sound of bird cries or sudden shafts of sunlight in the jungle with the flutes and seedy shakings of Indian instruments. It is the true music of the Third World with all the sores and rags, the rages and desperations turned into art, into essences: delirium of fiesta, mystery of Candomblé, agony of love. And it speaks intimately of all earthly things: perfume of flowers, the hot sting of rum in the gut, a stretch of deserted beach washed by breakers – sea spray on black rocks – a full moon riding high over a silent river, small towns baking in the sun, a young girl washing clothes knee-deep in a lake, a sandy trail through rolling fields of maize or pineapples or cashews. It is music that glitters and pulses, quick as raindrops, sweet as a laugh, inconsequential as a flower, hard as pounding feet. In its immediacy, in its precise attention to the surface of things it is as profound as a child's concentration.

For two months I have traveled through Brazil and heard nothing on the radios but the onanistic disco beat of imported American music. Tonight out of that chance that forms the past into a pattern of meaning, that creates endings; tonight for the first time I am introduced to the real thing and out of pure luck am listening to one of the great Brazilian artists.

When I glance up out of the depths of my own involvement I am startled to see that the poet, who is sitting beside me, has begun to laugh. He points to my arms; they are covered with goose bumps and the hair is standing straight out on them. I would like to smile back but hesitate to rearrange my face, which is tightly set against the emotion that I feel; once more on this interminable journey the power of music is threatening to bring me to the point of tears, and because I am the only one in the room who can hear the music, I am being observed by everyone with curiosity, as though by studying my reactions they could know something about Marlui's singing before actually hearing it. Carefully not smiling I look at Marlui and nod my head, and everyone watching me smiles with a kind of relief.

One denies old age by denying the past the power to order one's life. And it is the reconciling power of music speaking of lost chances, closed doors, old abandoned illusions, and finalities that makes, at least as long as the music lasts, these things acceptable. Protected by the music, secure within the safety of its armor, I venture a little further out into forbidden territory.

I will never go back to the farm and wander the dark trails. Listening to the music, once more, but this time hearing it within the context of its healing power, I am confronted with this fact. Filled with a wrenching anguish, I accept it. What Ramón had told me through the heavy screening of my kitchen that evening when he had banished me from the jungle to the bourgeois comforts of Quito, "You don't belong here," had had in Spanish other deeper meanings that until now I have been unwilling to unravel. He had said, *Usted no es de aqui,* "You are not of this place." When he had said it I had been filled with a terror that so threatened to topple the foundations of my life that I had almost immediately pushed his words out of my mind. If I didn't belong here, wherever "here" was, where *did* I belong? I was, if I interpreted this judgment in a broader way than it was perhaps intended, being painted out of my last corner. What had he meant? Where didn't I belong? Was he saying something that no one in Acapulco would have dared to tell my grandfather or, had my father gone to Rio to sell ice cream made out of air and artificial coloring, no one would have dared to tell him, that truth that I had already decided should have been spoken: Get out of here; your presence is ridiculous and immoral?

. . .

Four Texas gold adventurers had come to Rioverde in 1968 where I worked for three years as a Peace Corps volunteer. Brash and vulgar and funny they represented to me the very spirit of American exploitive free enterprise. They came with high-powered boats, dredges, rubber diving suits, cases of whiskey, boxes of tinned foods. They rented a room above the post office where the political chief of the town judged an occasional act of vulgarity or drunkenness and where on the first floor there was a tiny barred cell that was often occupied by friends of mine with excruciating hangovers. The gold hunters began hiring a few of the people: Rosa to cook for them, her daughter to wash clothes, Pancho to run the outboard motor, Clever to stand in the canoe and watch for snags. Later when they found the gold they would need everyone in town.

I had been doing my little Peace Corps act—bringing in pigs and chickens, new kinds of seed corn, a little tractor, trying to start a co-op, and the presence of these exuberant Texans was extremely threatening. To *me*. Rioverde was *my* town; I wanted to change it my way. Now there was too much easy money coming in, too many beer drinking parties in the new saloons that were opening up; Pancho was forgetting to give water to his pig; the town was going crazy on gringo dreams.

One evening on the dock I spoke to the leader of the expedition. He had just given me ten dollars to buy some rat poison that I wanted to mix with ground corn and put into every house in town. It would involve building twenty little boxes that rats but not chickens could get into; it was a very Peace Corpsish project. As we talked, up in front of the *Teniente Político*'s office, four of my Rioverde friends were arguing with one of the gringos about some supplies that they had hauled up from the dock. They had worked at this for about fifteen minutes and were whining that the dollar each that they had been offered was a niggardly sum. Wages at that time were about forty cents a day but surely rich Americanos could be more generous. "Jack," I said finally, "nothing personal, but I wish you guys would get out of town; you are really fucking up this place."

He looked at me as though I were insane and began to laugh and with one arm made a sweeping motion that included the tilting dock, the sandy street, the stunted palm trees being washed away in the high tides, the disgraceful houses with rotted walls and the roofs collapsing – the whole town with the little bamboo chapel that no priest would ever enter, the light plant that had broken down again, the hand pump in the middle of the street that offered brine to the people instead of water. Almost everyone in town was drinking, the street echoed with awful music, dark figures staggered in the shadows. "Holy Christ, you must be kidding," he said. "How can anyone fuck up a place like this?"

They went up the river in their boats, washed and dived for gold, lost most of their equipment when the river rose ten feet one night, and came back after a couple weeks, twenty pounds lighter, touched with malaria and beginning to go deaf from some evil little fungus that had begun to sprout in their ears. There was very little gold, they said; thank God they were doing this on other people's money. They went back to Texas.

When my Peace Corps contract was completed a year later I left the town, too. I had formed a farm co-op that dissolved three days after I was gone into a chaos of ugly accusations and terrible, half-insane suspicions, brother against brother, neighbor against neighbor; the town was shattered to its roots, and the police had to be called in to divide the co-op assets among a people who, but for my ordering presence, could not have worked together in a community *minga* for more than half a day without coming to blows. With the best intentions I had planted seeds of rage, jealousy, and vengeance in that awful little town that after ten years still bear fruit. In Rioverde I had written a book about what happened there, and it did not have a very happy ending. And it was my only monument; too bad that so many of us who need monuments end up building them ourselves.

And leaving the Peace Corps I had cried (as many of us did who had had our hearts broken by the Peace Corps experience), "But what are we doing down here? How do we dare?" And the director, who had also come to South America with the best of motives (but also enjoyed the thirty thousand dollars a year he was paid), laughed nervously and said, "Don't worry; Ecuadorians are tough; they're flexible enough to survive whatever we lay on them." It was probably true and though we would have been reluctant to admit it, we were much more irrelevant than we could have imagined. We forgave ourselves. Our intentions within reason had been pure and unselfish, and certainly if we hadn't much helped anyone, at least we had been profoundly educated to the sub-world of poverty where half the people in it died before they were three years old. We had been students, not teachers, taught by the most authentic teachers in the world, the dying children of the Third World.

One who has gone through the Peace Corps cannot help but love it for its good intentions at the operational level and for the occasional sweetness of the children who, working under its banner, come to live plainly for a time and light their incredibly tiny candles in a darkness that is made up in many cases out of their own flawed perceptions. The Peace Corps is a bureaucracy that at the country level often struggles to transcend itself. In Ecuador we had always been accused by the Marxist university students of being CIA agents, and while this, as far as I know, was never true, still, in an ominous sense we were agents of the United States government, and our mission, though we scarcely ever thought about it, was to defend on a naive and humanistic level the interests of foreign policy and free enterprise. We were that clown's part of foreign policy, the semilapsed bourgeois, who disguised our subservience with long hair, marijuana, dirty Levis, and big, ugly fifty-dollar boots. Trying to be apolitical we rejected both the rapaciousness of American business and the Communist tyranny, though in our hearts and though we had rejected him, too, we knew that Castro was the true father of the Peace Corps and that we had been recruited to destroy his power. We were stretched between two evil systems, neither of which was capable of addressing itself to the true problems of South America.

A little group of passionate volunteers moved into a mountain village near Loja where they set up a school to teach ABCs to the Indian peons who worked on the large haciendas there. They were Quechua-speaking Indians who wanted to learn Spanish in order to compete with the mestizo middlemen who were robbing them in corrupt and complicated business dealings. Unfortunately the text the volunteers chose had been written by either Ivan Illich of Cuernavaca or one of the radical Brazilian priests who had had to flee the country when the military took over. It taught not only Spanish but, hidden behind the words, forbidden and explosive truths:

> My name is . . . .
> I am a man.
> I am a human being.
> I have dignity.
> I have human rights.
> I am a farmer.
> The land belongs to those who work it.

Incredibly provocative to put such thoughts into the heads of animals, how naive the anger of the volunteers when the *hacendados,* distorting language to its insane limits, denounced the Peace Corps as *Communist* CIA agents. The school was shut down. If the Peace Corps was allowed a good deal of latitude to engage in radical schemes it was only because we did it so badly that we were no threat to the status quo. We could get involved in projects of nutrition, sanitation, and agricultural techniques; put down wells in waterless villages, form clubhouses for shoe-shine boys, but we had not been invited by the Ecuadorian government to live among the poorest of its citizens and incite them to revolt against the feudal injustices of a military dictatorship. And what could we have taught them that they didn't already know in the depths of their pounding blood? The Peace Corps, when it made a contract with Ecuador that allowed us to work here, had certainly promised that its volunteers would work within the confusions and corruptions of whatever representatives of the oligarchy happened to be in power at the moment. We boasted that we were "agents of change"; we were not; we were agents of order.

Those innocent Spanish-teaching volunteers who thought that incidentally they might slip in a bit of idealistic propaganda to a group of brutalized Indians about the dignity of man had, without realizing it, strolled into the very eye of the social tornado. It was as though they had opened up the door of the back room where the vats of arsenic and Kool-Aid were being blended for public consumption. It was bad enough to confuse brutes by telling them they were human beings, but they had gone too far, they were attacking the very foundations of civilization when they taught that land belongs to those who work it.

Land belongs to those who can buy it; everyone knows that. And it is this profoundly held belief for which men with land will die that promises to shatter the South American continent.

Put into wildly simplistic terms the ownership of the world's farm and pasture lands is the single overriding problem that, until it is justly solved, makes all the other problems unsolvable. A statistic: eighty percent of the farmland in Colombia is owned by five percent of the people; of this eighty percent held in private hands, six percent is being farmed. And what part of that six percent is devoted to export crops like coffee, bananas, marijuana, and cacao? Colombia is most famous for its crime rate and its millions of abandoned children; many people feel that after Nicaragua, El Salvador, and Panama have shattered in revolution and peasant uprising, Colombia will be next. Unless Brazil beats them to it.

Neither of the two great powers that control humanity has tried to confront the most fundamental fact, that the accumulation of land into a few hands can only result in catastrophic convolutions. Russia, with its communal system of publicly owned land and government controlled agriculture, ignores the simple truths about man's nature and the incentives that drive him to produce. The capitalistic system, out of which have grown the stifling mega-agro-businesses, have simply insured that less and less people will control more and more of the world's resources. Bankers and lawyers are the new farmers, and the dispossessed farmers are their hired day laborers. No wonder the cities of the world are ant-heap slums. No wonder tomatoes have a shitty flavor. No wonder the night streets crawl with rage and menace. Because it's good business half of America's farm output is fed to cows and pigs – and 15,000,000 people, mostly children, die each year of starvation. In Brazil land that used to be planted to black beans is now planted to soy beans that are sent to the United States for cattle feed; fifteen years ago it was estimated that forty-five percent of Brazil's people suffered from malnutrition; now it is seventy percent. This is referred to in business circles as "Brazil's Economic Miracle." The price of black beans triples, another thirty million live hungrier in order to chip away at Brazil's appalling (and still growing) foreign debt, a debt so astronomical that it can never be paid. Pauperizing a great nation for the insane pleasure of industrialization and a mechanized agriculture that will benefit none but a small percentage of its citizens is a madness almost impossible to believe. It is impossible to create a stable middle class in countries where populations are doubling every couple of decades, and it is naive to believe that a newly emerged middle class will be interested in solving national problems with solutions that will cut away at their new vulgar privileges.

And, ah, seduced by that ambiguous word "Development," how I had burned for a time, wanting to give poor Ecuador, sunk in its own careless and irrational ways, the benefit of my superior knowledge and my subtle perceptions. Development was a magic word in the mid-1960s. For disenchanted missionaries it took the place of "Christianity"; for disenchanted radical idealists it took the place of "Marxism," two words that like the word "love" give one an excuse to mess with other people's lives. It is still a magic word in the 1980s, but though development has now reached epidemic proportions and whole South American nations have been engulfed in the Americanization of their economies and their cultures, more and more people who had come here to bring progress, modernization, and development are beginning to realize the consequences of their noble acts. The development we have wished upon South America has been for the vast majority a sentence of death or, at the least, a steady plunge into a deeper poverty. South America is now a suburb of Miami; Latin Americans are our truck gardeners. A friend of mine says he walked for eight hours across a single planted field of marijuana in Colombia. Underdeveloped countries are often underdeveloped because the families who own them are perfectly satisfied with the way things are, and what can you develop in an agricultural country except its agriculture? But we are caught in our confusions between the conflicting claims of human pity for the dispossessed and the sacred claims of private property.

The terrifying explosions of populations, the faltering production of food, the inefficient use of land, the increasing costs of energy to run a mechanized agriculture, mass hunger, the growth of slums, crime, and human rage are all symptoms of one thing: the separation of man from the land.

And it is the passion of men to own the land they work that drives them into the tropical forests or into those marginal wastes that suffer from periodic droughts. This is all that's left; the rest has been bought up.

I suspect that from the very first, Peace Corps technicians borrowed from the agricultural colleges, USAID experts, or enlightened in-country farmers have suspected that the invasion of tropical jungle areas to commit agriculture upon them would create more problems than it would ever solve. But people who are committed to development are driven into strangely extreme positions and out of desperation to do something right for once will plunge into almost any new project that offers the slightest chance of success. Forbidden to attack the problems of poverty at their foundations, they are like doctors forbidden to remove a cancerous organ and who must treat the patient with chants and incense, lemon juice, rhinoceros horns, or acid squeezed from the pits of almonds.

About the same time that Brazil with a three-hundred forty-million-dollar loan from the World Bank began to build that network of roads through the Amazon that would destroy it, the Peace Corps became modestly involved in Ecuador in a similar plan. Half of Ecuador lies in the upper reaches of the Amazon basin; it is a tremendous area of virgin forests and great rivers. A few farmers had hacked out clearings in the Andes foothills at the jungle's edge; a few sad missionary towns timidly hugged the river's banks; a few geologists, shooting and shot at, wandered the lost trails looking for that oil that they finally found; a few military outposts guarded a wild frontier that was under a constant arrogant pressure from Peru. It

Witnesses, Seventh Day Adventists, Moonies, Children of God, the Macro-
biotic Vegetarians, Mahajari ji, the Divine Light Mission, and dozens of
others have dotted the countryside, from the coastal mangrove swamps of
San Lorenzo, through the Andes' sloped mountainsides of potatoes, barley,
and corn, to the lost villages along the Amazon with their meeting houses,
their cement churches, and their middle-class enclaves full of labor-saving
electrical equipment but safe behind barbed wire. An alliance of down-to-
earth fundamentalists operates HCJB, the most powerful radio station in
the world for spreading the Good News: Jesus loves you and God is kind
and just. Walk through the slums of Guayaquil or Salvador or Lima or Rio,
walk if you dare, through the Indian villages on the slopes of Chimborazo
and then say without blushing or blinking your eyes that God is kind and
righteous. What in God's name has God got to do with a continent brought
to its knees and strangling in its systems of corruption and injustice?

One would think that since most of the religious groups are so
marginally concerned with the physical degradation of the people they
hope to redeem that they would at least more fervently and sweetly burn
with moral charity for having been touched by God's passion for them. Not
at all. Most religious kooks burn with an appalling primal rage, and their
chief purpose down here seems to be to combat the pagan shamelessness of
the Catholic Church and its unholy alliances with the ruling powers. Talk
about the Catholic Church with a Protestant missionary and watch his eyes
go hard and glittery; watch his mouth go thin and mean. And vice versa. In
the little mountain villages where the priests are kings, Protestant proselyti-
zers are occasionally driven from the streets with clubs and stones, and a
few years ago in an isolated provincial town a couple of them were doused
with gasoline and set ablaze while a mad priest danced and cackled. Professional religious enthusiasts, as though they were looking at the world
through the wrong end of a telescope (a tunnel vision that is almost blindness) have one thing in common: loving God, they find it easy to hate man.
Or, if hate is too strong a word, they find it easy to regard man as fodder for
God's furnace, raw material to be consumed by God's inscrutable ways.
"We brought down twelve hundred Indians from the Tocantins to Belém,"
writes the old sixteenth-century Jesuit chronicler, "and through God's loving mercy, we were able to baptize the six hundred who died on the journey." Attitudes have changed in the last four hundred years but not much,
and hordes of missionaries still paddle up the smallest tributaries of the
Amazon looking for the last pathetic remnants of a people who once owned
the continent. "Yes, of course, we may bring them the measles or the tuber-

culosis that will kill them, but by accepting Jesus as their personal saviour they gain eternal life."

Made goofy by the Gospels, preaching weird and irrelevant concepts, buying converts with pots, beads, and machetes, let us give them the benefit of the doubt and admit reluctantly that if their truths are not our truths, still, their intentions are good. If they are not much interested in shoes for the feet of the heathen, they are, at least, interested in their souls. A lifetime of starvation, servitude, and sickness is such small potatoes beside eternal life. Christ has become a pawn in the Capitalist-Communist brouhaha.

Almost as inscrutable as God's ways are the ways of the World Bank, which, ostensibly engaged in the development of nations, ends up by removing five dollars for every dollar that is loaned. Looking for good intentions and finding none here, let us tip toe past the World Bank and its beneficiaries, the multinational corporations.

It is amazing that having known these things for years, it is not until tonight, moving within the spaces of the music, or more precisely, given the strange, cold perceptions of the writer to both move within the music and to stand outside it, I see myself as so closely related and so identically involved in all this suspect and half-arrogant activity. It had always been so easy for me to mock the missionaries; spit with rage upon the rotting body of Pizarro, baked chicken-brown in his glass aquarium; gaze scornfully at Lewis, the cactus extincter, and exchange little remarks with the charming manager of Ecuador's Coca-Cola company when we infrequently found ourselves invited to the same dinner party. Easy to judge my grandfather, repudiate my father, rail against the proliferation of the plastic hotels and their co-conspirators, the airlines. Easy to curse the multinationals spreading the new consumer's gospel – God, the machine, and his new product: Products.

But I had been like a secret masturbator who shrilly condemns this vice in others. Suddenly I see myself as joined fraternally with this whole shoddy and sometimes clownish crew. Cutting down jungle, preaching a mechanized agriculture that with all its emphasis on chemicals and machinery could never have worked, turning hunting grounds into pastures and driving the hunters into an insane despair, I had joined myself in brotherhood with not only mad king Ludwig of the Jari, but with every semi-kooky gringo on the continent. Free enterprise, Jesus Christ, soy beans and unpolished rice, Communism, transcendental meditation: they were all madnesses, substitute solutions to the staggering problems of continental poverty.

What we all had in common was a belief in Progress. We were all, some more corrupt than others, blindly kissing at the ass of Progress. None of us knew what Progress was, and in fact, since we were all working at an emotional or economic level that simply defined and dramatized our own prejudices and preconceptions, anyone's little project would inevitably be cancelled out by someone else's little progressive project.

And we had something else in common. In some terrible way, even the best intentioned of us have shared in some dark corner of the mind that conviction so honestly expressed by the Texas gold hunters: why not come down here and mess around, for how can anything that any of us might do be anything but for the best in a continent that is so completely fucked up. Beneath our love or pity or anger, on some level, be it religious, cultural, economic, social, or ethnic, we are moved by delightful little shivers of superiority and sad little shiverings of contempt for these corrupted nations who have so docilely allowed themselves to be dominated by the most rapacious features of an alien culture, these shell-shocked peoples who so ineptly drift toward a social chaos constructed out of their own ineptness and their inability to confront ultimate consequences. If we are joined together in a common humanity, still, our emotion for them is tinged with that patronizing something that the master feels for his slaves. How strongly I had felt this in the Salvador bookstores as I searched for a book by Ubaldo in those long rows of Steinbeck, Dreiser, Sinclair Lewis, and Erskine Caldwell, that not quite first-rate literature of the colonizers. The dominated Latin, insecure, feeling vaguely inferior and alienated from his proper destiny, reflects a self-loathing that is the easiest part of his conception of himself for us to accept; it is hard to respect anyone more than he respects himself.

Poor raped South America. We lie over her in a kind of post-coitus triste but beginning to feel the itch of a new engorgement. After Pizarro it was all so easy. We won't roll away from her yet; she still has the power to enflame our lusts, and her feeble efforts to roll away from *us* strike us as being not quite sincere. She has not yet been raped into madness like her black African sister.

If it is the music that has cracked me open, the river that has shattered my preconceptions, the black pessimism of my Brazilian friends who are predicting the inevitability of an ecological disaster that I accept as being true, it is the music alone that lets me accept my new vision with a kind of joy. I feel as though I were not fooling myself anymore; perhaps it is something like the satisfaction a man finally feels who stands before his peers and, for the first time knowing it is true, says publicly, "I'm an alcoholic." I now accept the curse that has been laid on me, and cursed, still know that I am guiltless: I was born bourgeois and will die bourgeois. In this game that I've been playing so seriously, perhaps all I've really lost is that final illusion that I could move out of my class, that I was free to make this decision.

Still, being bourgeois, if I had had the power to impose my often foolish will on desperate people willing to try any new scheme that seemed to be backed by science or technology, I was ultimately separated from them only by that power that I had. Everyone who has been addled by the Western presence dreams of being bourgeois, too. We all want to smell like roses, own chrome-plated radios, dress our children in frills and ribbons. And we all want the power to resist being pushed around.

We all use whatever little power that we have; it is that thing that allows us to lay a design over life, and who, owning a chain saw, or a driver's license, or a match and a can of gasoline — and nothing else — will resist the impulse to go out and carve curlicues over life's banalities. The men who make the chain saws that will turn the Amazon into a blowing desert are no more guilty than the Arcarios, those poor black peons, who for the few dollars they can earn to keep them alive, will cut down the forests that had been their homes. The poor are like people who must nourish themselves by consuming their own limbs, and out of their necessity will, perhaps even with a certain cruel delight, join themselves in monstrous projects made impressive by their hideous monumentality. There is a tribe of Indians who live on the upper Amazon near Peru with insights that are only slightly more searing; they have seen the future, and they know that they are powerless against it; they have begun to kill all their children on the day that they are born. But, of course, a moment's thought will rob this truth of its power to shock; we are all of us doing the same thing.

And Ramón? What of him and his brutal ways? Yes, he had had the right to drive me from the farm and uproot me from a life that was essentially melodrama. My efforts to be the hero of my own life had in the end cost everyone too much. Ringing the curtain down before the sword play and the solemn group before the catafalque was perhaps the purest, most unselfish thing he had ever done. But if he had had the right, I had had the right to resist him as long as I was able. By defining home as that place you couldn't be kicked out of, I had been the victim of another illusion where my true neurotic nature revealed itself. Remembering the regularity with which as an adolescent I had been kicked out of my father's house, I had clung too desperately to that little piece of turf. Ramón, in a sense, was my production. Not wanting to, but inevitably, I had made him into a bourgeois. That farm was not a home, it was a piece of property; I had put power into his hands, and with the best intentions he had used it.

In a larger sense home, that symbol of stability, is only one more concept being shattered by a crazy world where whole nations are stood against the wall and where millions are driven to clog the roads as they stagger toward another border and a temporary haven. There is no way to buy or beg continuity; there is no spot on earth from which one may not be driven. Home is where you are; home is where you find yourself. (Reading that sentence over and giving it a double meaning I note with a glow of pride that we have arrived at the edge of profundity.) It is that cubic space that the body claims – if roofed, that area where you store your dirty clothes and your books.

So. So what am I left with? I scratch around a bit, searching, for it is funny that feeling as naked as a blank page, I feel so good about it; I have been freed from an awful weight of rage and guilt, but it is not easy to be so unencumbered. Without rage and guilt I may end up as a man without qualities. I scratch around. What I am left with, I decide, is a conviction that each day I hold it will become more mathematically improbable: I am not going to die within the next twenty-four hours.

And I am left with the music.

For half an hour isolated by the earphones, head down and staring at the tape machine I have been listening to the music unaware of the others in the room. Now out of the corner of an eye I see Don's Guccis tapping out a rhythm that is very different from that music that I hear. His tapping toes create a powerful dichotomy. Glancing up I see that Marlui is singing. I hardly recognize her for a moment; she had been as I listened pure voice, nothing more than an instrument for the music's message. I had forgotten her great black eyes, the long straight hair, her look of openness and vulnerability. And now she has changed; bending over the guitar she observes her hands as they sweep over the strings or stretch at chords. Her face has become unnaturally calm, almost masklike. She has moved far away into the obliteration of the music and, incredibly tense, incredibly relaxed, seems to be as charged with energy as the Candomblé dancers when the African gods take possession of their bodies and the nerves beneath their skins snap and ripple with electricity. (It seems that touching them as they bend and sway to the drums one would be dashed to the floor in shock by contact with so much concentrated essence.) If the light were better, I imagine as I stare at Marlui, amazed, that I would be able to see that same stream of energy that I had seen one day streaming out of the sun like a golden rain.

And instantly, as I watch her, that phrase out of Loren Eiseley's book about Wallace, that thing that Wallace had gone searching for along the whole length of the Amazon, that little thing that had nagged at the edges of my consciousness for years, seems to stand explained in the figure of this woman with the tranquil face who is bent over her guitar and who with ease and mastery has given herself over to some inner emotion. What I am seeing, and for the first time clearly defined, is a manifestation of the potential moral beauty of man. I had seen it that very afternoon when the two fishermen had burst through the glitter of the river's flashing to hail our ship with their harvest of silver fish, their ton of *piarucu*. What mastery of their craft, what economy of movement, what an intense and private dialogue. Everything about them had celebrated their lives: they had always lived on the river; they had always fished, they knew and loved their work and through their work were passionately involved with life.

And I had seen something of the same thing – that same pure, intense letting go – that had washed across the faces of the three brothers as they sang and tapped their tambourines in Recife's nighttime mall; had seen it on the farm among the black dancers as they clicked into overdrive and went sailing away into the open spaces of a heightened consciousness.

Out of nowhere a new figure that I haven't remembered for almost forty years and whose name, if I ever knew it, has been long forgotten, begins to glow in my imagination. Watching him closely now I try to place him, try to make him repeat something that I had at the time considered of some great importance. He is kneeling before something as though praying. Who is he? Who is this guy – a fellow in flying dress, headphones clamped to his ears, red hair – violently red curling hair – a kind of stupid pugnacious face? This kneeling man? He is connected in some very logical way to the singers and the dancers and what I begin to remember is that for an instant, like that dying black man who had lain across his woman's lap, he had stood revealed as almost godlike, as man in some awesome culmination of his potential.

Christ. Like a slap in the face I remember. He is kneeling before a Norden bombsight.

I am crouching in the nose of a twin-engined training plane that is flying out toward the targets near the bombardier's school at Victorville, California. There is a red-headed cadet sitting just in front of me on the bombardier's seat and peering intently down and out to the desert floor. It is his turn to bomb, and he is nervous because he can't pick up the target. We are flying at seven thousand feet well above that industrial haze that pours over the hills and flows out of the canyons from San Bernadino, and looking down through it, all the pale desert colors washed out by haze, it is difficult to find the target, a circled whiteness laid over sand.

Sitting behind this guy I feel perfectly relaxed – or as relaxed as I can ever feel sitting strapped in some metal construction miles above the earth, hurtling above it, and given over to chance. I have already dropped my bomb; nothing spectacular; it had landed within that three hundred feet of the target's center and will not statistically shatter my credibility, and now, freed of anxiety, I have only to observe this nervous fellow as he prepares to drop his last practice bomb and do it either well or badly. I hardly know him and have no feelings about this performance, but watching him suspect, that tense and nervous as he is, I may be about to share in something weirdly slapstick.

It is our last flight as cadets, the first time we have flown without instructors. Tomorrow, newly dressed up as second lieutenants, mothers, wives, or sweethearts will pin wings to our chests, and, transformed by kisses and acts of Congress into officers and gentlemen, we will be sent to the South Pacific or to Europe and begin to drop real bombs on real people. It is the early summer of 1942.

We are less than a minute from the target when by chance I pick it out as it sprawls down there on the desert floor, almost invisible and impossibly close. I tap the cadet on the shoulder and point. Nodding his head he slides from his seat and kneeling over the bombsight takes it in both hands, swings it over onto the target, and snaps the switch that connects the bombsight to the automatic pilot. When I bombed I had been lucky, had picked out the target miles away, and had had a leisurely three-minute bomb run; this fellow will have about forty-five seconds.

In forty-five seconds it is hardly possible to manipulate all of the dozens of knobs, switches, and buttons – synchronize the cross hairs to remain motionless on the target, kill crosswind, establish true ground speed, open the bomb bays and the final switches that will allow the bomb to fall. Last week someone had bombed and killed two sheep fifty miles from the bombing range. I settle back to enjoy a comedy of errors.

But in that same instant when he had connected the bombsight to the automatic pilot, he had with some mysterious facility also connected himself to all this intricate and unfathomable machinery. He had flicked some psychic switch and had transformed himself out of his passion and his talent into that perfect interpreter and synthesizer of a half-million bolts, tons of aluminum – struts, cables, gauges, gyros, engines. More stunning:

he had *become* airspeed translated into ground speed, become altitude, temperature, wind drift, closing speed, even unpredictable error. As he kneels over the bombsight and his hands, as sure, quick, and intense as the fluttering wings of a bird, move over the knobs and flick on switches and caress this throbbing black box with the single moving eye, I can feel my own eyes burning with tears. I am in the presence of the reality of bombing and for the first time realize that we have not been trained to be technicians but killers. In his own way this performance is more flawless, more controlled, and liberated than any dancer's. The drone of the plane and the high whistling of air screaming through the cracks in the plane's Plexiglas nose make a perfect and ruthless musical accompaniment. Halfway through the bomb run, all in a moment, the cadet's flying suit turns dark, and it is as though another knob had been turned that had instantly emptied his body of its impurities. Literally, gallons of sweat pour from him.

Ten seconds before the bomb falls away he has done his job; his trembling fingers still linger over the synchronizing mechanisms, but he makes no further adjustments. When the bomb drops and the plane, released of its tiny weight, leaps an inch or two into the air, the cadet, still kneeling, turns his head and looks at something behind me. Sweat is pouring from his face, his mouth is open, his eyes wild and disoriented, his red hair dark and matted. The bomb gone, he is swinging back to the banality of reality, but for a moment, his face the face of a man ejaculating, he radiates the ecstasy of some pure fulfillment.

A full minute later, though it is hardly necessary, we kneel together in the plane's nose with the bombsight between us and watch as the bomb flashes at the target's center, a white rose with flame at its heart.

Now thirty-seven years later, emptied of every illusion but that conviction that I can extend my life by once more being involved in it and made joyful by the knowledge that I have been given new work to do (and every atom in my body hungering to embrace some new illusion), I make some final connection. It comes as a great discovery, this truth that has lived under my nose for years: man is not simply that animal who suffers; man is that animal who works. Man has a passion to use himself up, to lose himself in his own center, to become harmonious with nature by being allowed to express his own personal genius. We acknowledge this truth when we make a rich man of Mohammed Ali or when we value a single good day's work of Van Gogh at a million dollars. Man is most godlike when he sweats; the potential moral beauty of man lies in this simplest of things; man doing well something that he loves doing – the juggler juggling; the baker baking bread; the teacher before a class of children; a farmer hoeing out a row of corn. Even the trained killer who kills well fulfills, in some inscrutable way, his deepest contract with life and forgets for a time his own mortality, that stinking death that awaits him, too.

Hard knowledge to come to at the end of the seventies and in South America, this continent falling into the hands of the entrepreneurs, this continent given over to industrialization. It is becoming a place where man finds it harder and harder to lose himself in work that delights him or lends him dignity. Hard knowledge without sweetness; maybe, finally, I have come up with something tough enough to stand on.

•   •   •

It is late now, past midnight. No one has bothered to turn the taped music back on, and it is unnaturally quiet. The ship pulls a boiling surge of river behind it, and above the soft, slow diesel pounding it is possible to hear the sound of the water as it washes away from us and breaks against the river bank, tearing at earth and roots like a rush of rising tide. I am standing alone but about ten feet from me Hedrik, the wild Dutchman, isolated and thoughtful, leans over the ship's railing and stares down into the dark water. Above us the southern constellations wheel and burn. The poet from Manaus has made friendly contact with Beverly; they have been brought together by the music into a mutual enthusiasm that will fade under tomorrow's hot sun. They stand together on the other side of me talking earnestly. Leave it to the poet. He is telling her about the enchanted porpoises who turn at night into irresistibly beautiful men and seduce the river girls; he is inviting Beverly to check the back of his head for that hole that will prove that he is one of the river gods. Standing apart, watching the lightning burning at the horizon and twisting like threads, I listen to the poet without listening until the two of them stroll toward me.

"So; and only now I hear that you're a writer," the poet says. "This makes me feel very immodest. Not that being a poet is anything to boast about; still, everyone knows. I haven't tried to conceal my vice."

"The truth is I've only been a writer for about two hours," I say. "Perhaps tomorrow I would have told you."

"Ah, and is it the river that has enflamed your imagination to engage in something so unprofitable?"

"Yes, probably. But I've got the urge without the plot, like someone burning to make love and not a woman in sight."

"Well, if you have absolutely nothing to say, stick to poetry," the poet says. "But make it rhyme."

"That's easy for you to say; all Portuguese words end in vowels. But tell me, what was that good news you had about the Amazon?"

"Ah, yes, a thought that occurred to me. That happy ending to a horrid story, that all's well that ends well."

"So what are you going to tell me? That you were fooling? That the Amazon won't be destroyed?"

"Oh, no, fellow writer, the Amazon will be destroyed. There's no way to stop that. No one has the power to call a halt to something that will offend so many people. No, my news is not as happy as that."

"Well, then."

"Well, then . . . how can I explain? Look, have you never done something that was so awful, so against your nature, so senselessly destructive that you have never been able to think about it without shuddering? I mean real evil, real sin, something as senseless as destroying a continent."

"Yes," I say, almost eagerly, almost shuddering, remembering, "when I was a little boy. An old woman who invited me into her house one Halloween. Offering me cookies and ice cream. I stood in the darkness and threw an egg at her; it smashed against her face."

"Yes," the poet says, "something like that can color one's life, no? Did it solve a problem for you? Do you know yet why you did it?"

I had never once in my life wondered why I had done it; it had sprung from impulses so dark and confused that I had never dared search for its meaning. But now tonight on the river for just an instant I can see myself back there, a ten-year-old kid dressed in gray wool knickers, high wool socks, the khaki-colored sweater that grandmother has knit for me. I can see myself wandering through the residential streets of the Madrona district on that autumn night. Standing alone in the shadows of dark streets beneath the big trees that are almost leafless now. Piles of leaves ready to be burned or slowly smoldering. My pockets full of rocks and eggs. Rage in my heart. A half hour before, I had hurled a rock and smashed the windshield of a passing car. Hidden in a vacant lot, terrified but exultant, as the car's owner searched for me, screaming curses.

"I was a kid being crushed by grown-ups," I say, my voice beginning to break and rise in the grip of a fifty-year-old passion. "I had no power; I was in revolt against the grown-ups; they were all willing to see me destroyed. I had no one to defend me against my father."

Beverly and the poet, half-smiling, look at me without speaking. Hedrik, who is not part of this conversation but can obviously hear it, moves closer. "Oh Christ," I say, "I'm sixty years old and I still hate adults; I hate grown-up people. I still don't trust them."

"Ah, but who does?" the poet asks, and we stand together for a moment thinking of poor man and his naughty ways.

"But the good news you promised me. What do my old sins have to do with the river?"

"Perhaps this," says the poet. "That something good may come out of our sins. That maybe throwing that egg saved you from insanity. When the river is gone, when all the trees and the animals and the people are gone, when we stand in the wreckage we have made, man will be shaken with a shuddering that he has never felt before. He will finally face himself; he will finally realize that he must change. Perhaps by then it will be too late, but he will change. Our last days on this poor planet may be very noble ones. Very noble ones indeed."

"No, no." Hedrik says. He has moved to my side and stands almost beside me at the railing. I feel him as an immense presence as he bends down over the top of my head and whispers in my ear. His voice is either that of a prophet or a madman. "Man is man; he will never change. How can he? Why should he? We belong to God, and He has set us to an awful task. We still have tremendous work to do. Look up, look at the stars, have you ever seen them so bright? That is where man is heading, out there into the great spaces. Long after this planet is a lifeless desert blowing in the wind, we will be out there in our stainless steel projectiles. We will be out there in our millions and for centuries, searching out life and destroying it. We have a contract with God: He is using us to bring peace to the universe. We must go out there and one by one snuff out the stars."

Moritz Thomsen, born in 1915, lives now in Guayaquil, Ecuador. He served as a bombardier in the Eighth Air Force during World War II. At the age of 48 he became one of the early Peace Corps volunteers. His first book, *Living Poor,* chronicles his four-year Peace Corps experience of living in a small fishing village in Ecuador in the 1960s. He returned to Ecuador after leaving the Peace Corps to become a farmer on the Esmeraldas River, an experience he describes in *The Farm on the River of Emeralds.* He continues to travel and live in South America.

The cover art is "Parana" by Alfredo Arreguin,
Oil, 60 × 48″, 1988
Courtesy of Foster/White Gallery

Text and cover design by Tree Swenson

The book was set by The Typeworks,
using Meridien type, designed by Adrian Frutiger

Book manufactured by Edwards Brothers